A Norwegian Tragedy

A Norwegian Tragedy

Anders Behring Breivik and the Massacre on Utøya

Aage Borchgrevink

Translated by Guy Puzey

polity

First published in Norwegian as *En norsk tragedie* © Gyldendal Norsk Forlag AS, 2012. Norwegian edition published by Gyldendal Norsk Forlag AS, Oslo. Published by agreement with Hagen Agency, Oslo, and Gyldendal Norsk Forlag AS, Oslo.

This translation has been published with the financial support of NORLA.

Polity Press
65 Bridge Street
Cambridge CB2 1UR, UK

Polity Press
350 Main Street
Malden, MA 02148, USA

ISBN-13: 978-0-7456-7220-5

A catalogue record for this book is available from the British Library.

Typeset in 10.5 on 12 pt Sabon
by Toppan Best-set Premedia Limited
Printed in the USA by Edwards Brothers Malloy

For further information on Polity, visit our website: www.politybooks.com

Contents

Preface

A year ago today, on 24 August 2012, Anders Behring Breivik was found guilty of killing seventy-seven people, violating sections 147 and 148 of the Norwegian Penal Code, which cover acts of terrorism, and section 233, premeditated murder where particularly aggravating circumstances prevail. The prosecuting authority's plea that he be transferred to mental health care was not upheld. The court found Breivik criminally sane and sentenced him to preventive detention for twenty-one years.

Thus a chapter came to an end. The events of 22 July 2011 had not only been scrutinized in detail by possibly the most comprehensive court case in Norwegian history, but had also been thoroughly investigated by the 22 July Commission and almost endlessly discussed in the media. Nevertheless, there are still aspects of the case that have not been reported widely. The extent of the detailed discussion has perhaps also meant that the bigger picture has become fragmented. How can we understand 22 July 2011?

A single book cannot describe such a great tragedy, but a book can still go into further depth than an article or a television programme and attempt to create a narrative or analysis of the events. Ideally, then, a book may contribute to deeper understanding.

My work on this book took other routes than I had initially envisaged. I eventually encountered the dilemma of how much I should tell and where to draw the line. I made a different choice from most Norwegian journalists because I decided that some of the lesser-known elements shed light on the explosive hatred that had such deadly consequences. They have explanatory power.

This was not a simple assessment; rights came up against other rights. Those affected have the right to know as much as possible about the background to the catastrophe. Breivik and his family have the right to their privacy. With a case of such enormous dimensions, however, I concluded that openness weighs heavily as a consideration. This is why I chose to tell more about Breivik's background and family than was publicly known at the time, because the picture I would have painted otherwise would have been incomplete at best, if not false.

That decision left its mark on this book. I have written about the community that was attacked, AUF [the Workers' Youth League], and, in a broader sense, Norway. I have written about extremist reactions to the emerging new Europe, with a focus on Breivik's so-called manifesto. I have learnt a lot in the process. The events of 22 July showed that Norwegian society is strong, but also that some people are left out of it. The reasons for this are not always clear, including in this case.

The process of understanding what led to Breivik becoming such a radical outsider is important. Without knowledge of where the holes in the net of our society are to be found, it is difficult to mend them. On its publication in Norway in the autumn of 2012, this book caused a debate about writers' ethics and the roots of radicalization. Why do children from peaceful and prosperous societies end up as terrorists? While Breivik serves his possibly lifelong sentence, the discussion about the attacks on 22 July 2011 and the phenomenon of European terrorism continues. I believe that is a good thing, and this book is a contribution to that discussion.

Aage Borchgrevink
Oslo, 24 August 2013

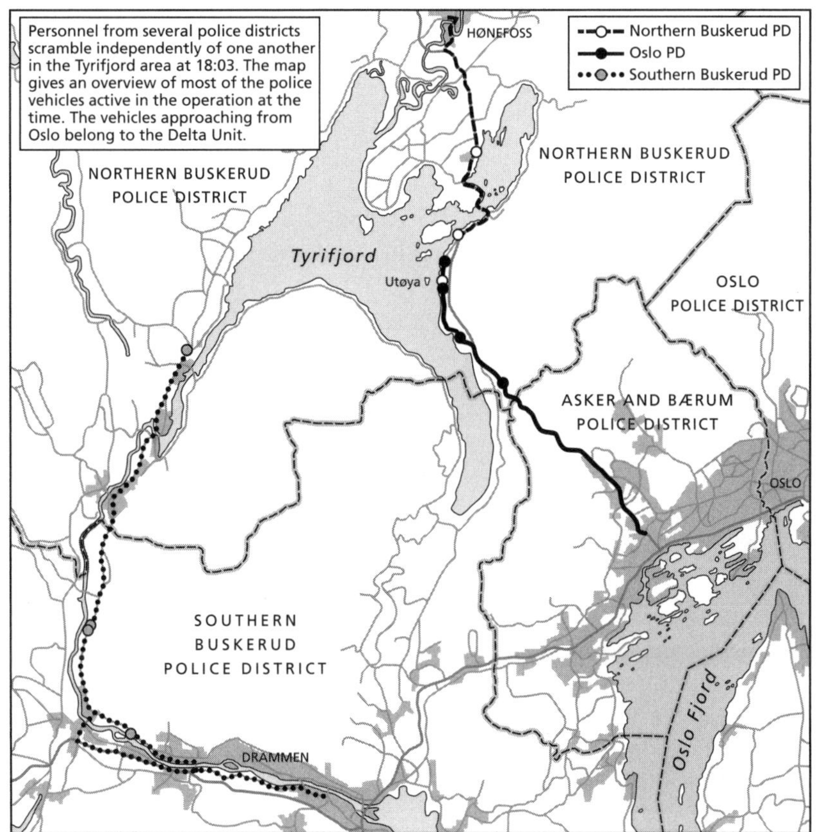

The Tyrifjord and surrounding area, 22 July 2011

Redrawn from 'Rapport fra 22. juli-kommisjonen' [22 July Commission Report], Report for the Prime Minister, NOU 2012: 14, fig. 7.3, p. 118.

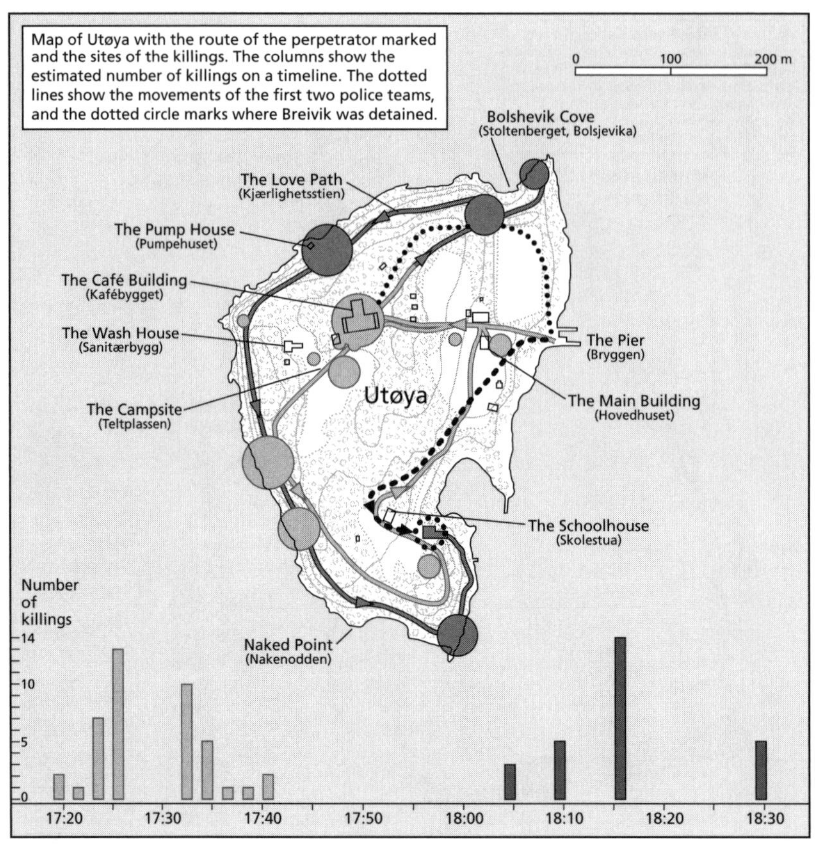

Utøya

Redrawn from 'Rapport fra 22. juli-kommisjonen' [22 July Commission Report], Report for the Prime Minister, NOU 2012: 14, fig. 7.5, p. 120.

1

The Explosion

The bomb exploded at 15:25:22. The blast reverberated through the city. The van disintegrated. A motorcyclist and a chance passer-by vanished in the white flash of the explosion. A fierce fireball blinded the nearest surveillance cameras and was followed by a cloud of smoke and dust. Pieces of the van flew like projectiles in every direction, axles and engine parts spinning through the air.

At the scene, cars were flung around, and the lamp posts bent like blades of grass. The buildings on both sides of Grubbegata bore the brunt of the shockwave, completely destroying their lowest floors. The pressure wave pulverized the windows in the floors higher up, passed right through the building and smashed glass in other buildings around the square in front of the high-rise H Block. Ceilings collapsed above the offices in the H Block and in the Ministry of Petroleum and Energy. Splinters of glass and wood whistled through the corridors and offices, drilling their way deep into wall panels and cupboards.

The blast sparked fires on both sides of the street and gouged holes in the asphalt. The bomb crater gaped open right through two levels of tunnels running under the street. These corridors were used to transport documents between the ministries. The explosion cut deeply, uncovering hidden passageways and exposing the very nerves of administration in Norway. There was a smell of sulphur, like rotten eggs.

Eight minutes earlier, at 15:17, the large, white Volkswagen Crafter van had turned in off the street called Grensen. It drove calmly up Grubbegata towards the government district and stopped on the right-hand side in front of a metal fence covered with a white canvas to hide the construction works outside R4, the building that housed the Ministry of Trade and Industry as well as the Ministry of Petroleum and Energy. The driver put on the hazard lights, as illegally parked vans often do, and made his final choice.

A couple of minutes later, the van rolled forwards again. It turned off to the left by the H Block, stopping outside the main entrance to the Office of the Prime Minister. A man in a dark uniform got out of the vehicle and walked on up Grubbegata. A security camera captured him on his way up the pavement: a man with a black helmet, a lowered visor and a pistol in his right hand, turning round and staring back at the van he had left behind. The time was approaching half past three in the afternoon on 22 July 2011.

It was a sleepy Friday in the summer shutdown.

At Tvedestrand, further south, a man stood on the jetty by his holiday cabin, studying the cloud banks hanging above the grey sea. It was the summer holidays, after all, even for the foreign minister. He decided to take his sons out trolling for mackerel, and went to change the hooks on his fishing line.

A young, dark-haired woman sat nodding off in a car heading in to Oslo. She was dressed up in red boots and red earrings and was tired after a night out with her friends.

The rain lashed down over eastern Norway – again. The summer of 2011 would go down in the history books as one of the greyest and muggiest in living memory. People in their holiday cabins stayed indoors; no point in going out into the mist. The grass was wet, and if you wore trainers your feet would just get soggy.

A woman lit a cigarette and took a break from preparing dinner in the kitchen. She had moved to a small coastal town by the Oslofjord after retiring from the Ministry of Foreign Affairs, but she still kept a small bridgehead in the capital: a studio flat in the West End. That evening, Tove was going to have some friends round.

A student from Stavanger and his friend, a girl from Oslo wearing a black turban, spoke quietly in his small room in Kafébygget [the Café Building]. Outside the window, the damp foliage glistened, blocking the view of the grey lake Tyrifjord. They were taking a short break together before the afternoon's programme.

At 15:21, the administrative secretary at the Electricians' and IT Workers' Union logged off the network and got up from her desk. Holidays at last. The union had its offices on the seventh floor of Folkets Hus [the People's House], the Norwegian Confederation of Trade Unions' building, which dominated one side of the square at

Youngstorget. To the left of Folkets Hus towered Folketeaterbygningen [the People's Theatre building], where the Workers' Youth League, among others, had their offices. The administrative secretary was a sprightly woman in her mid-fifties, a former Norwegian football champion. She usually cycled home, but that day she had taken her bike to be repaired. She was wearing light-coloured jeans, black trainers and a brown jumper. It had cleared up when she went out of the building. Since she was going to the metro station, she could walk either down towards Jernbanetorget or up past the government district and the entrance into Stortinget metro station. It was not far to go either way, but the secretary turned right and walked up the incline. She strolled along Møllergata and turned right up the alley leading to Einar Gerhardsens Plass.

In the meantime, the man in the helmet had crossed Grubbegata, walked down to Hammersborg Torg and got into a silver-grey Fiat Doblò. A man saw what looked like an armed policeman reversing the van out and driving down Møllergata in the direction of Hausmanns Gate. The strange thing was that the policeman was driving the wrong way down a one-way street. Was he completely disorientated? Why did the policeman choose to go that way? The man at Hammersborg Torg took out his mobile and made a note of the small van's number: V-H-2-4-6-0-5. Green plates.

In the government district at Grubbegata, there were people at work all day long, all year round. The buildings never slept, but on Fridays during the summer holidays most people left the office early. Normally, more than 1,500 people worked in the government district, but at twenty-five past three on this particular day there were only about 250 people in the buildings and 75 out on the street nearby.

At 15:24, the security cameras in Einar Gerhardsens Plass picked up a man in a white T-shirt walking towards the main entrance to the H Block. The man, in his early thirties, was possibly one of the people who usually took the short cut through the lobby, past the guards behind the desk on the left, on the way to the exit onto Akersgata. The lobby underneath the Office of the Prime Minister was open to the public. Less than a minute later, a motorbike stopped next to the Volkswagen Crafter. In the back of the large van was a homemade bomb weighing approximately 950 kg, consisting of fertilizer, diesel and aluminium. It exploded.

On the streets of the city centre, the pressure wave mowed down people on the pavements. A man was thrown onto the asphalt, as if by an invisible hand. He immediately got up again and tried to find his bearings. Some pedestrians lay in foetal positions, lifeless, while others immediately ran away. In a busy street, first one person, then three, and eventually the whole crowd ran in panic, as fast as they could, away from the site of the explosion.

A dying woman in light blue jeans was left lying by the fountain in Einar Gerhardsens Plass.

A cloudburst of glass rained down over the city. All around Youngstorget, shards of glass from the shattered windows smashed down onto the paving stones. Out in the square, a woman touched her head and stared at her hand, which was red with blood.

The centre of Oslo is compact. It is only a couple of hundred metres from the government district to the Storting, the main party offices and the biggest media centres. If a radius is drawn out another few hundred metres from the government district, then Norges Bank, the Royal Palace and the Ministry of Foreign Affairs also fall in the circle. It was possible to drive up to any of these buildings. When the raining glass had subsided, dozens of people lay, sat and walked around the centre of Oslo with blood streaming from cuts to their heads, arms and shoulders.

Within a few minutes, the pictures of R4 in flames, Grubbegata strewn with wreckage and the mangled H Block were being seen around the world. The pictures spoke for themselves. Devastated buildings, dust, smoke, people in shock and bleeding. Similar pictures had been broadcast many times over the past twenty years: Oklahoma City in 1995, Nairobi and Dar es Salaam in 1998, Moscow, Buynaksk and Volgodonsk in 1999, New York in 2001, Bali in 2002, Beslan in 2004, Mumbai in 2008 and, time after time, towns in Israel, Iraq, Afghanistan and Pakistan.

The damage being seen by television viewers around the world seemed to have originated outside the building. 'A car bomb?' wondered a man walking up Grubbegata as he filmed the inferno.

Over the course of the counterfactual hours before it became clear who was behind the bomb, many dark-skinned Norwegians in Oslo instinctively kept their heads down. The signature of al-Qaeda seemed to be written all over the Norwegian government district in fire, glass and blood. The explosion in Oslo struck like a bolt of lightning at the social and political landscape in Norway, splitting open divides like chasms. Could immigrants be behind it?

A foreigner watching the television pictures from the centre of Oslo while he commented on an English-language forum wrote that he 'did not know Norwegians looked like Arabs'. A well-known Norwegian blogger immediately answered: 'In Oslo they do. Arabs, Kurds, Pakistanis, Somalis, you name it. Anything and everything is fine as long as they rape the natives and destroy the country, which they do.'[1] Who was the blogger representing when he wrote that 'the left-wing government of Jens Stoltenberg that was just bombed is the most dhimmi [and] appeasing of all Western governments'? The term *dhimmi* describes non-Muslims who live under sharia, and in this case probably meant something along the lines of repressed and cowardly.

The notion of Norway as characterized by a sense of community and solidarity, as a harmonious island in a troubled world, faded. Had Norway suddenly ended up in some kind of revolutionary situation without most people noticing? The stench of the bomb was pungent. A layer of smoke descended on Oslo, obscuring the question of what was rotten in Norwegian society.

Shortly before four o'clock, I stood in front of the physics building on the University of Oslo campus and stared over the roofs towards the centre of the city. The cloud of smoke rose up from the government district and hung over the city centre for a while before slowly dissolving and disappearing. The surreal sight reminded me of burning villages in the Balkans and bombed towns in the Caucasus. Complicated local situations often lay hidden behind the suicide attacks and massacres I had investigated there. But here, in Oslo? It was hard to fathom.

I thought about my parents' accounts of 9 April 1940, when German aircraft swarmed over the city and Vidkun Quisling staged a coup d'état live on Norsk rikskringkasting [Norwegian Broadcasting Corporation; NRK] radio. Most of all I thought about the fallen towers in New York in 2001, and about the ideology that unites terrorists of many stripes in a common hatred towards Western cities and all that they stand for. The explosion was of such a magnitude that it appeared to be a declaration of war, an attack of geopolitical dimensions.

Yet this was only the beginning of the tragedy. Not only would the follow-up be more horrific than anybody could imagine, but the course of events would turn out quite differently to any preconceived notions. The man in the helmet was not dark-skinned, but white. Hmm, I thought, when I heard that: Chechen? Bosnian? Albanian? This must have originated in a distant warzone. No, it was not that straightforward. The man was neither Muslim nor a foreigner but one of my neighbours from the West End of Oslo.

In order to get closer to the origins of this atrocity, I would have to go not further away, but deeper. As I explored the dark online worlds of the past decade, fantasy culture and Oslo gangs of the nineties, I found that I kept on crossing my own tracks. What appeared to be political extremism, and in a way was, would turn out to have a complicated local dimension at its core here too. Some people had seen a monster taking shape, but their ignored warnings lay buried beneath layers of time, and witnesses were silent.

As I walked back through Marienlystparken [Marienlyst Park] with my mobile phone in my hand, I tried to find out how my friends and colleagues were doing in the city centre. The ambulances screeched down Kirkeveien from Ullevål Hospital. Sometimes, the solution is closer than you think, and hatred is written on the wall where nobody notices it. By chance, a friend of mine had seen a glimpse of it at a bar in the autumn of 2010.

2

Bacardi Razz

Skaugum

In mid-July 2011, the regular customer turned up for a last drink at Skaugum, an open-air bar at the back of the Palace Grill near Solli Plass in the West End of Oslo. It was the middle of the week, but there was little difference between weekdays and the weekend when everyone was on holiday. When the weather dried up, people flocked to bars and cafés like swarms of ants. The man pushed his way forward through striped shirts, hoodies and lace tops to order a Bacardi Razz, a sugary raspberry-flavoured rum that in Oslo's West End bars is often mixed with Sprite, decorated with a slice of lime and called a Butterfly.

The customer was quiet and polite as usual.[1] He was a typical West End boy, or man, of the sort that were two a penny at Skaugum, and he did not stand out apart from being less drunk and loud-mouthed than most of the others. He was medium height, blond and with an average build, in good shape. The bartender remembered the customer well from his days at Oslo Commerce School, one of the neighbouring buildings, in the late nineties. Over the years, as his hair slowly became thinner and his jaws rounder, he had continued to come back to the Palace Grill.

Most of the other boys from the nineties had got degrees and careers, grown up and settled down, but this regular customer had not followed the usual path from the Commerce School to a secure job in trade or industry. He did not have to pick anyone up from nursery at four o'clock and did not get up at seven to go to work.

Some take longer to find themselves, and an unmistakeable aura of interrupted studies and failed business ventures surrounded the customer at the bar. 'Get rich or die tryin', he had said to his acquaintances in the Progress Party youth wing early in the noughties, quoting the rapper 50 Cent.[2] But he was not much richer on this mild summer evening ten years later than he was back then.

Some of his businesses had made something, while others had gone quite badly. He had earned good money selling cheap phone call packages and fake diplomas, but his friends were still laughing about some of his ideas. For several months he had worked on his 'unemployed academic' project. He had developed a prototype of a pedal-driven billboard by putting together a bike and a newspaper cart. His idea was to take on an unemployed academic (of whom there were plenty, he thought) to cycle the vehicle with the billboard round Oslo: mobile advertising or, alternatively, ads-on-wheels.

It did not go well. The wind blew the cart over on the very first day, sending the billboard flying off to hit a woman. The 'unemployed academic' project was abandoned after its maiden voyage. Maybe his ideas were a little too big. The plan was not only about earning money but perhaps more about humiliating academics. Even though his friends thought he was enterprising, he was often strange and obstinate.[3] An odd eccentric who wore sunglasses around town, even though it looked peculiar in the evening, and who was perpetually vain, wearing a Canada Goose-branded down jacket in the winter or with his shirt collar folded up under his Lacoste jumpers. A metrosexual, as he said himself. Before he went out, he put on make-up. He was considering hair transplants and dental bleaching. He had a nose job done when he was twenty.

The man paid for his drink with a 200 kroner note, smiled and said that he did not need all the change.

The Palace Grill popped up in 1988, a casual alternative behind the neat West End façade of Solli Plass. My friends and I hung out there back then, pale university students in our dark leather jackets. By the summer of 2011, the Palace consisted of an American-inspired bar with a substantial selection of beers and whiskies and a reputable restaurant, as well as the outdoor bar in the courtyard called Skaugum, named after the crown prince and crown princess's family residence in Asker – maybe because the royals themselves used to show up in the courtyard there on occasion.

The place's alternative character gave way to an elegant West End watering hole where a composite mixture of local residents quenched their thirst. While the Palace Grill was frequently visited by A-list and B-list celebrities, cultural and media figures in their thirties,

Skaugum was where student hipsters, dark horses in the financial sector and more anonymous representatives of the West End's alcopop generation hung out under the open sky.

For almost twenty-five years, the Palace Grill had endured as a cultured alternative to the sleek concept establishments that stretched out in a golden crescent from Solli Plass up to the neighbourhood of Majorstua and then down Bogstadveien. There you could meet damaged West End characters drinking away the last remains of their grandparents' inheritance and saying that they would soon get their big break as designers, open a gourmet food shop or publish their manuscript that would solve all the world's problems.

This regular patron did not always go home quite so early or behave quite so well. There was something intense about him, which sometimes got out of hand.

At the turn of the year, he had been out on the town a fair bit and managed to get thrown out of the Palace Grill after having bothered one of the other customers. A TV star in his forties, known for his wicked humour and unrestrained behaviour, noticed that the thin-haired and blond regular customer was staring at him. The men nodded to each other, and the young, blond man came straight across to him. 'Anders Behring Breivik, nice to meet you,' the man introduced himself, speaking in his refined West End manner.

It was an uncomfortable conversation. Breivik immediately began lecturing about Muslims and immigration policy. The celebrity tried to signal that he was not interested. Breivik spoke about crusades and Knights Templar. There was something strange about him. It was difficult to put it into words, but it was something that could be felt. A kind of stiffness. A kind of flatness. Did he say he was writing a book? His face was almost expressionless, except for that artificial smile. His voice was toneless, his eyes stared and he blinked a lot. He sat on his chair as if he were sedated, not making a single spontaneous movement. It seemed as if his body were shut, closed off, like a condemned building.

The atmosphere eventually became so awkward that the celebrity called the bouncers. Breivik was led away, but he managed to turn round. 'In one year's time, I'll be three times as famous as you,' he said, before the bouncers pushed him out onto the street.[4]

Scenes like that are also two a penny in the West End of Oslo. There is often little distance between those who are famous and those who are not, but who would like to be. Celebrities must expect to be recognized, for good or for bad. Not all wannabes can master the codes of the West End, let alone the art of conversation. Groupies are not necessarily girls.

Breivik's parting remark did not appear especially likely and was more like typical hot air from an awkward bluffer with delusions of grandeur and an inferiority complex. Social skills are an art that requires constant practice, as Breivik himself thought, acknowledging that he had been out of practice for the past few years.[5] He was looking to boost his ego, being a bit of an attention whore, as he said. Maybe it was his lack of practice that made him go on monomaniacally about Knights Templar that evening, or maybe it was the combination of alcohol and anabolic steroids. Breivik took steroids on a regular basis.

Not only was he a monomaniac, he also spoke about something quite odd: knights. Although the Knights Templar have become a popular cultural phenomenon after having been resurrected in, for example, the computer game *Assassin's Creed*, crusaders have not been a common topic of conversation in Norway over the nine hundred years that have elapsed since King Sigurd I Magnusson led his military expedition to the Mediterranean.

In the manuscript Breivik was writing – the 'compendium' as he called it – the spirit of the age came in for harsh judgement. He called the superficial and money-orientated culture he saw around him at Skaugum the '*Sex and the City* lifestyle'. Over the last few years he had been concerned about the 'corrosive' effect of celebrity culture.[6] That was not how it was in the days of the Knights Templar.

The role of celebrities had changed as a result of the Internet, reality TV and social media. Breivik's generation was the spearhead in the democratization of fame. Carpenters and teachers – completely ordinary people – were suddenly perfect celebrities. Now that anybody could suddenly become famous, perhaps the pressure to do so also increased, and new arenas for showing off and for being seen were opening up, with blogs, chat rooms, Twitter and Facebook. The media's gaze used to be aimed at a select few, whereas the eyes of social media were, in principle, on everyone.

Unknown wannabes approached the celebrities in bars in the hope that a bit of their aura would rub off on them. A good celebrity story could increase the unknown individual's social status, like a character in a computer game who gets increased powers by acquiring a new weapon or a powerful spell.

Breivik took part in 'the game' to a certain degree even if he had secretly become critical of it, and to some extent critical of himself. 'I am not going to act like a hypocrite and pretend I have not been influenced by the typical *Sex and the City* lifestyle,' he wrote. 'I have been under the influence of this lifestyle as [have] a majority of my friends and even my own family members. I used to be proud of my "achievements".'[7]

In his compendium, he wrote about how this had changed. In September 2006, he moved out from his bachelor pad and back into his old room in his mother's flat. He and his mother had a complicated history. Breivik was a mummy's boy, but at the same time he was concerned about his façade: how things looked and what people would think. Even in his compendium, he became a little defensive when he described what it was like to move back in. His motivation, he claimed, was his lack of money.

> [J]ust before I started writing this compendium, I decided to move from my apartment in Frogner, one of the most priciest [*sic*] areas in Oslo, home to my mother. [. . .] The cost of renting my old apartment was 1,250 euro. My current accommodation expenditure (food included) is 450 euro [. . .]. This wouldn't have worked in my old life, when I was an egotistical career cynic as it would devastate my social image [. . .] (the pursuit to project a desirable façade to impress friends and potential mating partners). Sure, some people will think you are a freak for living with your parents at the age of 31 [. . .]. The only thing that matters is to ensure that you have enough funds and free time to complete the objectives necessary to execute your individual mission. As for keeping secrecy while living with another person; sure, you need many cover stories and you need access to the loft and/or basement storage areas.[8]

Things are not always as they appear. 'Your individual mission.' Even among the rich and the diplomats' sons in the West End of Oslo, there are people in cellars pursuing their solitary dreams, storing things in secrecy and surrounding themselves with layer upon layer of cover stories, like spiders in dusty bomb shelters.

The anonymous regular customer at the bar was in reality two people. In his compendium, at the same time as denouncing his former self, he described his transformation from a 'career cynic' to a knight equipped with a monumental mission. To signal the metamorphosis that was taking place, he signed the compendium not as Anders Behring Breivik, but as Andrew Berwick. Maybe he was not totally uninfluenced by the *Sex and the City* lifestyle after all, or at least by the desire to be seen and appreciated when he went out on the town.

The Consumer Zombie

Even though he might cling to celebrities, it was not easy to uncover any dark sides to the polite bar customer, but, one time he was at the

Palace Grill, he cracked. One Thursday evening in October 2010, he arrived at the bar early. Apart from a woman in her late thirties, Breivik was alone. Breivik was a social guy, in his own way, so he treated the woman to a beer and started talking with her.

'Knights,' he said, explaining what his book was about. The woman's friends came in and sat down. She was a literary researcher and began conversing with Breivik, who readily told her that he was inspired by chivalric literature.[9] He had never heard of *The Song of Roland*, but he knew that *Ivanhoe* was a novel about knights.

'My book's going to be big,' he said.

'What kind of genre is it', she asked, 'if it's not a novel?'

'It's a masterpiece,' Breivik explained.

The literary scholar tried to help him out and asked if it was fiction or non-fiction. Breivik answered with a reply that explained nothing at all. Either he did not understand the question and was not able to answer it, or he did not want to answer – mysterious. She did not understand what kind of book the strange guy's masterpiece was. When he said that he did not have a publisher, she stopped asking. Hardly an undiscovered genius, more of a slightly simple young man, she concluded, a show-off who had maybe done a few interrupted semesters at the Oslo School of Management.

The evening was young, and more of her friends were on their way. Breivik had not displayed his whole register yet. 'Novels about knights,' she thought, 'whatever next?' Without knowing it, she was on to something about the slippery salesman character at the other side of the table, but she had already forgotten his name.

History's most famous knight was never knighted by a monarch or a pope; he was self-appointed. Four hundred years ago, a man by the name of Alonso Quijano from La Mancha put a basin on his head and rode out into the world on an old nag he named Rocinante. The poor and childless man had read so many chivalric novels that he had begun to believe them. He took the name Don Quixote and was ready to fight bandits and save damsels in distress.

The conflict between the protagonist's fantasies about himself and other people's more level-headed opinions about the old man is the main theme of Cervantes' novel about the great narcissist of world literature, the Knight of the Ill-Favoured Face. With his lance lowered, Don Quixote charged at what he thought was a giant, only to be thrown to the ground by the sails of a windmill. To use an image from the psychiatrist Finn Skårderud, the narcissistic mind alternates between floating over the waters like an inflated Zeppelin and lying on the ground like the smoking wreckage of the *Hindenburg*.

Don Quixote's knightly character was constructed in a library in the early 1600s, while Breivik's knight, Andrew Berwick, was formed, dressed and armed on the Internet between 2006 and 2011. In spite of a difference in age of four hundred years, there are similarities between the two knights. Andrew Berwick also has a host of modern relatives. The Breivik/Berwick duo resemble characters described by many contemporary authors on both sides of the Atlantic, possibly because Anders Behring Breivik was even more a child of his time than many others. In a way, he had no real parents.

In his compendium – the 'masterpiece' – Breivik emerges as the consumer society's prodigal son, a loser in the capitalist battleground, a gamer who cannot distinguish reality from fantasies born online. The compendium describes two different people: a wakeful, political and active Justiciar Knight and a dormant, passive and unconscious consumer, almost like the plot of *The Matrix*, a film to which he frequently refers.

One of the pictures he has included in the compendium shows a face with its eyelids sewn shut and a scalpel approaching to cut the threads. This picture is related to his frequent use of opposed concepts such as sleeping vs. waking and living vs. dead. Both the sleeping and the waking Breivik could have walked right out of novels by Michel Houellebecq, Bret Easton Ellis or Chuck Palahniuk – a 'Norwegian Psycho', a person who is almost totally superficial and empty, whose best friends are not people, but brands. Breitling Crosswind, Chanel Platinum Égoïste and Château Kirwan '79 were respectively Breivik's favourite possession (a watch), his favourite eau de toilette and the wine he had put aside for a final party with two luxury prostitutes.[10] If a genre were to be suggested for the compendium, a notion of consumerist prose would come close.

Breivik writes about his miserable imprisonment as a cog in an enormous capitalist machine, in which people are seemingly free but in reality enslaved; in which people are seemingly part of a society but in reality are not bound to other people, not even to those who are enduring the same glossy hell as them, in the soft but deadly embrace of money. It is a self-portrait of *homo consumens*. Breivik, the dopamine wreck, is alive on the outside but dead inside. The smiling bar customer behind his glass, chatty and seeking contact, is empty, cold and dead beneath the surface. In his compendium, Breivik condemned the spirit of the age, in what at the same time emerged as a dark self-portrait. In the following paragraphs he writes 'you', but in all probability means 'I'. Breivik describes his former self as:

> a zombie where the highlight of your day is purchasing a 1,000 euro garment or a 100 euro sushi meal, or getting a blowjob from someone you met outside the toilet at a club that Saturday. On your way home you see a girl getting gang-raped by 4 Somalis. You don't offer it much thought as the slag probably had it coming anyway . . . Why should you risk your health for someone you don't know? And the poor Somalis are probably only acting out [*sic*] as a result of centuries of European colonialism. Poor fellas. Society should take responsibility and offer these underprivileged individuals better accommodations [*sic*] and more rights, perhaps affirmative action would ensure that they feel at home, that they finally would like us? How can we be so cruel and treat them this way?
>
> You work 9–10 hours a day, come home, eat, work out a couple of hours to keep fit, take your regular tanning, spa and Botox session and don't really have time for much else. Your concerns are not for the well-being of your family – close or extended – your neighbours, your kinsmen or countrymen, about the outlook for your country or your compassion for others, but rather the frightening scenario of being alone in this world. You don't want children because in essence you are a child yourself without responsibility or concern for anyone but yourself. Your only concern is how you can get your next dopamine fix, through and [*sic*] endless spiral of feeding your own ego.[11]

A zombie – in other words, the living dead. Here Breivik apparently summarizes his life in the noughties before he moved back to his mother's home in 2006, giving up the 'rat race'. He appears as the consumer incarnate, restlessly looking out for his 'next dopamine fix' in the form of a new piece of clothing or some plastic surgery. Dopamine is a pheromone at the centre of the brain's reward system – nature's own drug, you could say. It is activated by love, for example, but also, as with Breivik, by shopping. Breivik describes himself as a monomaniacal addict, as he was addicted to the bottle of red fruit-juice drink which allegedly went everywhere with him as a little boy. He is a child, as he says, not a grown man. Beneath his well-groomed exterior is a personality with no depth or substance. He is a puppet in the hands of forces that want him to work more, buy more and not waste time on other things.

Lurking in the background is his notion of sexually and physically aggressive immigrants, Somalis who gang-rape a girl, who represent not only a threat, but maybe also a fantasy of a different and more direct form of masculinity. The gang-rape represents the promise of fellowship in a group, the need for a violent reaction and an unaffected, sadistic hatred of women. Breivik's compendium portrays the process of the consumer zombie being cleaved open, giving rise to a violent, terrorist monster.

'I'm Going to Kill You!'

Either Breivik did not pick up the signals from the two women at the Palace Grill that his presence was no longer desired, or he did not care. He stayed sitting there, jovial and smiling.

When the third friend turned up, a beautiful, blonde, Nordic-looking woman, it was as if Breivik changed gear. He became insistent. He started off generous and courteous, although the group of friends made it clear that was enough. Breivik realized that being chivalrous was not working and began to boast. He ignored the first two women and repeated that his book was a masterpiece, but the blonde was not impressed.

Although he was talkative and generous in a calculated way, there was something strange and aloof about him. An icy shudder. Even though he was neither entirely ugly nor completely out of it, the chance of him chatting anybody up was out of the question, no matter how much he hassled them. The fourth friend arrived and, in an attempt to get away from Breivik, the friends went out into the courtyard.

Skaugum was closed and dark, but Breivik followed them. His positive chat-up techniques had been unsuccessful, and he now followed the blonde with an air of menace, stalking her. He went up close to her and glowered at her fiercely and intensely. It looked more strange than frightening. The fourth friend started dancing round him in the dark courtyard, waving her shawl and her dress, like a torero around a bull – or perhaps like a windmill in front of a knight? It was a comical scene.

'I'm going to kill you!' Breivik shouted.

The friends laughed and went back into the warmth and light of the Palace Grill. They spoke no more about the would-be author. If he had been a foreigner, they might have thought about his threat, but since he was just an unsuccessful white guy they laughed it off. What a freak. He did not really seem amorous either, just strangely obsessed with the blondest member of the bunch.[12]

Once again Breivik had been involved in an episode typical of Oslo's social life. Only someone who had read his compendium would have sensed a connection between Breivik's behaviour and a deeply ambivalent relationship with women, and especially with blondes who resembled his own sister and mother. This time, he was angered by rejection. He clung to famous men too, but it was women he threatened to kill. 'Traitor whores,' Breivik growled in the compendium.

In his diary entry from October 2010, which was a part of the compendium, Breivik gave a slightly different version of the incident: 'As for girlfriends; I do get the occasional lead, or the occasional girl making a move, especially now a day [*sic*] as I'm fit like hell and feel great. But I'm trying to avoid relationships as it would only complicate my plans and it may jeopardize my operation. And I don't feel comfortable manipulating girls any more into one night stands. I am not that person any more.'[13]

Perhaps this is the chaste knight Berwick talking, or maybe Breivik saw that it would be difficult to take girls home to his mother's flat? In the compendium, unseen by the outside world and surrounded by his cover story, Breivik lived out his fantasies. Dream and reality blended into one. His operation was no dream about a blonde-haired woman, but a nightmare of violence. 'Violence is the mother of change,' he wrote.[14]

A similar development from a lonely life of consumerism to a split life and terror is depicted in Chuck Palahniuk's 1996 novel *Fight Club* and in David Fincher's film of the same title from 1999. Palahniuk's protagonist is nameless, a sign of his fundamental lack of identity and of the notion that he is not an individual in a traditional sense, but a new type of subject: born of money and brought up with a life of shopping.

Although he does not realize it himself, Palahniuk's nameless protagonist develops an alter ego by the name of Tyler Durden, who is a free, active, politically subversive and alert character, just like Breivik's Justiciar Knight. 'We are a generation of men raised by women,' says Tyler. When Tyler eventually tells the protagonist that they are the same person, he also points out all the advantages of this fantasy – in other words, the advantages of himself: 'I look like you wanna look, I fuck like you wanna fuck, I am smart, capable, and most importantly, I'm free in all the ways that you are not.'

Breivik's many aliases and online nicknames might also be expressions of 'a confused identity perception',[15] just as his many cover stories suggest a confused perception of reality. A loved child has many names, according to a Norwegian proverb, but so does a person with no clear identity, as he or she can change his or her name at any time. *Fight Club* ends with the divided protagonist carrying out a massive terrorist operation, eventually bringing buildings down around him like a house of cards. The aim of the 950 kg of homemade explosives in Breivik's van was to topple the H Block, but, even though the bomb shook the government district, it did not manage to move the foundations.

Breivik's hedonistic past as a 'career cynic' resembles the background of many European jihadists, including some of the men behind 9/11. It is worth pondering whether it is easier for such zombies in consumer society to be radicalized, whether they have fewer aversions and are more open to buying into extremist and violent ideas online. The technological shrinkage of the world and the collapse of old value systems and symbolic narratives (such as religion, family and the nation-state) create a new man in Palahniuk's novel, not unlike the way in which totalitarian ideologies attempted to make a new communist or fascist man. The methods are softer and more subtle, but they still involve a form of invasion of or encroachment on the individuals who end up in the melting pot of consumer society.

This leads to a reaction, to rage, but there is no father to kill, no ideology to overturn or state to oppose. The consumer zombie's prison has no guards. This rage, then, either finds its expression in purposeless acts of terrorism and aimless urban vandalism or is turned inwards in the form of depression. Even if consumer zombies have no feeling of guilt towards others and are not troubled by conscience, they are still ashamed of themselves, in a kind of frustration about their own inadequacy in the marketplace. This shame is difficult to deal with because it cannot be relieved by confessing to others, and the solution is either another 'dopamine fix, through [an] endless spiral of feeding your own ego', as Breivik put it, or, as in *Fight Club*, carrying out a personal crusade.

The Herostratic Tradition

'In one year's time, I'll be three times as famous as you,' Breivik told the TV star. Even though reality TV elevated many ordinary people to celebrity status every year, the question remained: how would Breivik become famous? By writing to the newspapers? Breivik described himself to like-minded people online as a 'cultural conservative' intellectual, the opposite of 'cultural Marxists' writing opinion pieces for the papers. As a former paperboy, Breivik had worked out that newspaper carts could be used for mobile advertising. He also knew that a household deity turned up on the doormats of Oslo's West End every morning, and that god was called *Aftenposten*. People who got their names into *Aftenposten* were guaranteed attention at breakfast tables from Solli Plass all the way up to Holmenkollen. The only problem was that it was difficult to get in: 90 per cent of contributions were rejected at any one time.

Could he make a lot of money? That was difficult too. Be extremely handsome? Even after a load of operations, most of us still have some way to go there. Sport? You need talent. Blogging and social media? Some people managed. The extreme right-wing intellectual Fjordman, for example: a Norwegian man with a decent command of English who called Stoltenberg's government 'the most dhimmi [. . .] of all Western governments'. Fjordman made a name for himself not only in Norway but throughout Europe. 'Our own Fjordman is about to come in at third place among the most recognized/influential European anti-Jihad/anti-multiculti/anti-Marxist intellectuals/bloggers,' Breivik wrote enthusiastically in November 2009. 'I know it's hard to be a prophet in your own land but this is beyond all expectations. Congratulations Fjordman!;)'[16]

Fjordman was not to everybody's liking. He and those of the same opinion had been to some extent ridiculed in what Breivik called 'the mainstream media', but, within his niche, Fjordman was a big name. Fjordman was proof that culturally conservative intellectuals could find success outside *Aftenposten*. He was one of Breivik's great role models and, without knowing it, a kind of godfather for Justiciar Knight Andrew Berwick, Knights Templar Europe. It was a matter of finding your own niche. But Fjordman also had some kind of talent. What about those who did not?

The Fjordman phenomenon arose, according to himself, as a reaction to the terrorist attacks on New York and Washington in 2001. It would become the decade of terrorism, and so-called warblogs sprang up online like mushrooms. The shockwaves from 9/11 led to the faces of Osama bin Laden and Mohammed Atta being broadcast across the world. Europeans and Americans alike saw Islam in a new light. At the monitor in his bedroom, Breivik read *Inspire*, the English-language magazine of al-Qaeda, and watched videos of the terrorist network's bloodstained exploits.

There were many sides to the destruction of the twin towers, in terms of religion, society, politics and the media. The philosopher André Glucksmann also saw in the events in Manhattan an echo of Herostratus' ancient crime.[17] Behind the crime lay the criminals' desire to be seen, remembered and forever feared.

According to ancient tradition, Herostratus was an unknown citizen of Ephesus in Asia Minor. He was obsessed with his desire to be seen and remembered, but he had no gifts or talents. As a result, in the year 356 BC, he burnt down the city's Temple of Artemis, one of the Seven Wonders of the Ancient World. Herostratus was arrested, tortured and executed. The city of Ephesus made his memory taboo. His name would not be uttered or remembered: Herostratus would be punished not only by death but by being forgotten. Nevertheless, even the writers of the time overlooked the Ephesian ban, meaning that the expression *Herostratic fame* is a term that we still use.

Ancient writers saw two motives behind such meaningless destruction: the craving for eternal fame and the envy of mediocrity. The destruction was also a kind of art in itself, the expression of a pitch-black, negative aesthetic: burning the most beautiful thing on earth was awful, meaningless and astonishing at the same time. In the centuries and millennia since, many have followed in Herostratus' footsteps, professing the aesthetic of destruction, and many of them have also defined themselves, or been defined, as terrorists. Breivik's compendium was a veritable catalogue of expressions, methods and tales from the history of terrorism, and many Herostratic terrorists were not entirely unlike the man who boasted at the Palace Grill.

A few years after US incendiaries had obliterated Tokyo and the atomic bombs had struck Hiroshima and Nagasaki, Japan's most important religious building, Kinkaku-ji, Kyoto's Temple of the Golden Pavilion, also burnt down. The temple caught fire on 2 July 1950, and within a few hours the wooden building had been reduced to ashes. It was not the occupying US forces that had destroyed the shrine. The police arrested a twenty-two-year-old monk from the temple, Hayashi Yoken, who immediately admitted to the crime. A few months earlier, he had boasted to a prostitute in Kyoto that he 'might be in the newspapers soon'. Hayashi was known as a stubborn recluse, and during the court case it emerged that he felt that the other monks maligned and ridiculed him. He said that he was jealous of the beautiful temple and decided to destroy it in order 'to do something big'. The forensic psychiatrists established that he was paranoid and schizophrenic (the diagnosis was based, among other things, on the absurdity of Hayashi's crime). Nevertheless, Hayashi was sent to prison and to confinement in a psychiatric facility, where he died a few years later.

The best-known account of this incident is Yukio Mishima's documentary novel *The Temple of the Golden Pavilion*, the first draft of which bore the title 'Jealous of Beauty'. In Mishima's novel, the young monk is ugly, sickly and has a stammer. He is an outsider from early childhood. 'As can easily be imagined, a youth like myself came to entertain two opposing forms of power wishes,' Mishima's monk says. 'On the one hand I enjoyed imagining how one by one I would wreak punishment on my teachers and schoolmates who daily tormented me; on the other hand, I fancied myself as a great artist, endowed with the clearest vision – a veritable sovereign of the inner world.'[18]

The monk grows up in the shadow of the temple and eventually begins to hate it. 'Beautiful things [. . .] are now my most deadly enemies,' he says, before finally burning down the temple.[19] For Mishima, the fire is not only an expression of the stuttering monk's self-hate, his hatred towards beauty and his fantasies of power. On one level, the fire was a way of freeing himself from earthly beauty by destroying it, a kind of mystical and violent liberation related to suicide. But Mishima's fire is also connected to self-hate in occupied Japan, which in the early post-war period was indeed a burnt-out ruin. The burning temple was the ultimate gesture of powerlessness, the gospel of defeat.

Herostratus' successors throughout history have not been satisfied merely with destruction. Ancient writers pointed to a connection between destroying an iconic building and killing a prominent leader: both crimes are motivated by the perpetrator's desire to acquire the victim's fame. A number of assassins of recent times belong to the Herostratic tradition, and many of them have had similar psychiatric diagnoses to Hayashi. Some of them did also become celebrities themselves by killing or attempting to kill another celebrity, and are therefore celebrity killers in two senses. Some of the best-known cases are from the USA.

'I was an acute nobody. I had to usurp someone else's importance, someone else's success,' said Mark David Chapman after having killed John Lennon in 1980.[20] 'I was "Mr Nobody" until I killed the biggest Somebody on earth.' Before the killing, he had boasted to a girl he was chatting up: 'Something is going to happen soon. You're going to hear about me.'[21] Previously, he had told his wife that he was made to be famous, and that he was meant 'to be someone big'. During his court case, he was diagnosed as schizophrenic. The psychiatrists were of the opinion that he suffered from delusions of grandeur and also had a narcissistic personality disorder causing him to seek attention and fame to an abnormal degree.

Narcissism also seems to have affected Ted Kaczynski, known as the Unabomber. Kaczynski was an assistant professor of mathematics at Berkeley who retreated to a cabin in the woods of Montana and sent out letter bombs. Even though he was also diagnosed as paranoid schizophrenic, he was found sane and sentenced to prison for killing three people in connection with sixteen separate attacks between 1978 and 1995. Kaczynski wrote a manifesto that was published in the *New York Times* and *Washington Post* (in exchange for a promise to end his terrorist campaign), in which he gave voice to a kind of extreme right-wing ideology.

Kaczynski was opposed to modern society, especially to science and cold rationality. He described a conspiracy of 'leftist' forces consisting of communists and socialists, as well as feminists, minorities, homosexual people and 'political correctness' generally. He was motivated by revenge, he said, and sent bombs primarily to other academics. Apart from his ideological motives, Kaczynski's desire for attention and recognition was based on the fact he saw himself as 'someone special', someone more important than other people.[22] Kaczynski was characterized by his feeling of being a chosen individual, 'superior' to other people, and this suggested a possible narcissistic personality disorder.

According to Sigmund Freud, narcissism is connected to the child–mother relationship, an insecurity about one's own identity caused by the infant's separation from its mother being so traumatic that the child tries to re-create the original, symbiotic relationship. Psychoanalysts after Freud describe a narcissistic stage that young children must go through in order to construct a normal sense of self. Narcissism is a necessary starting point on the way towards a stable identity, but some people get stuck. People who are caught in the narcissistic stage alternate between being, on the one hand, angry towards anything or anybody that does not confirm their view of reality and, on the other, enraptured by grandiose thoughts of their own importance and excellence.

Just reading Kaczynski's manifesto was not good enough for Breivik. He plagiarized the article and wrote it into his compendium, with a few small changes.

Hayashi, Chapman and Kaczynski were all given quite similar and quite serious psychiatric diagnoses. The fact that they were nevertheless found legally sane and put in prison says something about the frequent place of Herostratic terrorists somewhere on a continuum between mental illness and religious or political extremism. The desire of narcissists to be seen as the special and exceptional people they are gives them a mandate to destroy and to kill. Other people and the rest of society have a merely instrumental role. They are tools that can confirm their grandiose self-image and exist solely in that function. From this perspective, the narcissist is in the right. As Hayashi said when questioned by police, 'I do not believe that I have done anything wrong.'[23]

Breivik also balanced the moral equations so that Berwick, the knight, had a mandate to kill and to destroy. 'In many ways, morality has lost its meaning in our struggle,' he wrote, giving himself the right to kill 'civilians'. While terrorism as a political tool is often imprecise, with the results of terrorist acts frequently being the opposite of their intentions, the success of Herostratic terrorism is independent of the crime's political consequences. Notoriety is achieved, even if the terrorist and his ideology are largely neither accepted nor respected. The ideology often seems a mere pretext. Whether or not the terrorist is liked is less important than being known.

When Breivik finally broke through the media sound barrier in Oslo city centre and was heard and seen, the response (as he had predicted) was almost exclusively negative, but not entirely (as he had also predicted), and he succeeded in achieving international fame, perhaps as the most famous Norwegian so far this century. An anonymous comment on the parenting website dinbaby.no, possibly meant as a provocation, but maybe not, put it like this: 'If I could choose to have sex with a celebrity, I would choose Anders Behring Breivik.'

The West End

It was around midnight when Anders Behring Breivik took a last sip of his raspberry-flavour spirits and put the drink aside. It was a short visit to Skaugum that mid-July evening. He did not return. He had a large and broad face from the front, smooth and pale like a statue. His gaze was distant and slightly indifferent, as if he were not all there. From the side, his face appeared oval, as if it belonged to another person. Who was the real Anders Behring Breivik?

On his way home from the Palace Grill, maybe he bade farewell to the part of town where he had lived almost his whole life, or maybe he just planned the route along which he would drive the Doblò on Friday afternoon, on his way out of the centre. In the second half of July, the nights were getting darker in Oslo, and the puddles on the asphalt glittered in the light from the street-lamps. The route Breivik took went through the middle of the West End, the better-off half of Oslo and Breivik's home of thirty-two years.

The West End is protected from what Breivik called the 'lesser privileged families'[24] of the East End by high property prices, sparse public transport and invisible walls. The idealized image of this marriage between wealth and culture, this dreamland with large gardens, is so strong that even people from the West End often believe in it, although the reality is certainly more complicated. From Solli Plass, Bygdøy Allé continued past the National Library, past the park by Norsk Hydro's offices and the memorial to the underground wartime press. The trunks of the chestnut trees vanished in the dark of night.

Towering at the top of Bygdøy Allé is the tall, dark outline of Frogner Church, where Breivik wanted to take his last communion before the operation that would cost his life – his 'martyr's mass', as he called it.[25] From the age of one and a half until he was three, he had lived in a flat on the hill behind the church, forgotten years that may have left more of a mark than could be seen on the surface. From Frogner Church, Bygdøy Allé turns slightly down again towards Olav Kyrres Plass and the Polish Embassy.

A few hundred metres away to the right was Breivik's old flat in Tidemands Gate, in Frogner, 'one of the most priciest [*sic*] areas in Oslo', as he described it. To the left was the taxi rank in Thomas Heftyes Plass, near Skarpsno, the fictional home of Wilfred Sagen. Sagen was the protagonist of Johan Borgen's 1955 novel *Lillelord* [Little lord], and is the ultimate West End character in Norwegian literature: the privileged rich man's son who became a Nazi.

At Olav Kyrres Plass, Breivik turned right and walked down Drammensveien towards Skøyen. At the roundabout by Skøyen station, Nedre Skøyen Vei went up the way to the low-rise blocks in Skøyen Terrasse. From there, the cycle path continued first a few hundred metres up a slight incline, and then down a steep slope among tall, broad-leaved trees to Nedre Silkestrå, a toytown-like car-free estate consisting of yellow-panelled low-rise housing from the early eighties with a view looking west towards Ullern Church. Anders Behring Breivik moved in there among the lilacs as a three-year-old in the autumn of 1982, together with his mother and half-sister.

From the roundabout by Skøyen station, Breivik followed Hoffsveien on towards Hoff. Maybe he threw a glance back towards Skøyen bus depot, where once he had become king of the number 32 bus? Hoff was still in the West End, but the detached villas here were mixed with flats and workers' houses. Factory workers had once lived here. They spoke a different sociolect from the indigenous population and built a People's House as a kind of socialist Trojan horse in the surrounding Conservative Party country.

Breivik set off on the last few metres home, crossing the tramlines by Hoff station and continuing past the Coop Mega supermarket up towards the anonymous low-rise building where his mother lived. When he reached home, he let himself into the ground-floor flat. Breivik went into his messy room. The computer was whirring. Long curtains concealed the window. From the wall, colourful, cartoonish and slightly disturbing faces by the graffiti artist Coderock stared down at him. The paintings were a memento of Breivik's own time as an 'artist' on Oslo's concrete walls, buses and metro carriages.

Breivik was tired after busy weeks with little sleep. The last week before the 'operation' was spent travelling back and forth to the farm at Åsta, a couple of hours north from Oslo, by train and taxi and hire car. He had already finished making a new Facebook profile, which said that he was a Christian and liked hunting, and set up a Twitter account in which he cited John Stuart Mill: 'One person with a belief is equal to the force of 100,000 who have only interests.'

This was only a part of the press pack that Breivik had prepared. The video was already done, ready to be uploaded, but the compendium, his 1,500-page pet project, the key to his distinctive split mind and one of the most remarkable testimonies that has ever been written in Norway, was still not ready. This enormous, disorganized manuscript pointed not only forward to his 'operation' but also, in a way, back to his childhood.

3

A West End Family[1]
Anders Behring Breivik's Childhood

'The Fatherless Civilisation'[2]

This time, Tove was furious. Jens could be so strangely insensitive. There were few faults to find with him, as he was a great husband in many respects, but he could sometimes be distant and rigid, principled in the wrong way – like now. Anders himself was not making a big fuss about it. The little boy with his milky, almost transparent complexion sniffled and his narrow eyes ran, but he was not whining.

'Come on!' said Tove.

She stomped off down the gravel path with Anders in tow behind her, slammed the little white wooden gate shut after them and walked over to the car. She sat down behind the wheel, while Anders crawled into the back. In the mirror, Tove saw him put on his safety belt. His face was red because of the allergic reaction, and he was possibly upset too. She turned out onto the road, changed gear and set off for Cabourg.

Behind them was the little white summer cottage, an old half-timbered farmhouse with a thatched roof. On the lawn outside, which was as straight as an arrow, Jens Breivik walked along pushing the mower. Although Tove had asked him to wait to cut the grass until Anders had gone home, Jens had stuck to his guns. The grass had to be mown, irrespective of whether it made his little son from Norway poorly and gave him the sniffles.

Normandy was at its most beautiful in the summer holidays, but Tove was seething with rage. When the little boy visited them, surely Jens could change his routine. Anders did suffer when he had his attacks. He was a sensitive boy and cried the time they drove over a mouse. Anders was not with them very often: sometimes at the holiday cabin in Telemark and here at the cottage in Bassenville. There was a farm nearby, and Anders was always thrilled to see the animals. He was sweet and well mannered, easy to deal with, confident and happy when guests came and played badminton with him. A wary and slightly meticulous boy who looked up to his father but stuck close to her, his step-mother.

The road wound between dense spinneys, past green openings and yellow fields on the way towards Caen. The first time Tove had met Jens Breivik was in London in the sixties, twenty years earlier. Tove had more or less done a runner from a summer job at a psychiatric hospital. She was in her early twenties and was fed up with the hospital. Tove thought it was the English doctors and nurses who were the real lunatics at the asylum. It was no place for her. She loved being in England but had to find something else to do. She turned up at the Norwegian Embassy to borrow the phone book, where she met a man staring at her with scrutinizing eyes. 'Can you type?' he asked.

It was Jens Breivik. That question would be the start of a career in Norwegian diplomatic missions that would last forty years and take her from London via New Orleans to Ankara and Shanghai. She met Jens again many years later, and this time they got married. That was in 1983. The same year, they ended up in court in Oslo in an attempt to obtain custody of Anders. For some time it actually looked as if the four-year-old might end up with his father and Tove in their diplomatic residence flat in Paris.

Tove looked up at the mirror again.

'Are you feeling bad?'

'Don't ask,' he answered, all grown-up.

'We're going to Cabourg,' said Tove. 'First to McDonald's and then to the beach. OK?'

'You're really nice, Tove,' Anders smiled from the back seat.

A Suspicious Smile

'Anders has become a contact-adverse, slightly anxious, passive child, but with a manic kind of defence, restlessly active and with a feigned, aversive smile [. . .]. It will be very important to take steps at an early stage to prevent the boy developing more serious psychopathology,' wrote a psychologist from Statens senter for barne- og ungdomspsykiatri [the State Centre for Child and Youth Psychiatry; SSBU] in

March 1983, in an application to Barnevernet [the Child Welfare Service] for Anders to be given a foster home.[3]

The team from the SSBU responsible for reporting on the case were extremely concerned. They were of the opinion that the boy was subject to a deficit of parental care and concluded that he should be taken away from his mother. This was a rare and dramatic recommendation from the SSBU, presented in slightly woolly professional terms. An 'insufficient care situation'?

The portrait of the four-year-old with a 'feigned, aversive smile' dates from around the same time that Jens and Tove got married in London. In this period, Jens also received telephone calls from Oslo.[4] It was his ex-wife's neighbours, who told him they had heard noises from her flat, and that the little boy and his half-sister were often home alone in the evenings. Something was wrong in the small family, which from the outside did not appear particularly unusual: a beautiful woman in her mid-thirties with two timid, blond children.

Anders Behring Breivik was born in Oslo on 13 February 1979 and moved to London as a baby. His father, Jens Breivik, was originally from northern Norway and came 'from a strict background with little communication in the family'.[5] He trained in business administration and economics at the Norwegian School of Economics in Bergen and became a diplomat.

Anders' mother, Wenche Behring, was a thirty-three-year-old auxiliary nurse from Kragerø in Telemark. They appeared to be a typical couple of the generation of 1968: a social climber from northern Norway who had made it all the way to the Ministry of Foreign Affairs, thanks to the revolution in education, and his princess from southern Norway. Both of them were incomers to Oslo with no close family in the area and, in a way, were true children of the post-war Labour Party state's social mobility and opportunities. As a diplomat, Jens Breivik served governments of both socialist and conservative persuasions, but he was an ardent Labour Party man himself.[6] The couple both had children from previous relationships; Jens had two sons and a daughter, while Wenche had a six-year-old daughter.

The marriage between Jens and Wenche was short-lived. Anders' parents separated when he was one and a half, and his mother moved back to Norway together with her two children, taking up residence in Jens Breivik's ministerial accommodation in Fritzners Gate, a short street just behind Frogner Church. Wenche saw her ex-husband as a monster, a 'devil' incarnate,[7] while he thought that she was 'mad' and impossible to talk with.[8]

The conflict did not end with their separation, and, in the years that followed, the little boy became a battlefield for his parents and eventually an apple of discord. Jens saw little of his son over the next few years, even when he was in Oslo, but he tried to support him and his ex-wife financially.

When Anders was two years old, in the summer of 1981, Wenche contacted the social care office to ask for help. She explained that she did not have any family or social network in Oslo, she was physically and mentally worn out, and she thought that Anders was a demanding child, 'restless and lately more and more violent, capricious and full of unpredictable quirks'. She often worked double shifts, she said, and took many night shifts to make ends meet. She asked for weekend respite care for Anders.

The application was granted a few months later, but the arrangement did not work well, and Wenche ended it because 'the home did not suit Anders'. The respite care family reacted badly to the mother, according to the SSBU report, seeing her as strange and difficult. They told the social care office of bizarre incidents.[9]

But this was only the beginning of an acutely difficult home situation. The relationship between Anders and his mother was full of violent conflicts and tearful reconciliations. Wenche was apparently quite unstable. She could be furious with the little boy one moment, only to shower him with affection immediately afterwards. 'Double communication' was how the SSBU later characterized it: she pushed the boy away and pulled him towards her in a way that was extremely confusing for him.

It seemed as if Anders was paying dearly for the difficult relationship between his parents: his mother took sides with his big sister and attacked Anders.[10] She treated him as if he were an extension of the despised Jens.[11] Even if the boy was neither mentally nor physically disabled, was he perhaps a demanding child after all? It was as if he had an unquenchable thirst. His mother was concerned about how he would gulp down his red fruit-juice drink and wondered whether he might be diabetic. She felt provoked by his smile, which she saw as inappropriate, condescending and disdainful. Since Anders was only three years old, disdainful and condescending were strange adjectives to use, but Wenche's frustration about the difficult connection with her son was maybe not just down to her alone.

In the autumn of 1982, Wenche and her children moved into a modern flat with five rooms in the Nedre Silkestrå housing cooperative. Jens had lent a hand with the deposit, perhaps quietly hoping that more spacious and pleasant surroundings might help to calm the situation. The family was in contact with the family welfare centre in Christies Gate several times, where they were especially concerned about Anders, as they believed that 'in emergency situations it would be tremendously difficult for the mother to deal with' her son. The mother described her three-year-old boy as 'aggressive, clingy and hyperactive'.

In early 1983, she contacted the family welfare centre again and was referred to the SSBU at Gaustad, where the small family was admitted for observation in the day unit for all of three weeks in February 1983. When they arrived, Wenche appeared disorientated, demanding and suspicious. She could not find the way up the hill from Gaustad, even though there was really only one road to take. She was preoccupied with money and demanded that the SSBU pay for taxis for her and her children throughout the rest of their stay. A team of eight people, including a psychologist and a senior consultant in psychiatry, observed how the family functioned together and how they functioned alone in other contexts.

Anders spent his fourth birthday with the SSBU. He was tested in many contexts and, among other things, spent a number of sessions in the supervised playroom. He went into a room with a sandbox, as well as boxes containing various toys, dolls and a drawing table. Against the wall was the 'world in a cupboard', a cupboard with many different little figures of animals and people, including people from different nations, soldiers and Indians. Through play, the boy would act out his inner world and show what he was thinking about while at the same time demonstrating how he related to the observer who was with him. Normally, children would find their way to the toys that interested them, take them over to the sandbox and play with them. All the toys made it possible for children to depict conflicts and situations that might characterize their own lives. But, over the course of the sessions Anders spent in the playroom, not much happened. Some of the time he would sit passively among all the toys. Other times he would wander about restlessly. He kept his distance from the specialist who was in the room with him.

It was as if the boy did not know how to play. When he played shop games with other children, it was 'the functioning of the till that interested him, not the game around it. [He] lacks imagination and empathy.' Although his language was 'well developed', the SSBU concluded that 'he has difficulties expressing himself emotionally [. . .] and is almost entirely lacking in spontaneity or elements of joy or pleasure'. An inability to express emotions is known by psychologists as alexithymia.

How could it be that this little boy, who otherwise had 'well-developed language', was not able to put words to his feelings? Was it because he was unable to articulate himself, or was it because he had nothing to articulate?

In child psychiatry, there has been an increasing focus on the concept of attachment.[12] In short, attachment theory is a theory of psychological development which claims that children undergo a critical phase of development in the period from when they are about six months old until they are about three. During this period, the brain develops quickly and the foundations are laid for how the child, and later the adult, will relate to other people. A child's relationships with its parents or other central care-givers are decisive factors in this developmental stage. When a parent comforts an anxious child, this gives the child security, but if the child seeks out its mother (or father) in order to be comforted, and experiences rejection, neglect or punishment, this creates insecurity.

If in this critical phase children consistently receive inadequate responses to their needs, the probability dramatically increases that they will be given a serious psychiatric diagnosis later in life. This phenomenon is known as a lack of maternal care (even though the primary care-giver does not necessarily have to be the mother – it could be the father or other adults). Play observation was one of the tests that indicated that Anders lacked basic security and had poor attachment; he was 'contact-adverse', as the psychologist wrote. He lacked a strategy for relating to his mother or other adults, and would wander around. In psychiatry, this is called a disorganized attachment pattern, a relatively typical form of behaviour when 'the harbour of security is, at the same time, the source of fear'.[13] There was nothing wrong with the boy's intelligence; he was not mentally impaired. His problem lay elsewhere, and was reminiscent of what would later be found in studies of Romanian orphans.

Anders was not given any diagnosis by the SSBU, but he was described as a 'divergent' child, and the picture the team painted of the little boy brings to mind partly what is today described as reactive attachment disorder (RAD), a relatively rare and serious diagnosis.[14] There is little research into how children with attachment disorders develop over their childhood and adolescence and on into adulthood. The little that has been done suggests that, although most have problems (it appears that there is a tendency towards narcissism and lack of empathy), there is considerable variation in the effects of poor attachment.

One of the interesting aspects of attachment theory, according to the psychoanalyst Peter Fonagy, is that it can explain transgenerational effects – in other words, why parents' (especially mothers') attachment patterns are inherited.[15] Fonagy also links empathy to attachment. He claims that attachment is a decisive factor in the development of a self-image and an ability to think about internal mental states, both those of others and one's own.[16] Fonagy calls this ability 'mentalizing'. As soon as a child understands that its mother is a separate individual from itself, it tries to anticipate or understand what its mother thinks and feels. The child mentalizes. This is the first step in the development of empathy, but, if a child does not feel that it is safe to imagine what its mother is thinking or feeling, this development will stall. A poor mentalizing ability can lead to misunderstanding social situations, a lack of empathy, and perhaps seeing oneself as empty or as a zombie.

The observation team from the SSBU described Anders as 'mildly pedantic' and 'extremely neat', thereby hinting at a nervous boy with signs of compulsive behaviour. But, although he was a 'slightly anxious, passive child', they still thought that he could function 'relatively normally' together with other children and with adults. The SSBU concluded that 'Anders has contact abilities', which ruled out extensive developmental disorders such as classic autism. Their concerns about him were due mainly to his home conditions – in other words, his relationship with his mother. Since Anders grew up without his father, his mother was his only carer.

Even though the focus of this old case was on Anders, it also painted a picture of an unsettled and possibly unbalanced woman. When the little boy's mother described him as 'aggressive' and 'clingy' – which he may have been, although this was not observed by others – perhaps she was also painting a kind of self-portrait. This self-portrait was confirmed by the SSBU, which described how she confused the boy by alternately pushing him away and pulling him towards her. The mother was 'uncritical', unable to see herself in the situation: everything was other people's fault. She was not able to set predictable boundaries and limits for her little boy. There was often a lot of noise at home, as if from partying, while at other times the young children were left home alone. Either one thing or its polar opposite. Black and white. Rage and remorse. For a child, unstable and unpredictable behaviour from their closest care-giver can be just as emotionally destructive as living with an aggressive or violent parent.

Psychiatrists call this emotional abuse, and research suggests that the long-term effects of such a 'deficit of care' can be just as serious as physical abuse. In later life, these children are at much greater risk of mental illnesses and suicide. Even when child welfare and child psychiatrists perform major interventions, the results are relatively poor. Children who have experienced poor attachment in the first years of their life will by the age of eight normally be restless and unpopular, with poor social skills. In adolescence, they will frequently become 'aggressive towards friends, also when they eventually fall in love, and they will often be rejected. They will nonetheless describe themselves as much more popular than they are, and there is much to suggest that they have particular problems understanding social interactions and reading other people's feelings.'[17] The consequences of poor attachment are not always easy to spot. Intelligent people may periodically be able to hide their problems, either partially or completely. Disciplined people unable to read social interactions can still train themselves in social skills. Sooner or later, however, the consequences are brought to light.

The SSBU thought that Anders was subject to a deficit of care from his mother. They recommended the most drastic measure at the disposal of child welfare: taking him into care. Taking children away from their parents into care is something that happens in Norway only in exceptional circumstances. It can be traumatic for parents and children alike, and is recommended only in emergencies. In 2006, there were 7,292 children living in foster homes and 1,386 in child welfare institutions,[18] which equates to approximately 0.5 per cent of children in the country. Many of them, however, were moved out of their homes without having to resort to compulsory care orders or intervention by child welfare. In 1983, it is likely that the figures were considerably lower.

Anders' situation was, therefore, quite unusual. He might not have been one in a thousand, but he was not far off. In a number of cases, a deficit of care can be situational. The mother might be temporarily depressed after giving birth or after a break-up. A difficult financial situation and a weak social network can make the situation even more challenging. Alcohol or substance abuse might feature. All these problems may be temporary or situational, but, if the SSBU reached the conclusion they did, this was because they did not think things would change in this small family, so the report entails quite an unambiguous judgement of the mother's ability as a carer. Anders' mother could not deal with him, she felt provoked and was practically falling apart, so the SSBU thought it would be best for everyone, including the mother, if he were placed in a foster home. Even though his sister did not present the same kind of challenge to his mother and avoided more of the conflicts at home, the SSBU recommended that child welfare keep an eye on her development too.

Anders' mother was on an emotional rollercoaster, although, according to the SSBU, she calmed down a little during the period she stayed at Gaustad. She requested a respite home but cut off the arrangement. She agreed to a foster home placement but changed her mind. She complained about a lack of support from Jens Breivik but did not say that he was helping the family financially. She wanted assistance from the boy's father but flatly rejected him when he came onto the scene in the custody case. Although she sought out help, she described the boy as the problem: she was worn out because he was 'demanding'. Anders may have been demanding, but there were two people in their relationship, and the mother was apparently incapable of self-reflection in any meaningful way. She was an innocent victim, as she saw it, and maybe in some ways she was.

In the SSBU account, the mother appears as a person with problems far beyond being worn out, isolated and in a difficult financial situation. If her problems were caused by her challenging situation or by depression after her separation and after Anders' birth, a change in behaviour or a glimpse of self-insight might have been expected. Psychologists link statements of the type 'I hate you, don't leave me' to what is known as a borderline or emotionally unstable personality. Such people can have normal intelligence but may appear in many ways like children – immature. These are people who often function poorly in relationships with their families, who have mood swings and poor impulse control, who see things in black and white, who are unable to put themselves in other people's shoes and who have little self-insight.

Immaturity in parents and a resultant deficit of care often originates in the parents' own upbringing, as Fonagy indicated. Many might have lost parents at a young age, while others will have grown up with depressed, violent or immature (borderline) parents of their own. According to the SSBU's generally carefully worded account, which was based mainly on information provided by her, Wenche Behring had herself had an 'extremely challenging upbringing, initially with physical illness and later mental illness in the form of her mother's paranoid delusions'. Her mother came from 'an affluent home' in the West End of Oslo but married a master bricklayer in Kragerø, a small town on the coast to the south of Oslo. Her mother caught polio while she was pregnant with Wenche and had to use a wheelchair, for which she apparently later blamed her daughter. Wenche's father died when she was young. She had a close relative who was disabled, which was a matter of stigma. Disabilities were to be hidden; it was important to keep up a façade.

It could, therefore, appear as if Anders Behring Breivik had a genetic disposition towards mental illness on his mother's side and also figured as part of a chain of attachment-related disorders spanning generations. His mother could almost appear as an aggressor in her relationship to her young son, but, from another point of view, she was a victim herself. Parental rejection is linked to aggression in adulthood. A rejected child stores anger and hatred almost like a pressure cooker that can burst at any given moment. Perhaps Anders' birth triggered a depression that brought anger and hatred to the surface. This chaos emerged when Wenche could not find the way to the SSBU.

Together, Anders and his mother wandered around like aliens on Earth, visitors from another planet who could not understand what they should feel or what they should do in the playroom. They were united in a deeply ambivalent relationship, occasionally escaping restlessly to seek confirmation from the outside world, but always finding their way back to each other.

In May 1983, child welfare backed up the SSBU's conclusion that Anders should go to a foster home. At the same time, Jens got in touch from Paris, trying to find out what was happening in Oslo. Concerned neighbours convinced him and Tove that the situation at home was excessively turbulent for the young boy. When Jens came on the scene, Wenche became intransigent. She opposed not only the compulsory care order but also the compromise suggested by child welfare of another weekend respite home for Anders.

In spite of the SSBU's unambiguous and robust recommendations that Anders should be removed from his home, his mother's refusal was the turning point in the case. Wenche Behring mobilized all her efforts in the fight against her ex-husband.[19] In August, when Jens gained access to the SSBU report in its entirety, the neighbours' warnings were confirmed. After having read the dramatic description of his son's conditions, he demanded custody of Anders. Wenche refused, and the conflict ended up in court that autumn.

'Do you like children?' the judge asked Tove in court in October 1983.

Maybe he was not convinced that Anders' step-mother would be there for him. The judge was an elderly man, a representative of the post-war generation, and possibly also of 1950s values and principles.[20] In addition, he was going by the judicial precedent by which the presumption of maternal custody applied in family law cases. According to this rule, the mother was seen as the principal carer. The child was in practice hers, while the father and the state child psychiatrists came second. Besides, the mother had contacted the authorities herself to seek help, and, if she was so terrible, why had the SSBU not asked for the half-sister to be taken away from her mother too?

On the mother's side, a nursery manager testified that Anders was functioning well at nursery. According to a source from the SSBU, this testimony was contrary to the report from the head of section in the nursery who had day-to-day responsibility for Anders, which apparently echoed the findings of the SSBU and described a boy with problems. The judge sat in his black robes listening to the testimony of the eloquent and much younger psychologist from the SSBU. The polite sitting hid a generational conflict in which the old view of family collided with the 1968 generation's individualistic opinion that the child should be the focus. The judge also had to decide to what extent the new technocracy of state child psychiatry should be brought to bear and how far the influence of the state should extend to the family. What was a family?

In spite of the SSBU's conclusion regarding a deficit of care and its unambiguous recommendation that Anders' situation had to be changed, the court ruled in favour of the mother. The verdict was in line with the strong position of mothers in family cases. Wenche had her revenge on Jens. The judge appointed two experts to report on the case (at the cost of the claimant – i.e., the father) and decided that Anders would stay with his mother for the time being. The report would be expensive for Jens, and the outcome would be uncertain.

Jens and Tove withdrew their claim, and their lawyer wrote that 'they would like to have Anders if his current situation is unsatisfactory, but they do not wish to tarnish his current situation in order to obtain him'. Jens underlined that his wish to take on custody of his son still stood. If the relevant authorities thought that Anders' situation was unsatisfactory, he wrote, it was their responsibility to do something about it. The SSBU commented on the judgement in a letter on 28 October 1983: 'We stand by our conclusion that Anders' care situation is so unsound that he is in danger of developing a more serious psychopathology.' At the same time, this implicitly states that the boy was already suffering from psychopathology, that he had mental problems to a certain degree, even though the SSBU did not make any clear diagnosis.

Such a note of concern on the SSBU's part was very unusual – yet another expression of how seriously the experts viewed the situation, and perhaps also an expression of their irritation at having been disregarded by the judge. As a result, the case went back to child welfare, which carried out another report in early 1984.

The child welfare report from April 1984, based on three visits to the family's new home, described what appeared to be a different family. Once again, Anders' smile caught the attention of the social worker, but it was ascribed the opposite value to the SSBU's 'feigned, aversive smile'. Anders 'was a pleasant, relaxed boy with a warm smile that makes him instantly likeable', wrote the caseworker. Anders and his sister were 'well-mannered', and Anders played nice and quietly with Plasticine and Playmobil. The SSBU had thought the boy did not know how to play, but now he was showing a different face. Or was it just a façade? His mother was 'in control'. She did not 'change her expression or get agitated in difficult situations' with Anders.

In this account there is an implicit description of how the mother had been seen before, as someone who changed her expression, who became agitated and who was not in control. A worn-out single mother, not very resourceful and practically without any support from her children's fathers. But the housing co-operative on the edge of Frognerparken [Frogner Park] was a delightful place in springtime, and the flat was very spacious for the small family. How much of this was a façade and what was behind it? Was the mother really in control of the small family at Silkestrå? And what was her little boy really like?

The young Anders' smile, like that of the Mona Lisa, is open to interpretation. The 'feigned, aversive' smile has now become 'warm', making him 'instantly likeable'. Anders had good reports from the nursery in Frogner Park. There was apparently nothing remarkable to observe about him. Since his home situation appeared stable, child welfare concluded that he should stay with his mother, but they introduced a cautious supervision measure, which meant monthly home visits. The caseworker indicated the possibility that new crises might arise, and that Wenche could be quite temperamental and indecisive: 'We base our proposal for supervision on the fact that the mother has repeatedly made requests asking for help in emergencies, e.g., help to have her children put into foster homes, weekend homes etc., and that she has then often changed her mind regarding the necessity and usefulness of this.' But even this measure was not put into action. Child welfare dropped the case, which had been based on a note of concern from the SSBU, just two months later. There was no particular reason except that the mother said she did not need any further supervision, intervention or help.

The years went by. The small family seemed to get on well. Had something serious really happened between them in the early eighties? Perhaps the SSBU team had been frightened of their own shadows. What was really hidden in their dossier? After all, it was the mother who had taken the initiative to ask for assistance and help. The thought of what might have happened if child welfare had taken the report from the SSBU more seriously, or if the judge had ruled in favour of the father, became an increasingly irrelevant 'if'.

According to Tove, Anders never mentioned this topic again. His memories of his earliest years had gone, he said. But, even if it is true that he has forgotten his early childhood, his experiences may not necessarily just have vanished. They could have consequences in the form of 'uneven development', according to attachment theory and to the SSBU. Childhood traumas can be like fermenting sourdough, a dark source of shame and hatred. Talking with the court-appointed psychiatrists in prison, Breivik stated that he could not remember his care situation being evaluated by the SSBU, but he knew that there had been a custody case and that it probably would have been best if his father and Tove had won, so that he could have lived with them.

Since those years, however, Breivik has mainly been keen to maintain his successful West End façade. For the most part, his description of his time at Silkestrå is like a rose-tinted sales brochure. Breivik later wrote about his childhood in his compendium: '[A]ll in all, I consider myself privileged and I feel I have had a privileged upbringing with responsible and intelligent people around me.'[21]

The Dark Sources

The place-name Hoff indicates there was once a pagan temple near Skøyen. A thousand years ago, the towering ash trees shielding Nedre Silkestrå were used to hang up sacrifices to the Norse gods, whether these were dead animals or perhaps people, but then the Norse religion was banished with sword and axe by an aggressive religion originating from the Mediterranean, namely Christianity. New names were coined, such as Abbediengen [literally 'abbey meadow'] and street names such as Konventveien ['Convent Street'] and Priorveien ['Priory Street'], after the monastic property in the area during the High Middle Ages. The area went from being a sacred grove where Thor and Freyr were worshipped to pastureland and a herb garden for the monks from the island of Hovedøya.

Nedre Silkestrå was just beyond Frogner Park and had the character of a paradise garden. Anders and the other children ran and cycled freely along the paths between the yellow houses or disappeared among lush thickets of lilacs and raspberry bushes. A tawny owl shrieked on dark August nights. The landscape was neither a sacred grove nor a monastic garden any more, but because of the rich deciduous woodland – with ash, elm and poplar – the municipality of Oslo had given the woods around Silkestrå the status of a protected biotope. Behind the wooden fences of Konventveien were beautiful villa façades of brick, stucco and painted panels.

Tending to façades is not an unusual activity among the tennis courts and fruit trees of Oslo's West End. The area's aura of success was reflected in wealth statistics.[22] The West End also glittered with cultural capital and the discreet inheritance of state-building patricians. Of course, success is measured not just in terms of the number of boats people own, the location of their holiday cabins or how many acres their gardens have. A career and a good education are also important. Christian Tybring-Gjedde, the leader of the Oslo branch of the Progress Party, lived at Smestad and had studied at Loyola University Chicago. The foreign minister, Jonas Gahr Støre, had gone to Ris Lower Secondary School, studied in Paris at the elite Institut d'études politiques, known as Sciences Po, and later worked at Harvard.

The higher up you are, the further there is to fall and the longer the shadows you cast. The West End is quite simply not a good place to fail. Breivik describes his West End background as being like a hallmark: 'I'm from the West side of Oslo, and most of my current friends are from privileged families (middle or higher middle class). There are many factors that separate us from lesser privileged families on the East side. The essential factors are the ethics and principles you adapt in your community.'[23]

Wilfred 'Little Lord' Sagen is the ultimate West End character in Norwegian literature. *De mørke kilder* [The dark sources] was the title chosen by Johan Borgen for his 1956 novel depicting this Norwegian Nazi. Wilfred grew up in a rich man's home where he apparently lacked nothing, apart from one thing. His father committed suicide when Wilfred was young, and even though the Little Lord has the perfect exterior, there is darkness within him. He has to be the best at everything. He plays the role of a polite, affable and promising young pillar of society with great talents, but in the evenings he sneaks out.

The gifted young pianist is a gang leader. Since he does not have any real heart or personality, only playing roles, he never grows up and never becomes an individual. Instead, he is split, or doubled, to borrow terms from psychoanalysis. The Little Lord re-emerges at night as a brutal pack animal. He beats up an old Jew and ends up being robbed by two working-class lads while on a drinking spree in the East End's Grünerløkka, in what is probably the first literary depiction of child thieves in Oslo. Borgen describes this Norwegian Nazi as the result not only of a split consciousness but also of a split city: the East End and West End are like night and day.

The psychological fall down into the abyss of Nazism has its sociological response in the fear of being declassed. The potential comedown hangs over the young Sagen heir like a sword of Damocles, and Nazism is his solution. The Little Lord's exploits in Grünerløkka took place almost a hundred years ago, but the city is still split today if you look at election results and research into living conditions. In the West End, life expectancy is longer, income is higher, the constituents are whiter and the election results are a deeper shade of blue – in other words, more conservative.

On an August day in 1986, Anders stood with his satchel on his back at Smestad Primary School. It was his first day, and, as he peered up at the large, yellow, brick building, he may have known that both King Harald and his son, Crown Prince Haakon Magnus, had been pupils there when they were young princes. Although Anders appeared to be a normal, happy boy who was good at school, according to his step-mother Tove he would later resent school. Like many of the children of parents from the 1968 generation, Anders was critical of what he regarded as their legacy. A shadow fell over his school years, but it is difficult to say whether that was in the late eighties or later.

At Smestad, as he later wrote, Anders remembered 'being forced to complete mandatory knitting and sewing courses':

> These courses were first implemented in various Western European countries as a result of Marxist revolution which started all the way back in the 1930s but had its climax around 1968. These mandatory knitting and sewing courses were implemented with the goal of deliberately contribute [*sic*] to feminise European boys in their insane quest to attempt to create the Marxist utopia consisting of 'true equality between the sexes'. I remember I dreaded these courses as it felt very unnatural and was a complete waste of time.[24]

As it appeared to Anders later, or at least as he described it in his compendium, there were many things that were the fault of the so-called '68ers.

The meticulous young boy, who knew about clothes and colour combinations from an early age and who lived with his mum and big sister, later felt that he had been 'feminized', as if he had been contaminated by effeminacy, softness and feelings. He saw a connection between the '68ers and decay not only at school or for the European man, but also with regard to morality and sexuality.

'An alarming number of young girls in Oslo, Norway start giving oral sex from the age of 11 to 12,'[25] he wrote – in other words, while they were still at primary school, which in Norway lasts until the age of thirteen. 'I feel shame on behalf of my city, my country and my civilisation. I loathe the post war conservatives for not being able to halt the Marxist Cultural Revolution manifested through the '68 generation.'[26] Although he viewed his childhood through blurry lenses and the factual basis of his assessment is dubious, the consequences for him – 'shame' and 'loathing' – could be just as real.

Breivik, a child of '68er parents, felt shame and loathing towards the thought of the Norway constructed by the generation of 1968, and the Norway towards which he later expressed such hatred was described largely as a gendered being: as a woman – emotional, unstable, promiscuous. Was this perhaps the nightmare vision of his own worn-out mother in the early eighties?

As I gradually went deeper into Breivik's compendium, I came closer to his own upbringing. The most emotionally charged sections deal with his anger and frustration towards women generally and his mother in particular. Breivik described how the decay caused by the '68ers had affected his own family. Both his mother and his father were apparently '68ers. His mother was also a feminist, he thought. 'I have had a privileged upbringing with responsible and intelligent people around me,' Breivik wrote, while at the same time having a bad word to say about all of them. The army officer who was his mother's partner while Breivik was a teenager was 'likeable', but also 'a very primitive sexual beast'.[27]

As for his mother and his sister, he left no stone unturned in describing how the moral decay let loose by the '68ers had influenced their behaviour and health. In a harangue about sexual morality and sexually transmitted diseases, he brought them in, describing their sex lives and subsequent health problems. He concluded by saying that his mother and sister 'have not only shamed me but they have shamed themselves and our family. A family that was broken in the first place due to secondary effects of the feministic/sexual revolution.'[28]

Parents' sins are visited upon their children. The description of his family is personal and brutal, written in a kind of moral rage. He was also a victim of moral deterioration, he thought, since his mother and sister had brought shame on him.

What according to Anders was a normal middle-class background emerges at the same time as a complicated family picture characterized by constant ruptures and great distances. The 1968 generation's concept of a 'fragmented family' is present to an almost caricatured degree: Breivik grew up in a maelstrom of half-siblings, ex-stepparents and various families with which he was half-connected. Tove was concerned about this aspect of his upbringing. It would be hard for any child, and it was remarkable that Anders took it so well.

'One day Jens will be proud of me,' said Anders, who always thought positively.

Strangely enough, the only one of Anders' close relatives who gets away more or less scot-free from the fury of the compendium is his father. 'The thing is that he is just not very good with people,' Anders wrote apologetically. But the reality was that Jens Breivik left his son to his own devices, especially after he separated from Tove. Throughout his upbringing, Anders' step-mother emerges as his only normal adult point of reference. It was when she came into his father's life that Jens took the initiative to seek custody of his son and, later, to spend time with him. When she disappeared, his relationship with his teenage son also came to an end. Jens broke off contact, which he later blamed on Anders. But Tove, who met up with Anders and with his half-siblings, understood some of the children's resentment towards Jens. They tried contacting him but were rejected. Jens Breivik was a distant and absent father. And this was a source of conflict, not just between Jens and his children, but also in Jens and Tove's life together.

The Cats of Ayia Napa

There was a squeak – a peculiar, raspy sound that appeared to be coming from somewhere far away, yet at the same time nearby. Tove was wide awake now, and blinked in the darkness of the hotel room. She heard Anders moving in the other bed. He was awake too. Tove switched on the bedside light, and there was that squeaking yet again. There was no question: the sound was coming from somewhere in their room. Tove and Anders looked at each other.

'What is it?' asked Anders. He was fourteen years old, no longer a boy and on the cusp of adolescence.

'I think', Tove said, 'I think there's something under your bed.'

Anders' bed was against the wall. Tove switched on the main light. They bent down and Tove carefully lifted the sheet hanging down from his mattress. There was something small and dark beneath his bed. A head and some paws. It was a cat, and there was something hanging out of it. The cat mewed again, a hideous sound, and Tove suddenly realized what was going on. It was giving birth. The small lumps next to the mother were kittens.

'Oh dear,' said Tove.

'Cool!' said Anders.

'Please, Tove,' Anders pleaded the next morning, 'do you have to tell them? Can't I just keep one of the little kittens?' But Tove was adamant. She went down to reception and asked them to remove the cats.

Anders was completely fascinated by the little family beneath his bed, so small and helpless, and Tove was not sure whether he had slept at all that night. He stared at the shivering blind lumps of life and watched the mother licking them clean and lifting them by the scruffs of their necks. The kittens made their first, trembling movements. Their small voices mewed. They crawled up against their mother, blind and seeking out warmth. Gradually, the small balls of fluff dried off. There was fur on the unprotected bodies lying at their mother's side, drinking their first meal. The mystery of life. The kittens lay against their mother in a fan formation, like a crystal formed of the will to live. None of them were bigger than the palm of his hand. Perhaps he wanted to give one of the small kittens a home in Oslo – care for it, give it warmth, look after it. Because what would happen to them here? Would their mother be able to look after her small family? How would the small kittens fare? Perhaps there was something exciting about such a defenceless creature. You could do whatever you wanted with it. But it was no use begging. The cat family was gone when they returned to their room that evening.

In the winter of 1993, Tove separated from Jens Breivik, but she stressed that she did not want to lose contact with his children, especially the youngest, Anders, with whom she had always got on well. She had sat him on her lap when he was little, treated him as her own child. She decided to take him with her on an Easter holiday to do something he would enjoy. While Anders' classmates at Ris Lower Secondary School sat in traffic on their way up to their families' holiday cabins in the mountains, he and his step-mother went on board a charter flight to Ayia Napa in Cyprus. All the packing and organizing had gone well, as Tove had always been on good terms with Anders' mother.

The days they were in Cyprus went by in a flash. They stayed at a hotel right by the beach, and the water was already warm. They had been taking holidays together for ten years, and Tove knew well what Anders liked to do. He was older now, and more daring. Tove watched in surprise as Anders zoomed about by the beach on a jet ski, sending the water spraying. Although he was a careful boy, he had another side too. At Smestad Primary School, he was one of the cool kids in the Skøyen Killers gang. He was active and quick-witted in many ways. Anders was adept at fixing all kinds of technical things, sorting out settings on TVs or video machines when they went wrong. He had evidently learnt something from the computer games in which he was so interested. Tove had a soft spot for the types who did well at school, and Anders reminded her a little of his father in that way: he knew a lot of things and used foreign words as if it were the most natural thing in the world. They travelled around a lot and only came back to the hotel in the evenings, tired and happy.

In Larnaca, they went up to the demarcation line, the border between the Turkish and Greek parts of Cyprus. There were watch-towers, barbed wire and barriers, remains of the war that had raged in the seventies. The border was like a weak echo of the iron curtain that had divided Europe into two ideological camps for forty-five years and had just been dismantled: a small and forgotten provincial version of Checkpoint Charlie. The churches on the Greek side stood directly across from the mosques on the Turkish side. Tove gazed across the border pensively, looking at the roofs on the Muslim side. Turkey: that was where she was headed. Her next posting from the Ministry of Foreign Affairs was at the Norwegian Embassy in Ankara. Another chapter of her life was around the corner, and Jens Breivik was no longer part of the story.

Anders was not very interested in the geopolitical drama visible with the ruins and the soldiers, as well as the backdrop of historical conflict between Christianity and Islam. Big, black sunglasses under his blond fringe. His white skin was exposed to the Mediterranean sun, but Tove made sure that he did not get burnt. On their way back to Ayia Napa, he went across to her. He reached out his hand. 'Here you go,' he said, opening his hand. In his palm was a small key-ring. Tove picked it up and peered at the picture in the plastic disc attached to the ring.

'Thank you!' she said happily. The picture showed a nude woman stepping out of a shell, partly wrapped in her long, brown hair. It had to be a Greek goddess. 'What's the picture of?' Tove asked.

'Don't you recognize her?' Anders said a little reproachfully. 'It's Aphrodite.' The goddess of love, no less. The boy was certainly growing, Tove thought to herself. He was entering puberty now.

There was only one time Tove got cross. She had hired a small moped for Anders on the condition that it would only be used while she was there, but boys will be boys. When she found out that Anders had borrowed the moped without asking and driven around by himself, she gave him quite an earful. 'That was really bad of you!' she said angrily. 'We had a deal!'

Anders hung his head. The boy was not used to boundaries. At home he did what he wanted to, and he was always good and easy-going with Tove. She had never needed to tell him off. Pranks had never been his style, but now he was getting a talking-to and was very sorry. He promised not to do it again, and Tove softened up when she saw his remorseful face. Borrowing the little moped with a shopping basket on its handlebars was no major crime, after all. It was the first time she had come into conflict with Anders, but he took it well.

Afterwards, everything was back to normal, and the usual light atmosphere quickly came back. Anders was open and chatty, but never confided anything, and he did not like to talk about sad or difficult things. 'Don't ask,' he had said that time she inquired whether he was feeling bad because of his allergy.

Tove drew a deep breath as their aircraft descended and started its approach to Oslo Airport, Fornebu. Their stay on the island of love had been a pleasant departure from everyday life, but now she was about to start a new life in Ankara. She would not see much of Anders for a while now. And how would the relationship between him and his father go without her? In any case he was not a child any more; he was a teenager now and would find his own path at Ris School. Who would have thought that this bright lad with his knowledge of Greek mythology had been treated as one in a thousand by child psychiatrists? But he was not completely grown up. Even on their way onto the flight, he had spoken about the kitten he could have taken home. It was as if he were obsessed with the little family that had come into being under his bed.

4

Morning on Utøya

Utopia on the Tyrifjord

600 metres is not far, but when it is 600 metres of water it suddenly becomes a gap to cross. In summertime, the lake island of Utøya lies like a green brooch on the wavy blue breast of the Tyrifjord. On the lake's eastern side, the land rises steeply up rocky wooded paths and red cliffs towards the forest of Krokskogen, where the trees on the edge look like grass on a roof shielding Utøya from the morning sun. To the west, the blue fjord stretches out for 10 kilometres towards gently undulating agricultural land and rolling woodlands.

The round blue shape of Norefjell rises on the horizon. In the winter months, the pale glow of Oslo is visible in the night sky like a static aurora, but otherwise the capital might as well be on another planet. The main town in the area is Hønefoss, which is a twenty-minute drive away north along the E16 road.

Utøya is big enough to accommodate caves, beaches, fields and woodland but small enough for a child to be able to cross the island in a couple of minutes, from the rushes in the small bay on the eastern side to the cliffs on the western side, or from Nakenodden [Naked Point] at the southern tip to Stoltenberget in the north, a rock named after Prime Minister Jens Stoltenberg and his father Thorvald, himself a former Labour minister. Couples could easily disappear in the thickets or hide in the caves on the western side.

From the air, the island looks flat, inviting and heart-shaped, but, for boats coming from the west, the island is steep and unapproachable. The sediments in the rock faces resemble wooden growth rings or pages of a thick book. Utøya is a land in its own right. Independent, self-sufficient and isolated from the world, like a miniature Norway, or every child's dream of a secret paradise without adults, a land they can discover, build and govern all by themselves.

On the morning of 22 July 2011, Anzor Djoukaev was woken by the sound of rain falling on his tent canvas. He was at the Hedmark county branch's camp, at the end of the campsite in the field. His sleeping bag was wet. He edged his way towards the tent opening and glanced out at the greyness. His shaved head made the raptor-like features of his face stand out. A Caucasian eagle on a Norwegian islet. There were many routes to Utøya. Anzor was seventeen years old, and it was his third time at the summer camp run by the youth wing of the Norwegian Labour Party, Arbeidernes Ungdomsfylking [the Workers' Youth League; AUF]. The weather did not look very promising, but he knew from experience that it could change quickly. The football tournament was due to start at half past eight, but Anzor decided to skip it. Water dripped off a pair of socks left on the guy-ropes. It was simply too wet. He sighed, crawled carefully back onto his ground mat, adjusted his sleeping bag so that he came into contact with the wet parts as little as possible and lay down to sleep again.

Around Anzor, the other boys were snoring. Once again, they had gone to bed in the early hours of the morning, after another sleepless summer night. Not much sleep, too many friends and too many girls. Luckily they could sleep during the lectures. Around the Hedmark camp, dozens of colourful tents shone in the grey morning light. Hundreds of teenagers were waking up to a new day, and the early birds were already shuffling off in their Crocs to the showers and the toilets in the wash house, with their toothbrushes and sponge bags in their hands and their rain jackets slung over their shoulders. The wash house was built on piles raised slightly above the ground and was supplied with water from the pump house down by the water's edge a hundred metres away.

About a thousand young people from across the country were visiting the camp during the week, which meant a lot of showers and many thousands of litres of water each day. There were many routes to Utøya. Anzor had arrived on Tuesday evening, more or less straight from Chechnya. Utøya was the highlight of the summer. He thought everyone was nice there. There was no backstabbing, conflict or bullying.

The idea that landscape forms character is a central tenet of the Norwegian mentality, and this notion is still in the best of health, possibly because it cannot be disproved, even in an age when many Norwegians spend more time in virtual landscapes on screens than in forest, field and fell. In any case, there was no doubt that Utøya had set its mark on the AUF, making the group one of the most robust creatures among the fauna of Norwegian politics. The AUF is older than the state of Norway. One of the organization's precursors, Norges Socialdemokratiske Ungdomsforbund [the Norwegian Social-Democratic Youth League], was founded in 1903, two years before Norway became an independent state. The AUF celebrated its fiftieth anniversary as early as 1950, since the Oslo local branch had been founded in 1900. Its fiftieth birthday present from Oslo og Akershus faglige samorganisasjon [the Oslo and Akershus Trade Union Confederation] was neither flowers nor a case of wine. It was an island: Utøya.

To be gifted paradise seems like fantasy, a dream present – until you think about the maintenance costs. It took time to work Utøya into the organization and into its budget. The committee report from 1958–60 stated that Utøya represented a 'disproportionately large burden on the organization's labour capacity and finances'. Pictures hang in the corridor in the island's Café Building of voluntary work from the early sixties, with pale and muscular young men bent over their spades. At the same time, Norway was changing. In 1960, half of Norwegian voters were workers. Fifty years later, the traditional workers made up only 18 per cent. While 3 per cent had received higher education back then, the figure has now risen ninefold, to 28 per cent. The number of public-sector employees had more than tripled from 200,000 to 730,000 people. Whether or not it was owing to muscles shrinking proportionately as a result of the revolution in education, AUF members nevertheless began to tire of intensive collective work on the green island.

In the late sixties, the situation had become so desperate that the AUF tried to sell off Utøya. The summer camp in July had been the main event on the island right from the start, but it took many decades before it was established as one of the core events in the social-democratic calendar and the crowning argument in AUF recruiters' persuasion of new generations of youth members: 'And then we've also got a summer camp with football, swimming, concerts and hundreds of cool people – on an island!' But the Trade Union Confederation turned out to have been far-sighted. The combination of politically engaged youth and a fairy-tale-like summer island generated a whole that was greater than the sum of its parts.

Utøya would become the place where the politics of the future were hammered together at political workshops, but, more than that, it was perhaps where Norway's governing caste was formed. The Labour Party has been the dominant political force in Norway since the Second World War. Support for the AUF's policies from its mother party has not always been great, but Utøya became the place where many future social democrats spent their first time away from their mums and dads, the place where they had their first kiss and met their future friends – and sometimes husbands and wives. The loyalty and discipline that characterize the Norwegian Labour Party and distinguish it from the fragmented organization, frequent defections and bitter leadership battles of its main competitor, the Norwegian Conservative Party, were formed on Utøya. In Norway, where the number of registered members of organizations is approximately six times the population, it goes without saying that the strongest organization will dominate the field.

Utøya at Its Best

The political and the personal were poured into the Utøya mould in equal measure, beaten out through discussions, warmed by the summer sun and bathed in the Tyrifjord at night. Not everyone on the island would become prime minister, but all Labour Party prime ministers since Gro Harlem Brundtland had learnt the ropes on Utøya. 'The paradise of my youth' is what the current prime minister, Jens Stoltenberg, called Utøya. The highlight that Friday was to be the visit by Gro herself, known as the 'Mother of the Nation', who led the Labour Party from 1981 to 1992 and for Norway personified 'the Marxist utopia consisting of "true equality between the sexes" ',[1] as Anders Behring Breivik later expressed it.

It was the first time in ten years that Gro had come to Utøya, and the older AUF members wondered whether the younger ones on the island would come to hear her talk. In one of the bedrooms in the wash house, Ida Spjelkavik planned her day as she put on her trainers and got ready for that morning's volleyball game. Ida, twenty-five years old and from Trondheim, was the AUF's international secretary. Perhaps as a consequence of her background as a presenter on student radio (where she hosted a foreign affairs programme) and on NRK, Ida had a calm and natural air of authority that put those around her at ease. As steady as a rock, I thought when I first met her in 2010, but as accommodating as a summer's day. Her bright eyes, round face, blonde hair and cheerful laugh made her a natural focal point for the international volleyball team, which included visitors from Uganda, Georgia, Swaziland and Lebanon.

There were many routes to Utøya. The international visitors were interested in Gro, who was a high-profile international leader, but would the fourteen-year-old Norwegians remember who she was? Ida was not sure. And how would the workshop on Western Sahara go later on in the day? It was conceivable that not all of the island's guests were as passionate about international solidarity as Ida was.

Utøya had been at its best the day before, Ida thought a little bitterly, as she struggled in the mud on the volleyball court a few minutes later. The rain was lashing down and the clouds hung over the treetops like a jagged and cracked row of teeth. There was no Utøya without mud, but on the volleyball court it seemed as if the mud rose up from below the surface of the earth like cold lava, swallowing grass and trainers alike. The international team was making little progress against the Norwegians that day, Ida realized, as the ball smashed down at the international team's feet, sending the rainwater splattering.

The previous day there had been a debate about the Middle East with Jonas Gahr Støre, the lean foreign minister who was idolized by parts of the AUF. The Middle East was the main international issue for the AUF members, who took the opportunity to challenge the foreign minister. Why not boycott Israel? Why could Norway not recognize Palestine straight away, with the governing authorities asking for recognition and all countries in favour of the two-state solution?

'I don't believe in boycotts,' Støre answered, explaining to the youngsters sitting on the grass why he saw isolation as both the wrong strategy and an ineffective one. 'People have to talk to each other', he concluded, 'even if they disagree – and especially when they disagree.'

A heavy-set girl in her mid-twenties looked around to see what the young people thought about the boycott question. In the Storting, Stine Renate Håheim represented not only Oppland county but, in practice, the AUF members too. She was the youngest member of the Storting's Standing Committee on Justice but a grand old lady on Utøya. The island had left its mark on her in the sense that the football tournaments had wrecked her knees. Stine compensated with her inspired leadership of the cheering section.

Earlier that summer, Stine had joined Freedom Flotilla II in Athens, with its shiploads of activists planning to break the Israeli blockade of Gaza. The project was not without its risks: nine activists had been killed when the Israelis boarded their ships the year before. Palestine was the international issue that Håheim was most passionate about: occupying another country was not right, shooting at civilians in Gaza City was not right, nor was the blockade of the Palestinian ports. It was the fight for justice that led her to join the AUF as a fifteen-year-old. Every time something has been changed in Norway, she thought, the Labour Party has had a role to play. Håheim was an eloquent person who had found her calling at Utøya, just like Anzor and Ida. Her burning engagement could shine brightly there.

The Freedom Flotilla had received considerable attention from the media, and that was something, but the expedition itself was a fiasco. Due to a sawn-off propeller shaft and strange decisions by the Greek port authorities, the boats never left Piraeus that summer, so Håheim was spared the ordeal of encountering the Israeli special forces at sea. Instead, Comrade Håheim (as she called herself on her blog) sat on the grass on Utøya, attentively following Støre's analysis of the Netanyahu government's likely reaction to the application for UN membership being prepared in Ramallah by the Palestinians. Håheim had a pinch of *snus* under her lip, the kind of tobacco snuff popular in Norway.

Further up the grassy slope, Anzor dozed in the sunshine. His thoughts circled off high up into the sky, but the lad from Lillestrøm nodded in agreement when he thought he heard Støre support a boycott of Israel. Attitudes, expectations and bias affect your understanding, and Anzor misunderstood the foreign minister on this point – otherwise the 2011 summer camp would have made even bigger headlines than usual that evening.

It was part of the nature of the AUF to criticize its mother party. From the very start, the militantly anti-militarist youth had admonished the Labour Party for lacking revolutionary vigour and pandering to the parliamentary system. The conflict peaked in the early twenties. Should the Labour Party remain a member of the Soviet-led Comintern and choose to follow a revolutionary line, or should it participate in the democratic institutions of non-socialist Norway? The AUF members saw themselves as the spearhead of revolution, genuine communists, and they were activists by nature. One of their leaders, Einar Gerhardsen, who would later become prime minister, turned up outside the premises of *Aftenposten* in Akersgata and threatened the editors with dynamite. He was prosecuted and convicted for his conduct.

In November 1923, the youth organization broke away from its mother party and endorsed the Moscow-loyal Communist Party of Norway, which was formed by dissenters from the Labour Party. Among the minority who stayed to create a new organization, named the Left Communist Youth League, was Einar Gerhardsen from Oslo. But, while the communists would be a footnote in Norwegian history, the split heralded a century of social-democratic hegemony: the century of the Labour Party. The war changed the Labour Party's stance on defence and alliance politics, but the AUF remained a left-wing ideological stone in the shoe of the pragmatic governing Labour Party.

During the so-called Easter Rebellion of 1958, when the AUF branch known as the Sosialistisk Studentlag [Socialist Student Group] proposed a resolution criticizing NATO and the deployment of nuclear weapons in West Germany, another group of AUF members disappeared off to the left. In protest against Norway's membership of NATO, the excluded AUF members and their sympathizers established the Socialist People's Party. Traditionally, the AUF's anti-militarism resulted from the perception of the army as a tool of the upper class. Although the war changed the relationship between the army and the Labour Party, a latent scepticism remained in the AUF towards the use of force and the alliance with the USA. The mother party's attitude towards the AUF resembled that of a proud but slightly patronizing parent who thinks that her children's piercings are a bit ridiculous, that their opinions are sweet, but that her offspring will turn out well in the end. We all grow up eventually, after all.

'The youth organization is much more capable than the Party and the trade union movement when it comes to schooling socialist-minded and socialist-inclined women and men,' the late Haakon Lie once said. Lie would go on to become an influential secretary of the Labour Party from 1945 to 1969.

Forty years later, he dismissed the AUF as 'half-educated scamps' when they interfered in the debate about the EEC referendum in 1972. Utøya nurtured utopian socialists rather than pragmatic social democrats. The attitude towards the AUF as an optimal cadre factory but a political lightweight was most clearly expressed by Haakon Lie, but he was probably not the only one with that view in the Labour Party.

'We Must Be Vigilant Now'

After the Middle East debate was over, Ida had led the workshop about the world's newest state, which was introduced by Liv Tørress from Norwegian People's Aid. The sun was still shining on the grass and on Spjelkavik's 'global group'. Tørress's stories from the war in the country now known as South Sudan, and her thoughts about future developments, attracted a large audience. To top it all, Jonas Gahr Støre came and perched on one of the logs at the Oslo branch's camp, where the international guests had gathered in the afternoon.

Støre had asked Natia how things were in Georgia and had asked Sam about the situation in Uganda, but Ida thought that what made the greatest impression on the international guests was not Støre's wealth of knowledge, but the simple fact that a foreign minister in trainers was speaking to them on equal terms, quite informally and without any bodyguards or advisers.

In the background, the team from Norwegian People's Aid shuffled about. The organization did not only contribute experts from its comprehensive international humanitarian work for the international workshops. The team from Hadeland in south-eastern Norway also comforted the young ones who missed their parents, put plasters on those who grazed themselves on the rocks and brought ice packs to those who got injured on the football pitch. While other state-supporting parties had militia or paramilitary wings, the Norwegian Labour Party had its own humanitarian organization. Norway in a nutshell, Ida thought, this odd country out, on the very edge of the world map.

Ida Spjelkavik and 'the global group' with Foreign Minister Jonas Gahr Støre on Utøya, 21 July 2011; from left to right: Ritah from Uganda, Tamta from Georgia, Thabile from Swaziland, Natia from Georgia, Jonas Gahr Støre, Bassel from Lebanon, Sam from Uganda, and Ida Spjelkavik (photograph by Tore S. Bekkedal)

Norwegian People's Aid also had its roots in an age with more conflict. The organization's baptism of fire was in Finland during the Winter War of 1939–40, but in the summer of 2011 the wars were further away, in Afghanistan and Libya. On Thursday 21 July, Norwegian People's Aid had national representatives from Palestine and South Sudan. They were there to give substance to the notion of international solidarity.

The summer camp on Utøya is situated not only in the middle of the Tyrifjord but also in the middle of the slow news season. An appearance there almost guaranteed space on the evening news, and there was an election looming in September. In that respect, there was a certain logic in the Labour Party leaders dividing the days between them, interrupting their holidays to pop in and see the AUF. But Utøya was also one of the places where Støre could bring himself up to speed with political activists. As the foreign minister drove back to his holiday cabin in Tvedestrand that afternoon, he sorted his impressions in his head. So many different faces. All those young people would build a common future for themselves and for the country. Who would these young people become, and what would they do when it was their turn?

One of the exciting things about the AUF was that the participants on Utøya not only represented the whole country but increasingly came from all over the world. In the football match, he had played on a team with a girl from Somalia. She had hurt her foot, and, even though she had been bandaged up by the people from Norwegian People's Aid, she was still limping afterwards.

Støre got home in time to join his family for dinner with some friends. The evening sun was warm and languid. It was completely calm. On the way home to their summer cabin, Støre and his family steered their boat out onto the clear waters of the fjord. An enormous sunset blazed away on their right. One member of the family shook her head and muttered that the blood-red sky did not bode well. 'Red sky at night . . . ,' thought Støre.

That same day, an article by Støre was published in *Bergens Tidende* and *Stavanger Aftenblad* under the title 'Urolige tider' [Uneasy times], in which he wrote: 'When I read about great historical events, I often ponder what the people of the age were thinking immediately before history took an unexpected turn. In the early summer of 1914, leading politicians said that there were no clouds in the sky of high politics. A few weeks later, the First World War was under way.'[2]

Støre's uneasiness was linked to what the long-term political consequences might be of the crises in the eurozone and in US government spending. He envisaged a growing anger, the final form of which nobody could foresee, and he called for alertness:

> I fear the social unrest that will come when new generations cannot get jobs [. . .] and ordinary families have to face the bill for financial and political indulgences for which they never voted. [. . . L]arge parts of Europe and the USA will see this as deeply unfair. And they will seek out ways to express their anger.
>
> We do not know today what such frustration will lead to, but the result of what we are seeing over the course of this summer makes me uneasy. I am glad that the Norwegian economy is in order, but we must be vigilant now.[3]

Over his years as foreign minister, Støre had led Norwegian efforts in Afghanistan and defended Norway's military involvement in the war in Libya. As an adviser for Prime Minister Gro Harlem Brundtland in the nineties, he had built up an international section in the Office of the Prime Minister. He had later followed Gro to Geneva as her chief of staff when she led the World Health Organization. Støre had seen how the world had shrunk after the end of the Cold War. Internal affairs could become foreign affairs over the course of a couple of messages on Twitter or a blog post. Caricatures from a Danish newspaper went around the world, causing a commotion from Chad to Chechnya, due to the efforts of some enterprising activists and smart politicians flirting with fear and conflict. Foreign policy hit home in the form of sanctions against Norwegian business, coffins from Afghanistan or a Norwegian population with roots in other parts of the world. If there was flooding in Sri Lanka, the waves reached all the way to Oslo and Stavanger.

There were two ways to see this development, either as a threat to the traditional Norway or as an inevitable development that enriched Norway, if it was handled properly. Støre stressed the latter view. In domestic politics, Støre had promoted integration as a major issue and launched the concept of 'the new Norwegian we' to create a more inclusive Norwegian identity that was not focused exclusively on ethnicity, names and skin colour, and which accepted that people did not need to be only one thing. They could be Norwegian but also Sikh or Muslim, Norwegian but also Polish or Chilean.

While Støre had been Norway's most popular politician since 2005, he was at the same time the most hated among opponents of immigration and extreme critics of Islam. 'The most dangerous man in Norway,' according to Anders Behring Breivik. 'Must we now follow Foreign Minister Jonas Gahr Støre's order to the Norwegian people to "adapt" to the New Norway and the Greater We?' asked a leaflet from the organization Stopp islamiseringen av Norge [Stop the Islamization of Norway]. 'Is that what you want? Have you been asked?'

It was not just those sceptical towards immigration or critical of Islam who disliked what Støre stood for. At half past six in the evening on 14 January 2008, Støre was in Kabul. During a meeting with the leader of the Afghan Independent Human Rights Commission, he heard a bang outside the hotel. The explosion was followed by salvos of shots and further explosions. The security guards in the room ordered everyone down onto the floor, including Støre. The guards drew their weapons and moved into position by the doors. In the lobby, which was on the floor above the meeting room, a man in a police uniform stormed in through the entrance door armed with a Kalashnikov assault rifle. Another terrorist was left lying in the courtyard outside, killed in the exchange of fire with the hotel guards. A third died in the lobby when he set off the bomb in his vest. The terrorist shot at everything that moved. A Norwegian photographer came out of the lift and saw a policeman point a weapon at him. The photographer threw himself to the ground and avoided the shots. Two other Norwegians in the lobby were hit, Bjørn Svennungsen from the Ministry of Foreign Affairs and Carsten Thomassen, a journalist from *Dagbladet*. Thomassen later died of his injuries. An American diplomat was also killed, together with three of the hotel staff. While the attacker searched for more victims in the gym on the ground floor, Støre was evacuated to a bomb shelter at the bottom of the hotel complex. A few minutes later, the attack was over and the four terrorists were either killed or taken prisoner. It was never clarified whether Støre was the target of the Taliban's attack. He travelled home uninjured, but with the experience of having seen fanaticism at close quarters.

The AUF summer camp was a polar opposite to the hatred shown at the Serena Hotel. Together with the typically Norwegian faces of AUF members such as Ida Spjelkavik and Stine Håheim was not only the eagle-like face of Anzor from the Caucasus but also an abundance of faces with Arab, Tamil, Persian, Latin, Albanian, African, South-East Asian and Polynesian features. On the surface it looked as if Støre's 'new Norwegian we' was taking shape. The question was perhaps whether there was a deeper reality behind it, or whether Utøya was a kind of saccharine, state-subsidized utopia in the Tyrifjord that would fall apart the day it became real.

Ida and Stine had been going to Utøya for more than a decade and knew that determined long-term work led to results. They did not feel part of an abstract new Norwegian we, made up in a column in

Aftenposten. On Utøya it was just 'we'. Back in the nineties, the AUF defined its aim of becoming the most inclusive, multicultural organization in Norway. That entailed positive discrimination in favour of minorities when it came to choosing positions and duties in the organization. Since Utøya was the way into the AUF, a low-threshold event, everything was arranged to facilitate the participation of young people from minority backgrounds. Pork was not served at the summer camp, so everyone would eat the same food (unless they were vegetarians). An alcohol ban was already in place, and the shower rules were changed to make it clear which facilities and times were for the girls and which were for the boys. The AUF actively recruited in places with many immigrants, and some of the Utøya participants still lived in reception centres for asylum seekers. The children of first-generation immigrants were beginning to take part, and some of them were leader types who brought others in with them. After Mani Hosseini got involved in the AUF, there was a wave of new Kurdish members in Akershus county. Similar things happened elsewhere.

Through its hard work, and by building on the internationalist foundation of the labour movement itself, Marx and Engels' slogan 'Workers of the world, unite!', the AUF was reforging the Norwegian labour movement. Utøya's rainbow race might have looked artificially perfect, but it also communicated that the labour movement was drawing energy from the growing pains Norway was going through in connection with immigration and integration. Many of the second-generation immigrants on Utøya had experienced discrimination, poverty and conflict and had a more concrete relationship to the values of the labour movement than many of the typically Norwegian children of the welfare state.

Stop Them with Spirit

Utøya is about fixing things that are falling apart, that suddenly go wrong, stop working or simply do not turn up. There are holes in the tents that must be mended, cold water in the showers and rice that must be cooked if the potatoes are finished. Utøya is about always being prepared. Utøya is about improvising. In that respect, Utøya is not only a paradise or every utopian young socialist's wet dream, but also training in the ideas that characterize the mother party: problem solving, the will to govern and pragmatism.

The memories had begun to fade of the time when the AUF was an action group, with members who had travelled round the countryside in the thirties to beat up the paramilitaries of Nasjonal Samling

[National Unity], the fascist party founded by Vidkun Quisling, and who had participated in all sections of the resistance movement during the war. Sixty-five years of peace and prosperity had made both Norwegians and AUF members into people with 'many friends in common, and no enemies',[4] as the author Erlend Loe put it.

In spite of the tough leadership struggle in the autumn of 2010, when Eskil Pedersen beat Åsmund Aukrust in the ballot, with 175 against 173 votes, it was a harmonious and calm group of two young women and two young men who led the AUF. It might almost seem that Utøya was too good to be true.

Drinking?

'No, practically none at all,' said Anne-Berit Stavenes, the leader of the Norwegian People's Aid team on Utøya.

Fighting?

'No, not here. Utøya is a paradise. The week we spend on the island is a holiday for us too.'

At about ten o'clock in the morning on 22 July 2011, the AUF published a report on its website about the new memorial at Utøya. Ida and Eskil Pedersen had taken part in the unveiling two days earlier. A modest plaque had been screwed into the trunk of a birch tree straight across from the kiosk at the Café Building. The text was almost invisible when the sun shone on the bright metal, but in the rain and mist on Friday 22 July the letters stood out like dark cracks on the smooth façade. The sparse text honoured the memory of 'the AUF members who gave their lives in the struggle against fascism in the International Brigades during the Spanish Civil War of 1936–9', listing the names of four young men from Lørenskog, Trondheim, Førde and Kabelvåg who were killed in Spain in 1937 and 1938.

Martin Schei, from Førde in western Norway, was only eighteen years old when he left an AUF course on Utøya and – without saying goodbye to his parents or family, and contrary to the mother party's line of neutrality – set off for the recruitment office in Paris. In Spain, he joined the Spanish government forces in the fight against Franco's rebel army. He fell a few months later in September 1937, during the Aragon Offensive. Schei reached the age of nineteen. Beneath the names of the fallen are some lines from Nordahl Grieg's 1936 poem 'Til ungdommen' [literally, 'To the youth']: 'The grenades roll silently / on conveyor belts. / Stop their drift towards death, / *stop them with spirit!*'[5]

From land, Utøya has many faces, depending on the season, the weather and from where it is observed. Sometimes the island looms in the rain like a dark secret on the leaden grey waters of the fjord. At other times, it can only vaguely be seen as a mirage in the mist, a glimpse of something dark revealing itself and disappearing so quickly that from land you are left wondering if you really did see something out there.

For most people, the island was just a fleeting flash of green down in the massive Tyrifjord, which thousands of commuters drove past on weekdays and tens of thousands of tourists from Oslo went past at weekends on their way up to their cabins in the mountains. During the daytime, the rushing sound of the E16 road could be heard out across the fjord, but, at night-time, all that could be heard on Utøya was the lapping of the waves and the wind in the trees. Except when the summer camp was on.

The quiet guests at the campsite on the other side of the water from Utøya did not associate the AUF with calm and objective political discussion but with a smörgåsbord of noise: cheering from the football pitch, roaring music from the stage and the rock tent, often through the night, screaming and yelling from the teenagers in the water. The noise died down in the wee hours of the morning and was a little less loud when it rained, but otherwise the young ones kept going throughout that whole week in July.

5

Morg the Graffiti Bomber[1]
Anders Behring Breivik's Youth

King of the Number 32 Bus

Morg, Spok and Mono squeezed up against the wooden fence. The three fourteen-year-olds in dark clothing gave the occasional cautious glance over the side. Night descended over Skøyen bus depot, but the watchmen were still in the area. The boys had sneaked away from home at around midnight and fetched their spray cans, mostly nicked from the shelves of nearby petrol stations. If a can cost 90 kroner and you needed at least five cans to spray a piece, it goes without saying that tagging could quickly turn into an expensive hobby.

Mono was tense. If they were caught, all hell would break loose. Not only would they get a bawling from their parents or be grounded: there were rumours of watchmen who beat up taggers. Muscle-bound hunks who broke boys' arms and noses. Their boss was a former foreign legionnaire with a photographic memory. Oslo's most notorious security guard. He knew the names behind every tag and gave the boys two chances. If you were caught a third time, you would get a beating. At night-time, it was full-blown guerrilla warfare along the tracks and concrete platforms of Oslo Sporveier [Oslo Public Transport Administration]. But at Skøyen bus depot it was the three taggers who had their eyes on the watchmen, not the other way round.

Mono was not a particularly experienced tagger but, unless you were a total nerd or a complete snob, most people went out at some point to have a go. It bothered Mono that his tags looked so bad.

Had he not practised enough? The other lads drew sketches during lessons and drafted larger pieces in their bedrooms, painstakingly made, often intricate and very colourful street murals. Spok and Morg were quite experienced. Morg spent many hours painting a piece in a pedestrian subway under the ring road up by the Radium Hospital. The colourful piece was still burning on the cold concrete wall for a long time afterwards.

For the big boys, though, it was not a question of colours or pieces in godforsaken holes half-way to Bærum. 'Put your name on the train': they had to put their tag – in other words, their nickname or brand – somewhere it would be easily visible, where it was difficult to get to and where you would get some cred. 'Rockin' it'. Many of the West End taggers were, or became, skilful artists, but aesthetics were not the most important thing for these fourteen-year-olds. Excitement, joining the big boys at their game and being seen by the population of Oslo: that was what it was about.

'Now we're going to be big!' Morg smiled. It was a few months after he had borrowed the moped in Cyprus without asking. This raid was something quite different.

Three shadows glided over the fence and blended into the darkness between the buses. The dull bus roofs looked like the backs of sleeping fish. The watchmen had gone, and there was a window of time that would stay open until the morning traffic started. That was as long as no guards, random policemen or infuriated everyday heroes turned up unannounced. The street lights glimmered on the buses' windows and metal bodies.

The three busmen slipped in between the vehicles and graffiti-bombed the sides of the number 20 and 32 buses. This was their chance to become kings of one of the bus routes that crossed Oslo from east to west. The boys had time to paper the buses with throw-ups – in other words, more elaborate versions of their tags: Morg and Spok in bold with black outlines and filled with colour. Mono groaned. Why did his attempts always turn out so bad? People would see that he was a 'toy', a wannabe, an amateur.

There were crews of taggers, groups who worked together, at many of the schools in the West End, but the three lads at Skøyen bus depot were not members of any crew yet. It took time to collect enough points to get in. The toughest crews were from the East End. Downtown was more wicked than uptown. If you bombed on Karl Johans Gate, the main street in the city centre, you were king.

Morg went 'all city', as it was known, 'bombing' all over town. He planned his missions like a general from his bedroom. He was going to be the greatest. If Spok put twenty cans in his bag, Morg took a stock of a hundred. Spok came into contact with the 'GSV' crew from Vålerenga. The abbreviation GSV meant many different things, including '*grise sporveiens vogner*' ['mess up public transport carriages']. There were many foreigners in GSV, including Pakistanis who were linked to the criminal gangs beginning to stir in the West End of Oslo.

After the western and eastern metro systems were joined up at the end of the eighties, hip-hop culture was one of the factors that led to bridges being built over the divide between east and west in Oslo. Hip-hop turned things upside down: now the west looked up to the east. Better to be a gangster with cred than an artist in an overcoat or a daddy's boy in dockside shoes.

Morg was struggling to get into a crew. Maybe he was trying too hard, overambitious. The older boys smiled at him, while his peers kept a distance. He was Asperger-like, a weirdo, according to a tagger from Hovseter.

Mono cannot forget one time when he and a friend were on their way downtown from the basketball court in Njårdhallen sports centre at Makrellbekken. It was the best court in the West End since it had a chain net, just like in the film *White Men Can't Jump* with Woody Harrelson and Wesley Snipes. In the underpass below the ring road, they came across Morg, all alone on a Saturday afternoon. He was writing on the walls, 'Morg, Morg, Morg.'

'What's up, Anders?' asked Mono. Morg answered him in 'Kebab Norwegian', a multi-ethnolect slang incorporating words from many immigrant languages. '*Schpaa*,' said Morg, meaning cool. It was as if he were pretending to be a Pakistani from GSV, but he was dead serious.

Mono later realized why his tags looked so awful. It was strange that he had not worked it out before. Perhaps graffiti was not entirely his thing. Tagging was a lifestyle, sneaking out at night, nicking spray cans from the paint shops. You acquired an eye for the city's surfaces: is that wall suitable for throwies? The joy of a 'burner'. Scratching spotless surfaces, leaving your mark on the façades of Oslo's West End. Money and more money for teamwear (Chicago Bulls was the usual; Michael Jordan and Scottie Pippen were the names that mattered), hoodies and tagging trainers. Chevignon jackets in winter, and never a day without a baseball cap.

The real pros went to Denmark and bought consignments of cheap spray cans in Copenhagen. You came to know the names of crews and taggers, toys and kings, the pacts that existed, which areas were no-go zones and who had grassed on whom. A science for the initiated, but meaningless for the other metro passengers with their heads in the newspaper, looking up indifferently at the splashes of colour rushing past the window. Almost all of them were caught eventually, and the fines were getting steeper and steeper.

'Taghead!' proclaimed an angry information campaign by the public transport authorities. The Winter Olympics at Lillehammer were approaching and the façades of the capital had to look spotless. In Oslo, a teenage tagger was given an immediate custodial sentence of seven months. The taggers responded by 'bombing' seats and windows. Morg collected emergency hammers and, according to his own accounts, wrecked ticket machines with a bolt gun. The public transport authorities signed a contract with private security companies to smash the tagging community. Zero tolerance. The municipality took a hard stance, which resulted in practically criminalizing a generation of youngsters. In total, 1,136 young people were reported for graffiti in the nineties, including not only Morg and the high-profile criminal David Toska but also the famous actor Aksel Hennie.

This war also affected the tagging communities internally. Grassing was the lowest of the low. It was rumoured that one of the Ris lads had grassed on some of the best-known taggers from Oslo's West End. At the same time, Mono's parents became concerned. They found out that Mono was stealing. Morg and Spok's year group was notoriously wild and a party never went by without fighting. Mono remembered one Friday at a house party in the Vinderen part of town. Some strangers gate-crashed the party, as they always did. This time it was taggers on the look-out for the Ris lads.

'Motherfucker!' shouted one of the guests. He was Norwegian but used Kebab Norwegian slang. The stranger suddenly spun round, flooring one of the Ris taggers with a roundhouse kick. That was just the beginning of the reprisals. It was said that Spok was beaten up in the fields at Ekebergsletta, while Morg was left alone. He was never quite at the centre of events, a peripheral figure.

Mono was already out of the country by then. When Mono was sixteen, he lived with his diplomat parents in a city in the Middle East widely known for terrorism, conflicts and attacks, but for Mono the Middle East was an oasis of calm after his time at lower secondary in Oslo. He gave up tagging. The three busmen had got away from their operation at Skøyen bus depot without a scratch. For a few days, Morg was king of the number 32 bus. Mono shook his head at the thought. For the life of him, he could not understand why he had tagged the number 20 bus with his right hand, when he was left-handed.

A School with Class

As you take the metro line heading up from the city centre towards Holmenkollen, a large, white brick building appears on the left-hand side between Vinderen and Gaustad station. Unobtrusive birch trees surround the prominent building like pale servants standing at attention. The elegant yard in front of the school looks exactly like the driveway in front of a manor house. A daydreaming metro passenger could easily imagine horse-drawn carriages and open-top vintage cars stopping here in a bygone era, dropping off well-dressed gentlemen and ladies with stoles before the couples proceed to the entrance, arm in arm on their way to the ball . . .

Both my mother and my brother went to Ris School, and I was offered a place at Ris Upper Secondary School in 1985.

The large windows of the old building have many stories to tell. The school was requisitioned by the German occupation forces in May 1940 and initially housed Austrian Alpine troops, mounted combat units that were billeted in the school's hippodrome, the brick building that has recently housed the R.O.O.M. furniture shop. The Austrians were later replaced by Wehrmacht reserve units.

The hippodrome was the scene of one of the Nazis' biggest events in Norway. On 30 June 1941, Reichsführer Heinrich Himmler visited the school at Ris to receive the oath of allegiance from the first Norwegian recruits who had volunteered for the 'Wiking' division of the Waffen SS to take part in the crusade against the Bolsheviks – in other words, the attack on the Soviet Union. Hundreds of young people in black were marched up in the hippodrome under flags with the swastika and SS banners to listen to the Reichsführer's speech.[2] Down in the city centre, the legendary resistance fighter Max Manus was sneaking over the rooftops, looking for a place from which he could shoot Himmler. The assassination plans were not carried out. The thought of German reprisals acted as a deterrent.

Lessons at Ris were moved to Ullern School, where a tense relationship arose with Ullern's headmaster, who was from Nasjonal Samling, the fascist party. The teachers from Ris were good Norwegians, according to local historians: 'The teachers were patriots to a man, as were the pupils. There were perhaps some collaborators here and there, but they were soon frozen out and stopped going to school.'[3]

The granite memorial outside underlines the attitude of Ris School during the war. Carved into the memorial stone are the names, dates of birth and dates of death of thirty-three young men and one woman, as well as the places where they were killed during the war. Many were aircrew; some died on distant battlefields in Europe, while others were shot in Akershus Fortress or killed fighting the Gestapo in Oslo. On sunny autumn mornings, the memorial cast a long shadow across the moist grass and damp asphalt outside the school where the pupils went past on their way from the metro station.

Many of the best-known resistance heroes of the war lived along the Holmenkollen line, the metro line that goes through Gaustad station, by Ris School. Max Manus's house was at Gulleråsen and had a view across the fjord where he had blown up German ships during the war. Gunnar Sønsteby, the most highly decorated Norwegian citizen, lived further up towards the edge of the forest, not far from the small lake of Bånntjern. Those of us who grew up there felt their presence, the living memories of the resistance, even though we were born many decades after the war. The memorial stone carries the following inscription: 'They could have continued their normal lives, they had to go, they were called.'

The memorial stone at Ris Lower Secondary School

The sacrifice of these thirty-four national martyrs meant that Norwegians could still be proud of being Norwegian, even after a war in which large parts of the population remained passive and a significant minority actively supported the Nazis. The memorial stone tells the pupils at Ris School a story of honour. They too, if required, are expected to sacrifice their lives for their country. If you attend the patrician Ris School, you will learn to think big. Monuments like this form the glue of national communities and can be found all across Europe. At Thermopylae, a stone still stands to mark the spot where Leonidas and his 300 Spartans fell in battle against the Persian King Xerxes in 480 BC. The inscription on the stone reads: 'Go, stranger, and to Lacedaemon tell that here, obeying her behests, we fell.' 2,500 years have passed since Thermopylae, but the memory of the Spartans' martyrdom lives on, perhaps because it can be seen in a context that still gives meaning. The Spartans allegedly fell in the West's struggle for freedom against the invading hordes from Asia, where Greek democracy (certainly not especially advanced in Sparta, which was governed by priests) stood against despotism, free Greeks against Persia's slaves.

300, a cartoonish epic in which Leonidas is portrayed by a well-trained Gerald Butler, was in any case listed by Anders Behring Breivik as his favourite film on the Facebook profile he set up on 17 July 2011. Winston Churchill and Max Manus were other favourite figures of his. The echo of the struggle against foreign occupation, carved in stone outside Ris School, reverberated all the way into Anders' social media profiles.

Ris School has been renovated and rebuilt several times since the municipal council took over its dilapidated buildings in 1945. The wooden floors and doorsills had been worn down by the German soldiers' jackboots, while toilets and sinks had been smashed and destroyed. My mother finished school in 1945, but over the years she had spent at Ris Gymnasium she had hardly set foot in the building. The school has been restored and rebuilt, but every May its aura as a nest of resistance is brought to life when wreaths with Norwegian flags are laid by the monument to the school's war dead.

I chose to renounce my place at Ris Upper Secondary School in 1985. Down jackets, headbands and Alpine skiing were never my thing. There were also some weirdos there who listened to heavy rock and were interested in weapons, but that was not my thing either. Social class was a reality at Ris. My cousin told me a story about a children's birthday party at nearby Slemdal. One of the boys turned up at the party with his hair slicked down, driven by a private chauffeur. The chauffeur passed the ten-year-old a bag with his indoor shoes and a present for the host. 'Thank you, Jensen,' the boy answered. 'You may leave, Jensen.'

My brother went to lower secondary school at Ris in the seventies and told me how one of the boys in his class was known only as 'the pig farmer's son'. Teasing and conflicts went on at all schools, but they took on a unique upper-class twist at Ris. My mother told me similar stories from her childhood when she went to Slemdal and Vinderen primary schools in the thirties. Among the wealthy children there were also the sons and daughters of gardeners, drivers and butlers. The children were in the same classes when they were small, but everyone knew that the servants' children would not go further than middle school. Ris Gymnasium was reserved for the upper-class families. In addition to the difference between the financial and the cultural elites, or snobs and freaks as they were known in the eighties, there were historical class differences in the West End. They were understated, but real.

A lot had changed since my mother went to Ris during the war, and the class differences had apparently been ground down in the post-war period. The Labour Party state and the '68ers had brought to an end the time when people stood cap in hand and when little lords gave orders to their chauffeurs. As for designer clothing, Ris was not the only school in Norway where the fashion police ruled, but something lingered in the restored buildings.

One of those who applied to go somewhere else after finishing at Ris Lower Secondary School was Jonas Gahr Støre from Gråkammen, a short distance away. Although many of his friends were staying on at Ris for upper secondary, he saw Ris as constricted, characterized by a conservative social set that was not very open to new ideas. A marshy lake with no new water flowing in and no outflow, nothing for a restless soul.

Støre ended up instead at Berg Upper Secondary School, near the neighbourhood of Tåsen, a school with a more varied and diverse range of pupils, attended by young people from across the city. It had an international curriculum. Støre wanted space, a wider stage for expressing himself than the hippodrome at Ris. He wanted to be many things, not just one thing. To be free. Why did Norway have to be a small country anyway? Why could it not be bigger, in the sense that it could be filled with great variation and changes, surprising viewpoints and unfamiliar spaces? A place where everyone had the chance to choose their own life, instead of being defined by traditions and customs. Støre was interested in revue theatre, and in politics too.

In spite of an individualistic inclination, Støre appreciated social democracy and the notion that everyone had equal rights and equal options in life. Freedom is best enjoyed in an open, egalitarian and inclusive society. Hierarchies lead to oppression both for the master and for the servant, both for the slick-haired ten-year-old and for his chauffeur. Støre left Ris and considered joining the AUF but thought the organization as it existed in the West End was a little dynastic, a little sectarian. The driving forces were Jens Stoltenberg, the son of leading Labour Party politician Thorvald Stoltenberg, and Hans Jacob Frydenlund, son of foreign minister Knut Frydenlund. Støre looked further to other social sets, other cities and other countries. First he went to the Norwegian Naval Academy in Bergen and then to Sciences Po in Paris, where he found his political direction in the mid-eighties.

The Bomber from Ris

Whatever happened to the pig farmer's son? Not everyone who left Ris School set out on the path to being foreign minister.

In the mid-eighties, a former pupil of Ris Upper Secondary School ended up in Ullersmo Prison after a dynamite attack on a mosque in the Frogner neighbourhood of Oslo. Witnesses thought it was a miracle that nobody was killed in the attack, which stunned the whole nation. 'Jens Erik' was also convicted of crimes for profit. In the nineties, he distanced himself from right-wing extremism and became a central figure in the 'Exit' project, which helped young people wanting to leave neo-Nazi groups. Today he is a normal family man as well as a keen runner in his spare time. Perhaps the energy of his youth is not entirely gone.

He started at Ris Upper Secondary School ten years before Breivik started at lower secondary, but there are some parallels in their stories.

Jens Erik was an outsider. Going to Ris was a painful experience. Nobody was directly malicious towards him or consciously shut him out, he would later believe. On the surface, it was not a particularly negative situation, with no bullying, but it was as if he did not quite fit in. Sport was the focus of attention at Ris, but Jens Erik was no sportsman, at least not in cross-country skiing, tennis or orienteering, which were the main disciplines in the local sports club, Idrettslaget Heming. Team sports were not the big thing on the hill below Holmenkollen, where Norway's most famous skiing competitions take place. Jens Erik had attended lower secondary school in Molde, on the west coast of Norway, where he had been used to being one of the best in the class without having to make too much effort. At Ris he was suddenly the worst at everything. The standard was high, but perhaps his academic decline was just as much a consequence of his unhappiness. In his second year he failed in physics, which should perhaps have alerted the teachers since he had been a good pupil to begin with.

'Is everything OK, Jens Erik?' one of the teachers asked him, to which he naturally replied: 'Of course!'

The school's commitment went no further than that. The pupils had to work things out for themselves.

When Jens Erik got off the metro at Gaustad station in the mornings, having come from the direction of the city centre, all the other pupils would be coming the other way, from Holmenkollen, Gulleråsen or Gråkammen. Jens Erik had the feeling that the others came from a small and closed community in which the families knew each other and lived according to set rules that nobody else understood, as if they had always lived there. While the others had holiday cabins by the sea or in the mountains, Jens Erik lived with his single mother at a not especially glamorous address downtown.

Every day, he could sense the unspoken class differences. Jens Erik went home from school by himself. He was interested in the history of warfare and found a journal at the library published by the Institutt for norsk okkupasjonshistorie [Institute of Norwegian Occupation History], which was run by veterans of Nasjonal Samling. In this publication, it was the pupils on the Ris memorial stone that were the baddies, while the goodies were the headmaster of Ullern School and the Austrian Alpine troops. Perhaps this version of events appealed to Jens Erik, who was 'frozen out and stopped going to school', almost like the collaborators during the war.

There was a telephone number in the journal, which Jens Erik called. Suddenly he had friends and a political mission. Jens Erik dropped out of school in the summer of 1984.

The extreme right-wing groups took care of outsiders. They accepted the odd ones. Ideology and politics were not really that important for Jens Erik. The important thing was to be accepted. He wanted to be part of a group. It was the same story as with Johnny Olsen, who was convicted of murdering two men in the Hadeland area in 1981, or the groups in the Nordstrand and Bøler neighbourhoods of Oslo in the nineties, members of which murdered the Norwegian-Ghanaian boy Benjamin Hermansen in 2001. These were outsiders, some of whom had also been robbed or harassed by gangs of immigrants in the nineties. Crime was a part of the package, as those who went into extreme right-wing groups had already crossed a number of boundaries. One day, Jens Erik was driving together with his new friends past a mosque in Frogner.

'Someone should see to blowing that place up,' the leader said.

'OK,' said Jens Erik.

A few days later, he was given some dynamite and a blasting cap by some of the group leaders. Then one night he went out to place the bomb. You do as your group tells you.

According to the school, R–I–S stands for respect, initiative and serving each other. Some are left out, though, and among them are people who have been behind some of the most notorious terrorist attacks in Norwegian history.

Growing Pains in the Nineties

Anders Behring Breivik encountered another side of Oslo when he started at Ris Lower Secondary School in 1992, aged thirteen. The new pupils were lined up outside. The headmaster came out of the school building, wearing his combat dress as an army reserve captain. The headmaster had been on refresher training and greeted the new class like a sergeant at boot camp. It is uncertain whether the headmaster's military style really helped to improve the school. Sometimes the tannoy crackled and the headmaster would announce: 'Whoever's left a Mozell-branded fizzy pear drink bottle on the steps has five minutes to remove said bottle.' Many in the classrooms would giggle and impersonate his lisp, and even some of the teachers would shake their heads.

Even if the headmaster was not always respected, though, he was feared. The pupils he did not like would have a hard time at school. The pupil body had changed since the eighties, too. In the early nineties, the lower secondary unit from Smestad School was transferred to Ris. New pupils came, from Hoff and Skøyen, who often had a different social background to the youth from the grand houses of Slemdal and Vinderen. The school community became more open and varied. The variety that Støre was looking for in the seventies came to Ris. The first pupils from immigrant backgrounds appeared in the schoolyard. The new Norway was on its way.

But this new diversity, as well as the increasing level of contact between the West End and the young people further east, was no straightforward matter. Violence and juvenile crime became widespread in a different way from before in the West End of Oslo. The number of reported violent incidents in Oslo rose by 22 per cent in a four-year period in the nineties,[4] suggesting that Mono's experience of his time at Ris was not just plucked out of thin air. The problem of class, which had possibly never been completely absent, reappeared, but in a new and confusing form. The cap in the hand of the poor boy now did not belong to him; it belonged to you, and he had stolen it. The idea of honour resurfaced. Young people in the nineties had to look after themselves and their possessions. In the process, they discovered the concept of honour: in other words, they took it from the gangs who beat them up.

Hip-hop culture had arrived in Oslo in earnest, offering new opportunities to young people who previously would have been left out. The pig farmer's son was reborn as a hip gangster, and the girls saw him in a different light. The growing pains of the most recent, international wave of immigration were tearing through the city, and the new pupils at Ris Lower Secondary School stood on top of demographic, social and cultural fault lines without realizing their significance. It was as if Oslo itself were a teenager, awkward and uncomfortable, with knobbly knees and bones aching from its sudden growth, short-tempered and moody due to the tempestuous hormones sweeping through its body.

My younger relatives and friends' children frequently spoke of fights and thefts around this time, often involving young immigrants. The author Aslak Nore summed it up it thus: 'For young people in Oslo in the nineties, theft was a central rite of passage, almost on the same level as confirmation and their first kiss.'[5] It was in the nineties that the consequences of immigration and the multicultural society first manifested themselves in the West End.

At both Smestad School and Ris, a growing number of pupils came from foreign backgrounds, first and foremost from Pakistan, and some of these youngsters had links to gangs further east in the city. The gangs were better organized and more determined. Teenagers started turning up and loitering in the West End of Oslo, on the lookout for snobs to rob and girls to chat up. The immigrant boys were feared and mythologized, and this fear descended on the schoolyards when the gangs came in from the suburbs. This had the strongest effect of all on the taggers, who often allied themselves with what the Oslo rap group Karpe Diem called the 'West End niggers' – young people from minority backgrounds with links to the city's gangs. This gave the East End lads access to parties and girls, while those from the West End got protection. But it was an arrangement that bred contempt, and many of the taggers would pay for it sooner or later.

These security pacts were based not on equality but on hierarchy. The gangs in the Oslo area viewed respect as a zero-sum game: in order to get more respect, you had to take it away from others. In normal social transactions, as we learn at school, respect is based on trust; people have mutual respect for each other, and both parties come out stronger. That is not how it works with gangs. For them, respect is about inspiring fear and exercising power over others. When this type of respect becomes a central social value for which young people compete, it is a recipe for conflict. Youngsters would throw insults at each other. 'Gaylord!' 'Your sister's a whore!' Those who put up with the insults lost all their respect. Those who fought but were given a beating lost a little respect. Those who fought and won took respect from the person they beat.[6] The gangs derived their ethos from criminal cultures, even though they often referred to traditions from their home countries.

'*Izzat*,' the Pakistanis would say: 'honour' in Punjabi.

People who submitted in order to get protection had no respect and so could not expect that their agreements would be honoured if the conditions changed. According to the researcher Inger Lise Lien, the Norwegian boys often came out of this game worse off. They also had to accept that the Norwegian girls went after who was coolest on the streets and so preferred the boys from foreign backgrounds. To some of the Norwegian boys, it appeared as if they had been left as losers, pale dorks ousted from the sexual market, snubbed by history – in their own city.

One solution was to start their own gangs only for Norwegians. Many of these groups became violent and semi-criminal, and many of them were characterized by white pride music and extreme right-wing attitudes. An extreme right-wing group also emerged at Ris Lower Secondary School in the nineties, ten years after Jens Erik had dropped out.

This is not the whole story, of course. In many respects, integration has been successful in Oslo, and the same young people who cursed those with other skin colours, whether white, black or brown, often had friends, girlfriends or boyfriends of different ethnicities. Still, these conflicts in youth culture left their mark. Even fifteen years later, thirty-somethings who had grown up in the West End still described their Pakistani friends and classmates as treacherous vermin.

'It always ended with the Pakistanis stabbing you in the back,' sighed a former tagger from Røa, in the West End. A guy from Tåsen spoke about a Moroccan classmate at Sogn Upper Secondary School who allegedly explained to the Norwegian boys that the immigrants had come to Norway to fuck their women and steal their money. 'He repeated it as often as he could. How do you think a seventeen-year-old would react to that?'

A lad from Bærum started a rumour that the 'B Gang', a notorious Pakistani gang, was deliberately colonizing the West End with Pakistanis strategically moving to live in new parts of town. With eyes in the schools and on the streets, the B Gang could stake out the refined houses of the West End and rob the promising youth of the area. This rumour was probably just as distant from reality as Breivik's idea that Oslo's eleven-year-olds engage in oral sex en masse, but it is an accurate expression of the feeling among sections of the West End youth in the nineties of being besieged by the invading hordes from Asia.

On the other hand, the immigrant children did not have an easy time in the West End either. The rap duo Karpe Diem's single 'Vestkantsvartinga' [West End nigger] does not describe a dark-skinned superman, a Muslim Tony Soprano in a Norwegian chicken run. The song deals with just how isolated immigrant children were in the sea of white boys and girls, with their expensive brand-name clothes, holiday cabins at Kragerø, good marks at school and condescending attitudes towards those who were different. A former player on the boys' team of the Ready Football Club said that the dads of the West End team Heming, from Slemdal, cheered on their team by shouting 'Come on, Norway' when they played against a largely black team from the East End.

The city may no longer have been quite as socially divided as it once was, but the social fusion was not without pain. Oslo was going through a hard time. Its young people were facing new dilemmas and choosing different paths. The parents and teachers of the 1968 generation had passed down a pleasant mental ballast to the teenagers of the nineties – the thought that different cultures can enrich each other – but this did not seem very meaningful when a gang of bullies from Somalia, Turkey or Pakistan ran off with your watch.

Anders Behring Breivik landed in the middle of this chaos. During his time at secondary school, he was supposed to find out who he was, who he wanted to be with and what it was all about. Who was Anders Behring Breivik?

There are some striking similarities between Breivik and Jens Erik. Both lived with their single mothers who were incomers to Oslo (and so did not have much of a social network) and were slightly below their classmates in terms of financial status and where they lived. They were immigrants to the West End and were lacking the key to the locked manor-house door. No entry for the working class. Neither of them were sportsmen; Anders was actually quite clumsy but managed to do enough practice to become 'average plus' in ball-games, according to one of his friends. Both of them were interested in the history of warfare. They were good pupils but perhaps not top of the class. Both of them sought out criminal groups, and both dropped out of upper secondary school.

The big difference at Ris between 1982 and 1992 (apart from the difference between its being an upper secondary and a lower secondary) was that the social make-up had become more varied by 1992. In addition to the snobs, the Nazis and the rockers, hip-hop had come to Ris. Breivik became a hip-hopper. He would play not at being a Nazi but at being a gangster. The single-parent boy from Skøyen was more justified than many others in identifying with the lads from the East End suburbs. He tagged, spoke Kebab Norwegian slang and bought American hip-hop clothing from the Jean TV shop downtown at Arkaden shopping centre. The slang for white Norwegians was 'potatoes', and Anders later described himself as 'the cool potato'.[7] Like other cool potatoes, Anders had his own security pact, a Pakistani friend with connections to the legendary gang superheroes in the East End.

Breivik's friend 'Rafik' had also come from Smestad Primary School. He was one of Breivik's neighbours. At Ris the two boys were inseparable, according to the other pupils, together in their outsiderness. Even though Anders always wore expensive clothes, the snob culture, Old Ris, regarded the pair from Smestad as losers and wannabes. Anders was slim and pale. His friend was a Paki. They came from the 'slum' down in the hollow below Frogner Park. They were scorned. It was worse for Rafik, who was one of the first from a non-Western background at the school and was tormented because he was different. Perhaps he was subjected to the same amorphous exclusion as Jens Erik, but, according to some of his fellow pupils, there were also more directly racist smears. It was not the neo-Nazis who were the worst tormentors but, just as much, the polo-shirt brigade from the fanciest postcode areas of Oslo.

Perhaps Rafik learnt something from his first year at lower secondary. By the following year he was another person; the caterpillar had turned into a black butterfly. Those who had tormented him would soon see. He spoke about his cousins in the East End.

One of the hip-hoppers from Ris met him on the metro one day. He said hello to Rafik, since the two boys had got on fine during the first year. Rafik was together with another boy, and he ordered his classmate to go with them and steal from some snobs up at Midtstuen. The hip-hopper could act as a guide for Rafik and the gangster from the East End. If he said no, there would be trouble. The other boy looked at him menacingly. They were serious. The hip-hopper pulled open the doors of the metro carriage and squeezed out at Gaustad station before the two young thieves had time to react. He ran through the streets of Ris and Vinderen, racing home. He did not speak to Rafik again after that day.

It was rumoured that Rafik's relatives were in the B Gang. Other pupils from Ris saw Rafik bringing thugs from the East End to exact revenge on those he thought were racists. The boys at school began to keep a distance. People who had previously felt sorry for Rafik, who had ignored him or looked down on him, now became afraid of him.

So Rafik was Anders' 'security pact', his connection to the gang culture. Through Rafik, Anders had an opportunity for contact not only with GSV, the crew from Vålerenga, but also with one of the toughest gangs in Oslo: the B Gang. These were the most dangerous boys, with the most expensive cars and the best-looking girls. In any case, Anders thought this was a golden opportunity for 'the cool potato'. He intensified his tagging, took risks, honed his ghetto style. But it all led nowhere. It is not enough just to think that you are cool; you have to convince others too.

Anders later claimed that he had been betrayed by Rafik and beaten up by his friends. Rafik thought that they simply grew apart, as teenagers do. Anders gradually came to think that Rafik had been carrying out jihad, that the juvenile crime of the nineties was Islamic holy war against infidels. In police questioning, Rafik said that Anders had constructed his past. He had no connections to the B Gang. Not only had Anders fabricated incidents that had not happened and retold urban myths with no basis in reality, he had also interpreted the whole package in a context of religious conflict that he had plucked out of thin air. What had happened in the nineties was a matter of juvenile crime, not jihad.

Other pupils from Ris thought that Rafik remained friends with Anders while he had no other friends but left him as soon as some new friends emerged. It was a typical situation: two outcasts will find their way to each other, but if one of them has a chance to be part of a group he will leave. A common fate is not the same as friendship.

Whatever happened, Anders did not relinquish his style from Ris or, perhaps, his idea that he was 'the cool potato', the West End tagger with friends in the B Gang. When he started at Nissen Upper Secondary School in 1995, his classmates reacted negatively to the fact that he spoke Kebab Norwegian and dressed and behaved like an immigrant from the ghetto. A genuine, tough hip-hopper? What a joke.

Anders did not take the point. He was in the same boat as the immigrants, at least in some respects, so why could he not talk and dress like them? It slowly dawned on him that a wannabe Paki was just about the least cool thing you could be at the cultured Nissen School. Perhaps the culture clash at Nissen was one of the reasons why Anders applied to transfer to Oslo Commerce School and toned down his hip-hop style. He saw no more of Rafik. He had no security pact any more, if one had ever existed. His old tagging friends had gone. He tried to adapt, but it was as if he never quite found his niche. Either things went completely wrong or nobody noticed him.

He attended Oslo Commerce School for a year and a half without being noticed. But he left his name behind him at Skøyen bus depot and on the façades of buildings from Ullern to Kolbotn: Morg.

The Aesthetic of Destruction

For the metro passengers who saw the letters daubed on the walls every single day, it was not clear what the taggers were really trying to convey. Most of us cannot even decipher what the taggers have written. 'GSV'? Or was that 'CLN' written on the wall? The letters just ran into each other anyway. Word porridge. What was the point?

'I'm not a graffiti artist, I'm a graffiti bomber,' the tagger Cap says in the film *Style Wars*. This US documentary from 1983 deals with different schools of graffiti in New York and is the taggers' bible. The graffiti writer Cap, who is white, is the villain of the idealistic and multicultural graffiti world shown in the film. Cap does not paint burners or intricate pieces; he is destructive. His aim is to tag *more* than the others. Not big or beautiful pieces, but to leave his mark everywhere – on every wall and every carriage.

When Cap sees a wall where a crew has spent hours or days working painstakingly on a piece, he immediately writes 'Cap' on top of it. Simply and quickly, in red and white. Happiness for him is destroying what is beautiful, because everything beautiful deserves to be erased, forever. No colours, nothing attractive, just destruction for the sake of it – in order to say 'fuck you', to say 'no', to say 'don't'. Cap does not see any friendly community of idealistic graffiti artists; he sees no rainbow race creating warmth together, with keen colours on cold concrete. Graffiti is war, and Cap wants to dominate and subdue the others.

While the others are organized in crews, Cap is a one-man army, alone against the world. Sometimes he cannot even be bothered to write, just spraying wavy lines along the sides of carriages and walls, so-called spaghetti. The other taggers in the film accuse him of being talentless, jealous and desperate for publicity, but Cap just answers: 'I'm a king of bombing.'

Cap articulates the same aesthetic of destruction as that described by Mishima in *The Temple of the Golden Pavilion*. By destroying what is beautiful, you create a peculiar, terrible form of beauty. In a way, you also take the power of the piece you destroy. You diss the tagger who made it, and, in the zero-sum game for respect, you take respect away from him.

Graffiti was a big thing in the West End of Oslo during the nineties. Perhaps the municipality's campaigns and their associated fines, incarcerations and brutal security guards contributed to spreading the view of graffiti as vandalism and as warfare not only among Oslo's citizens, who were initially quite indifferent towards the paintings on the walls, but also among the taggers themselves. It was not only a matter of writing your name in the city, especially in difficult spots where many people would see it and where there was a danger of being caught; it was also a matter of destruction, bombing metro stations and billboards or maybe capping – in other words, ruining other people's pieces.

Cap's spirit crossed the ocean when the taggers started 'lining', or crossing out, other tags and throwies, painting wavy lines along the train windows and beating each other up. One of the larger crews was known as TSC, the Spaghetti Crew. Some crews detested colours and wrote only in silver and black. Oslo would become the silver city. Another factor that contributed to the nineties tagging culture in Oslo becoming so tough and brutal could be that the general level of youth violence was higher in the nineties than in the eighties or the noughties.[8] This meant that there were two ways to gain prestige as a tagger: you could be good or you could be crazy.

Anders followed Cap's formula in not going for big or beautiful pieces, but for more. He bombed across the city. In February 1994 he was back at Skøyen bus depot. While the Winter Olympics were being held in Lillehammer, the boy who wanted to be king was caught for the first time. This time, it was the guards who had their eye on the taggers, and Morg, the bus tagger from Ris, was reported for the first time. His case ended up with mediators. Morg 'did not plead guilty but declared himself willing to repair the vandalism', according to the police report. Anders was unable to admit guilt. He 'defends himself intensely when he does something "wrong"', Ris School reported, pointing to incidents when he had been late, had forgotten his homework or was confronted by his teachers for other reasons.

For Anders, his tagging was a way of living out his identity as a lower-class gangster. It was also an instructive experience, and possibly a formative one. A tagger is a salesman trying to sell himself as a tough guy, an advertiser with an eye for which surfaces are best suited to spreading his message, and an artist, since the aesthetic of destruction is still an aesthetic. Tagging was his first encounter with crime, and the first time he bombed the city. Perhaps, most of all, it was also an opportunity to be part of a secret community, a kind of fraternal lodge for the initiated.

In 'Fra vugge til grav' [From cradle to grave], a song by the hip-hop group Klovner i kamp [literally, 'clowns at war'], a group member known as Dansken ['the Dane'] describes his past as a tagger:

> Me and Dr S drew sketches in our rooms as kids
> And walked up and down bombing the streets where we lived.
> We bought Multiple T, stashing the cans in our bags
> And ran from everyday heroes, cops and guard skags.
> But I was a jammy dodger and life's not fair
> So it was always Dr S who ended up getting snared.

A tagger who did not fit into any crew could fall back on Cap's idea of being a one-man army. During this period, Anders started doing exercise. He got up early in the morning to do a session before school. He also did his newspaper round, so as rebels come he was an extraordinarily disciplined boy. He was able to get fit, to put on the 'game face', as he would later say. Having been a slender boy, he gradually became strong and muscular, but he was still no tough guy and perhaps thought with horror about what would happen if the guards caught him a third time.

Figuratively, taggers are a cross between terrorists (who 'bomb') and hit men using 'silencers' on their spray cans – in other words, magnets under the cans to keep the little mixing balls still, so they do not make too much noise. When the young Aksel Hennie ran around the city at night with his bag full of spray cans, without knowing it he was practising for the lead role he would later play in the 2008 Norwegian epic *Max Manus: Man of War*, about the eponymous resistance hero from Oslo. Spok and Wick were Anders' two closest tagging friends, and both were well-known West End taggers with connections to a number of crews. Anders described himself as 'the glue of the gang',[9] the one who organized the group and built alliances – not a figurehead, but the one who led from behind the scenes. Other West End taggers thought that Anders was trying to command and control Spok and Wick, who responded by distancing themselves from him.

Anders was a typical teenager, extremely self-confident and extremely insecure at the same time. There was something dissonant about him, something persistent. He was working his socks off to be cool, but either you are cool or you are not. Rafik left him, and Spok and Wick disappeared. But Anders would not give up.

The second time he was caught, it was by the police, not security guards. On 23 December 1994, the fifteen-year-old arrived at Oslo Central Station all alone on the train from Copenhagen, and the police found forty-three spray cans in his bag. The vagrancy the SSBU had talked about had now taken on international proportions. Copenhagen was where cheap paint could be bought, so many Norwegian taggers would go there, and Anders had treated himself to a real Christmas present. Two weeks later, he was caught again. This time he was filmed by security guards writing on a railway underpass at Storo. The guards gave people two chances. According to the rules of the game, he would get a beating the next time he was caught.

In their report, the police were taken aback to discover that the boy 'was in possession of a metal-tipped emergency hammer'.

At this time, child welfare came back on the scene, ten years after they had dropped his case. There were some discussions between the caseworker, Anders and his mother. It turned out that he had travelled to Denmark on his own once before. His mother was worried that her son would become a criminal, but Anders played it down. In February 1995, the fifteen-year-old wrote a letter to child welfare to announce that he would no longer co-operate with them after having been 'exposed' at school. Grassing is the ultimate sin for a tagger, and he alleged that child welfare had grassed to people at school about his situation. The school pointed out that it was Anders himself who had told them about his child welfare case when his class were discussing tagging and ethics, but Anders was adamant.

At the same time, his mother withdrew her consent enabling child welfare to obtain information in relation to the case. Perhaps she was not worried any more, perhaps she did not like things coming out that put her family in a bad light, or maybe she was just following some kind of internal pattern. She asked for help and then pulled out. She gave her consent and then withdrew it. The same pattern repeated itself from the saga of the respite home in 1981 to the court case in 2012. Neither mother nor son attended their next appointments. Child welfare shrugged their shoulders and dropped the case, stating that it appeared as if the small family had 'made up'.

His trips to Copenhagen were not the only thing that Anders was known for at Ris School. Like most boys, he was involved in a couple of fights, in which he both beat up other people and was beaten up himself, but the incident many former pupils remember is the time he punched the headmaster. The military-style headmaster had apparently accused Anders of committing some violation or another, but nobody remembers any more whether it was to do with tagging or a fizzy pear drink bottle left on the steps. Perhaps the headmaster saw honour and respect more or less the same way as the gangs did. Anders denied having done anything wrong.

'Alright,' said the headmaster. 'Then hit me, if it's true that you didn't do it.'

It is unknown what the headmaster really meant by that, but Anders did as he was told and punched the headmaster in the chest – hard. Maybe in a way the headmaster was like the judge in the custody case ten years earlier, a man from the fifties with old-fashioned values and slightly simplistic solutions to the difficult problems facing Ris School. Many of the other pupils would probably have liked to see Anders hit him even harder.

At the end of their time at lower secondary, the whole of class 9A went on an end-of-term trip to a cabin on the island of Hvasser, near Tjøme in Vestfold county. They were going to swim, have a barbecue and reminisce about their time together. On the train down to Tønsberg, Anders gave a sly smile. Something was rattling in his bag.

'Shit, Anders! Have you brought spray cans along now?!' His classmates shook their heads.

'Of course,' said Anders. 'We're going to Tønsberg, after all.'

It was as if he was unable to appreciate that this was neither the time nor the place. His classmates explained to him that it would be impossible for him to do anything in Tønsberg in the quarter of an hour they had before getting their bus. This was not a tagging mission but an end-of-term trip. An end-of-school trip! Was he going to tag the rocks on the shore or something? Forget it, Anders. But the spray cans did come in useful after all.

As twilight fell on the bonfire where class 9A were gathered on the island, out came the cans from the bag. One by one, Anders threw them on the bonfire, where they exploded with thunderous roars. The flames from the explosions reached up high into the warm June air. Three years at fucking Ris were over with a bang, and Anders' career as a tagger was as good as over too, at least as far as he was concerned.

Tagging had given Anders training in planning and carrying out illegal acts. His bedroom at Silkestrå had become a war room where material procurement and operations were planned in detail. One of his friends later said that Anders carried the idea that 'your reputation follows you' on into his adult life.[10] Tagging gave him a modus operandi, and, maybe most importantly, tagging was the first time that Anders created an avatar for himself: Morg.

Taggers have a signature, a persona if you like, which is the name they write. Morg was Anders Behring Breivik's alias, his first virtual self. Morg was a bad boy, a one-man army, a criminal rebel and an artist with a code of honour. Just as a narcissist creates an inflated self-image, Anders had created Morg, and he used Morg to market himself. For a number of old acquaintances from his tagging days, Anders was not 'Anders' but 'the guy who used to write "Morg"'. They had forgotten his name, if they had ever known it, but they remembered his tag.

Taggers choose their names for various reasons. Their names should be cool, they should express something, show attitude, and they should look good when they are sprayed on walls. Morg was not a bad tag. It was easy to remember and slightly creepy, since it sounded like the English word 'morgue'. It also contains a reference to the Marvel comics of the early nineties, and that is probably where Anders found his name.[11]

The company Marvel Comics has been in business since 1939 and is best known for superheroes such as Captain America, Spiderman and the Fantastic Four, but the Marvel Universe also contains a host of supervillains. One of them is Morg, known as the executioner. His weapon is a double-edged axe, an executioner's axe, which he used to behead his own people. Morg is a traitor: when his people were defeated, he went into the service of the victors and was assigned the duty of executing his own people, which he performed mercilessly.

To describe the stories and characters of the Marvel Universe as cartoonish is putting it mildly. They are almost impossible to relate to the uninitiated, but it is easy to see how Morg could fit into 'RL', real-life stories. He would not have been a name on the memorial stone outside Ris School. Morg the executioner was on the same side as Heinrich Himmler and the headmaster at Ullern School during the war.

The illustrations of Morg depict a swollen, reddish torso with muscles like inflated balloons. His shoulders and upper arms bristle with lizard-like spikes for use as defensive and offensive weapons. Beneath his thin hair, his face is distorted in a skull-like grimace. His enormous, double-headed axe hangs in front of his crotch like a colossal phallus.

If you take away the exaggerated and comic aspects of the Marvel Universe (even though caricature is the whole point), if you, heaven forbid, were to view the comics as a kind of reality, or reality as a

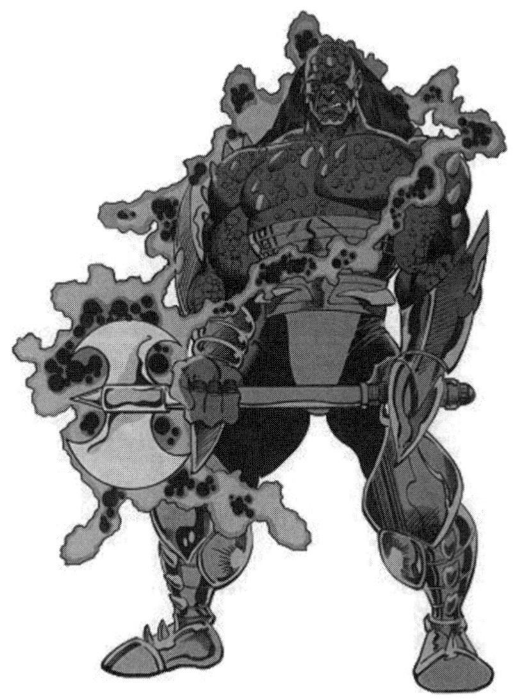

The supervillain Morg

kind of comic book, then the figure of Morg is sadism incarnate. The only thing missing is an SS badge. The supervillain has some of the characteristics of Cain, the brother-killer, and represents the same aesthetic of destruction as professed by Cap. Anders had an emergency hammer, but perhaps it was Morg with his axe standing there at Grønland police station in January 1995, denying he had been tagging, even though he accepted the fine of 3,000 kroner. Morg can also be bought online as a plastic action figure.

Anders would cultivate a considerable number of avatars over the years, but Morg was his first.

The Tåsen Gang

One day, while Anders was in year nine at school, there was trouble during the lunch break. Visitors came to Ris, and some of the lads from Ris turned pale. They knew they had crossed one of the city's invisible boundaries, and now they were worried about what the consequences would be. The gang that was paying Ris a visit was made up not of Kurds or Albanians but of Norwegians. It was not from one of the East End suburbs of Oslo but from Tåsen, in the north of the city, a white middle-class neighbourhood not far from Ris.

The Tåsen Gang was gaining recognition and respect all across Oslo because they took a stand against the immigrants and the powerful gangs. A couple of years later, the villa gangsters from Tåsen had become legend: the lads who were tougher than the immigrants. Child thieves on the metro's Sognsvann line and gate-crashers from downtown who turned up at parties between Kringsjå and Blindern risked getting beaten up by the Tåsen Gang. But this time, the gang was out for revenge.

The weekend before, some of the lads from Ris had been at a party with girls from Tåsen, thereby stepping quite some distance into the Tåsen Gang's territory. The fourteen- and fifteen-year-olds from Tåsen were already notorious maniacs and bullies and were now going to beat up the lads at Ris, teach them a lesson and then hurry back to their own lessons at Tåsen School.

Anders must have noticed the anxiety in the eyes of the young aristocrats from Ris who knew that they did not stand a chance against the lads from Tåsen, and perhaps this sight made an impression on him. The Tåsen guys had entered the schoolyard, looking for their victims, when the situation took an unexpected turn. Out of the main building rushed the headmaster. He caught hold of a couple of the Tåsen kids and quickly and resolutely reduced the tough guys to a group of normal boys leaving Ris School slightly crestfallen, with unfinished business. Behind them were some relieved boys from Ris, and a pensive Anders Breivik.

One of the Tåsen lads who were there that day, 'Dekor', laughed about the incident. 'That's what it was like sometimes. Even those of us who were so damn cool got beaten sometimes. Initiative is everything in situations like that, and that headmaster at Ris sure knew how to sort out people.'

The urban myth of Anders' generation about how ruthless the immigrants were was to do with a Norwegian girl who was battered by a Pakistani gang in Frogner Park. The boys allegedly cut up her face with a knife, as the pimps in Naples used to do to brand their whores in the nineteenth century. Breivik mentioned this story in his compendium, as well as an alleged rape of another Norwegian girl by a group of Pakistanis. He also wrote about a number of incidents in which he got into trouble with immigrants and 'wannabe Pakistanis' (which presumably means Norwegians), the result of which, with a couple of exceptions, was that he had to run off, was beaten up, or both.

In one of these cases, Breivik accused Rafik of being involved in an incident in which Breivik was punched on the steps at Majorstua. Again it is uncertain how much of this is true, and his friends raised doubts about a number of these incidents. Rafik told people he knew that he did not know about any rape incident, and that there had not been any dramatic break between him and Anders. When they would meet each other later, it was always on good terms.

In Anders' compendium, the Oslo of the nineties is characterized by contempt for women, a gangster mentality, racism and a kind of violent sexuality in which sex with the Norwegian 'potato whores', whether it was willing or unwilling, was a symbolic rape of Norway as a nation and a humiliation of Norwegian men. Hundreds of Norwegians had allegedly been killed in jihadi attacks, he claimed, while right-wing extremists were responsible for only one killing: the murder of Benjamin Hermansen. In addition to his own experiences, Anders had 'heard of and witnessed hundreds of Jihadi-racist attacks, more then 90% of them aimed at helpless Norwegian youth (who themselves are brought up to be "suicidally" tolerant and therefore are completely unprepared mentally for attacks such as these)'.[12] Although this situation was exaggerated and presented in quite absurd terms, it was not entirely plucked out of thin air (if we are to believe researchers), so against this background maybe it was not so strange that Anders changed course while at upper secondary school. Not only did he leave Nissen School for the Commerce School, but he also went from being a 'wannabe Pakistani' to coming into contact with the Tåsen Gang.

Some people can speak without even opening their mouths. 'Dekor' is such a person. His face is not one that you forget. It tells a story as soon as he sits down at the table: a story about the city of Oslo. Dekor also has a physical presence that you cannot get away from. You can feel him from a distance, as if he were standing right next to you when he is really on the other side of the table, eating his salad. Dekor is towering in height, even when he is sitting down, although he has evolved over the years from a fierce Viking towards being a friendly teddy bear. He is calm and attentive, and his jaws show no signs of the steroids he used to take. He talks slowly in short, concise sentences, occasionally dragging his words out, as if caressing them before sending them out into the world. He has the air of an artist who enjoys attention and likes telling a good story.

Maybe the Tåsen Gang was partly theatre, like black grouse trying to ward off their rivals, a gang of over-energetic boys, some diagnosed with ADHD, improvising ever wilder performances and relishing the associated attention. Clowns at war. Their stage was composed of streets and newsagents' shops, parties and schoolyards in the north and west of Oslo. Dekor's father was in show business and a band manager, among other things. Dekor was a driving force in the Tåsen Gang: the craziest, the strongest and the one who had the wildest parties.

'I was actually a bit of an outsider at school,' Dekor explained. 'Didn't have many friends, wasn't cool. But when I started lower secondary, it was a turning point in my life. I walloped one of the cool kids. He went straight down. Suddenly I was the cool one. "Wow", I thought, "this works." In a way, you could say that was how it started.'

It was fighting that would become a trademark for Dekor and eventually for the other lads in the group that became known as the Tåsen Gang, but it was fighting 2.0 compared to the normal fights at parties that I remember from the eighties. It was immigrants who taught them.

When they were fourteen or fifteen, the conflict with the immigrant gangs began, including the Pakistanis in the 'A Gang' from Bjølsen and the Young Guns. Dekor remembers this as a series of humiliations. The gangs would surround their victims, taking their caps, pushing them around and spitting at them, preferably while the girls were watching. The Tåsen lads decided to put a stop to this degradation. Things like that should not happen, so they fought back. The Norwegian boys were used to fighting one on one. The problem was that, when they did that and won, the rest of the gang would jump on them and give them a real beating. You learn from experiences like that.

The Tåsen Gang began to fight as a group. 'I've got fifteen psychopaths behind me' is a line from the song 'Alt som ikke dreper' [What doesn't kill us] by Klovner i kamp. The rap group had its origins in the Tåsen Gang, and the gang's motto was 'What doesn't kill us makes us stronger'. You had to bear pain, laughing off a punch in the face. When the immigrants started using knives, the Tåsen Gang armed themselves too, with bats, stones or whatever was to hand. One of the lads became known for beating up people with ashtrays, and broken bottles were a recurrent theme.

One of the lads became a specialist in neo-Nazi music, and, through Sogn Upper Secondary School, the Tåsen boys got to know the neo-Nazis from Bøler. They had some parties together, but, although Dekor and the others once tagged the school at Sogn with slogans such as 'Pakis go home' or 'Norway for Norwegians', the Tåsen Gang never became an extreme right-wing group. At Sogn they actually managed to spell 'Norway for Norweigans', which became a local joke at Tåsen. This racist stunt caused the conflict with the immigrant gangs to flare up again, as the school at Sogn took in pupils from across the city.

Dekor became an expert in fighting, and his philosophy was simple: 'Initiative. Initiative is everything. It doesn't matter how big you are or how many of you there are. If you just make the first move and go straight at them, you'll win. Even if you go at them and get a beating, you haven't lost. OK, you get beaten up, but you still won because you showed initiative.'

Gangs are about fellowship, respect, territory, parties, rules and stories: more or less like tagging. Dekor, Dansken and several of the other Tåsen lads were taggers. Crime is the logical consequence of gang activity; breaking the laws of society strengthens the group's internal bonds. The Tåsen Gang did a few small jobs, but they never competed with the Pakistani gangs or the Tveita Gang, which were involved or became involved in serious crime. The Tåsen Gang started stealing cars, for fun and not making any money out of it. Dekor acquired a universal Ford Escort key from a garage, so they could take as many Escorts as they wanted. 'That's how we learnt to drive,' he explained. 'We did handbrake skids on the pitch at Voldsløkka and would zoom around on the gravel there.'

Apart from some minor burglaries of newsagents, Dekor and his friends were not particularly interested in break-ins. The Tåsen lads liked doing things when they would be seen – for example, they might go into a 7-Eleven shop and help themselves to things from the shelves en masse so all the staff could do was watch. Dekor specialized in hit-and-run raids at petrol stations and paint shops. He would storm in like a thundercloud, grab spray cans, Tectyl and whatever he needed for his tagging, then disappear just as suddenly as he had appeared. Initiative and shock tactics were his trademark. 'Later on we started dealing, mainly at Sogn and the schools in the West End,' he explained, 'and then we soon realized that it was better to earn money than to spend it all the time. But we never went very far as drug-dealers.'

Drugs first entered the scene when they were in their late teens, mostly hash and cocaine, and anabolic steroids.

The Tadpole Mafia

Anders turned up in Tåsen aged seventeen or eighteen, probably in the summer between his second and third years at the Commerce

School, according to the Tåsen lads' back-calculations. Some of Anders' tagging mates from Ris had played with Dekor in Lyn Football Club, and it was through these connections that Anders turned up at the legendary parties at Dekor's place. Admittance was not offered to just anybody, but the Tåsen lads had heard of Morg. Anders had graffiti-bombed the city centre, on Karl Johans Gate. It was not easy to write your name there, and Anders won respect for that story.

To tell the truth, it was not by tagging that the Tåsen Gang made their name. 'Our clique painted trains with silver sleek and buses with black brushes,' Dansken rapped. 'The sight of a new fresh coloured burner gave life essence. / I got lessons, but my talent didn't improve with patience / The explanation, sorry for painting, not my vocation.' Perhaps because the Tåsen Gang's tagging skills were so bad, they let Anders bomb with their crew, RTM, which stood for 'Royal Trade Mark' or '*Rumpetrollmafiaen*' ['The Tadpole Mafia']. A loved child has many names, as the Norwegian proverb says, and so does a crew of taggers. Dekor thought that Anders was a better-known tagger than he was, even though Anders did not have any major talent either. Skøyen's own Munch he was not, but you can get far in tagging if you make some effort and are bold, like Morg. At Dekor's parties, Anders also demonstrated another ability that won him respect with the villa gangsters. A couple of the lads were good at arm-wrestling, but Anders beat them both.

'He was fit,' one of the Tåsen lads remembered. 'There weren't many of us who did weights back then, but Anders did.'

Before long, Anders had established himself as a kind of Tåsen Gang hanger-on. One night in June, the police caught him again, this time for driving a moped without a licence and with a blood alcohol level over 0.1 per cent. He joined the Tåsen Gang for their parties and went out bombing with RTM. This must have made an impression on Anders. He was not exactly the coolest in the class at either Ris or Nissen, but now he had been accepted by the toughest lads in town. He had not been successful as a 'West End nigger', but so what? All those nights he had spent at some godforsaken concrete underpass or metro station half the way to Bærum were finally paying off, all those nights he had spent his hard-earned paper round money spraying out 'Morg, Morg, Morg, Morg, Morg'.

The Tåsen Gang were showmen and they were Norwegians; their ideals were heroic and things were simple: either you had cred or you were a nerd. If you lost your status, you were finished; the gang did not accept losers. The immigrants who used to be heroes were now enemies. Bloody Muslims, and fuck those Norwegian girls who got involved with immigrants. 'We called them Paki whores,' Dekor explained.

One night during the magical summer of 1997, Anders went alone with Dekor, Mr Tåsen himself, to graffiti-bomb Vestgrensa station. This was a sign of how far he had come. In the old days, at Skøyen bus depot, he had dreamt of belonging to a crew, being part of a gang and being respected. After four years of hard struggle, he had made it from there to Tåsen. Morg the executioner had finally pulled it off. The two boys vanished into the midnight darkness, down towards the city through empty streets, past gardens with fruit trees and trampolines. Down in Bjølsen, on the A Gang's patch, they bombed walls and bus stops as a message to Rashid and the other child thieves from Pakiland. Perhaps a message from Morg to Rafik too, and to all the others who had let him down over the years. When he was with Dekor, he had nothing to fear. His reputation alone was enough to keep people away. Anders had been caught for tagging twice before. True, that was a long time ago, but perhaps he was worried about being caught a third and final time.

He told Dekor stories about Security Concept, the company that the public transport authorities were using for their tagbusting campaign. People came all the way from New York to study Oslo's fight against graffiti, and on the front line for the municipal council was a former mercenary soldier, a man who was rumoured to be able to break bones with his bare hands – an articulate smart guy with officer training who was polite in a psychopathic way. You were safe on the streets, but if you went near any public transport facilities, the guards might be hiding in the bushes anywhere.

The alpha male Dekor pricked up his ears in interest. Perhaps he suspected he would run into the mercenary sooner or later.

Morg and Dekor walked on into the dawn light, past Ullevål Hospital and the towering outlines of the oak trees in John Colletts Allé, and up to Damplassen. It was warm, as if Oslo had become a friendlier and safer version of its usual hard and moody self. Their spray cans rattled in their bags, and they had already made a sketch of the piece they were planning. At Vestgrensa station there was a wall at the back of a nursery school that was visible from the metro. The wall was that night's big target, but first Morg and Dekor did a round of the metro station.

There, on the concrete walls and wooden fences, Morg officially became a part of RTM, the Tåsen crew. The two boys' tags fitted into the crew's name. First, Dekor sprayed 'dekoR', then he added a 'T', before Morg finished it with 'Morg', so that 'dekoRTMorg' was written on every surface of the now closed station, in many cases with a piece of spaghetti (a spray-painted line) at each end. Day was breaking as the boys drew up the outline of their piece on the wall. They had already been working at it for a while when Morg looked around. The first metro train would be along soon, and so might Security Concept too . . . Suddenly it was too much for Morg. 'Let's go,' he said.

The two boys felt danger approaching. Security guards? The mercenary himself? At night, paranoia can set in at any moment and get even the biggest, strongest and craziest tagger going. Even the tough Dekor. The two boys ran back to Tåsen, where Morg was staying the night at Dekor's place. Shortly before the two boys fell asleep, Morg said: 'If we carry on like this, we're going to be really famous.'

The End of Morg

In his compendium, Anders wrote that he stopped tagging at the age of sixteen, but that is probably false. According to Dekor, they were eighteen years old that night at Vestgrensa station. Maybe there was a reason why Anders wished to alter this point from his past. Apart from his tagging, he was not especially prominent in the Tåsen Gang. He was no tough guy. When his face appeared in the newspapers in the summer of 2011, his old friends did not recognize him.

'I've got a good memory for faces, but I didn't recognize Anders' face,' said the man who used to be famous for his ashtrays. 'Maybe because he was so anonymous. I really only remember one image of him from that period.'

There was often trouble and fighting at Dekor's parties, and on one occasion Anders was involved in such an incident, which he describes in his compendium. According to Breivik, the altercation was an example of an encounter with violent jihadists during his youth:

> (Time: 23:30) – Assault and attempted robbery – Us 10, them 12 Moroccans. Location Tåsen, Oslo.
>
> They were robbing (collecting Jizya) and beating local kafr/Norwegian kids at Tåsen Center, they had done this on numerous occasions. They didn't live there but travelled to Tåsen from a Muslim enclave on [*sic*] Oslo East. I was at a party on [*sic*] Tåsen when we heard they had just beaten one of my friends' younger brothers. We went there to chase them away from the neighbourhood. They had weapons, we had weapons. I was hit with a billiard [cue] in the head. Result of the fight: we made a deal with them, they promised they would never return and harass the Tåsen youngsters again.[13]

There are a number of interesting facets to the account of this incident. For one thing there is the use of religious terms such as *jizya* (a tax that was levied on non-Muslims in, for example, the Ottoman Empire) and *kafr* (an infidel) in relation to an ordinary incident of child delinquency.

It might appear as if something dawned on Breivik during the period when he read Fjordman's essays in the time after he had moved back to his mother's house in 2006. He began to understand his youth in the Islamic terms with which the online counter-jihadist milieu was so preoccupied. Theft by juvenile delinquents became *jizya*, lies became *taqiyya* (Koran-sanctioned deception to hide religious affiliation), while peaceable Norwegians became *dhimmi* (non-Muslims who live under sharia). The petty-criminal subculture of the nineties was reborn as a religious conflict.

But it was not only his use of terminology that showed that Anders had removed himself from the chaotic streets of Oslo and constructed his own virtual reality. The Tåsen lads who were involved in the same fight have a slightly different version of the scuffle at Tåsen's small shopping centre in the summer of 1997. 'We were having a party at my place,' Dekor recalled.

> Then there was a phone call from a good friend of mine, a guy who was a year younger than us, who said he'd been robbed at the shopping centre. We gathered a bunch of people from the party and ran over there with some bats and pool cues. We stormed into the youth club at Tåsen, Action 22, which was in the basement of the shopping centre. 'Come on then, you fucking Pakis!' we shouted. But there were so fucking many of them, there were more of them than us. So we lost the initiative. People thought 'uh-oh' and just stood there, a bit perplexed. There was some brawling back and forth, and I got a smack from the guy who was the leader of the other gang. One of them took a pool cue off one of us and hit him with it. It wasn't Anders though, but the guy who liked white pride music. I think it was a red-haired Moroccan who did it, a crazy guy who came to Norway as a child straight from the mountains of Morocco, so people said. So we decided to leave it at that and went back to the party quietly and calmly. So we lost that time. Fights were always different. But there was no mention of any deal that they wouldn't come back. Things didn't work like that.

While Anders usually portrayed himself in a good light, he also often claimed he had been beaten up when it was not true. He claimed that Muslims broke his nose and hit him on the head with a pool cue. Maybe he felt a need to fabricate examples of jihad, maybe he was just expressing his feeling of humiliation, or maybe it was a kind of masochistic fantasy that came to him later. Instead of remembering his mistreatment as a young child, Breivik exaggerated trivial adolescent incidents. Psychoanalysts speak of 'projective identification', by which suppressed memories of childhood abuse might be transferred to other situations.[14] By constructing a victim narrative in which Muslims are the assailants and he is the victim, perhaps Breivik was creating a picture of suppressed cruelty that he would later relate to as if it were real.

The Norwegian vigilantes of the Tåsen Gang were not quite as dominant as Anders wished to believe either. 'We were shit-scared of the immigrants too,' as one of the lads said.

The members of the Tåsen Gang were not, after all, as hardcore Norwegian and racist as their reputation suggested. Most of the boys had immigrant friends, and their hostility was directed more at concrete individuals or gangs than against specific skin colours, religions or ethnicities. Anders was a good school pupil and was intelligent, but he struggled to understand the 'social game'. He never became a cool hip-hopper, he did not realize it would be wrong to tag on his end-of-school trip, and he did not understand that the situation in Oslo was more complicated than a black-and-white conflict between Norwegians and Muslims. If Anders had hung around longer with the Tåsen Gang, perhaps he would have remembered those months differently. It was not his lack of fighting skills that meant he lost all his brownie points with Dekor and the other lads. Neither was it his hip-hop past, as the Tåsen Gang listened not only to Nazi rock but also to 'nigger music', and some of them were even rappers.

In the summer of 1997 Oslo was blessed with sunshine, tanned bodies, warm water to swim in and house parties. The boys went diving in the fjord from Panteren, the cliffs on the west side of the city's Bygdøy peninsula. They were being watched from the rocks below by girls in bikinis. It was the perfect setting for a flirtation or a first kiss, or to try out more serious ideas. Anders had not had many dealings with girls, but that summer he met a girl who hung out with the Tåsen Gang, 'Elin'. This must have been like hitting the social jackpot for him. After his lean years spent at Ris and Nissen, he now had a gang, a crew and a girl. It finally seemed as if he had made it socially, before the end of his strenuous teenage years. The ashtray man remembers seeing Anders and Elin walking hand in hand. Hand in hand?! Yes, hand in hand. That was the only clear memory he had of Anders.

The reason that left such an impression was that, in so doing, Anders sealed his fate with the Tåsen Gang.

Gangs are primitive organisms with clear rules about what you can do. This showed that Anders understood nothing of the rules that applied in the gang. 'His error was that he hooked up with one of the Tåsen girls who was unpopular with our gang, one of the ugly girls,' Dekor explained.

> I remember thinking, 'Huh? I thought he was cool, and then he ends up with her?!' That made him lose all of his kudos. The ugliest girl of the lot. That made him lose face. He'd probably been regarded as quite cool since he dared to go out tagging and had done graffiti in the city centre. 'Woah', we thought when we heard that, 'he's a tough cookie.' But then he ended up with Elin and wasn't quite so cool after all.

Dekor laughed at their ruthless reasoning as youngsters, but back then it was real. Either you had cred or you were a nerd. If you lost your status, you were finished; the gang did not accept losers. This was basic social gaming knowledge in the Tåsen Gang. Morg did not understand the social game, so Anders left Tåsen probably at some point in the late summer of 1997, when he was starting third year at Oslo Commerce School. His relationship with Elin did not last long. She soon found another boyfriend, a Pakistani. She had become a 'Paki whore', according to the Tåsen Gang, who got into trouble again, this time with friends of Elin's boyfriend.

The gang gradually split up towards the end of upper secondary school, with the boys spread out at different schools and some having ended up out of town. For some of the boys, things snowballed into parties and drugs, and a couple of them ended up as junkies. The hip-hop group Klovner i kamp achieved nationwide fame, and most of the other lads did alright in various creative professions. The one who always put on neo-Nazi music at parties moved to the ethnically diverse neighbourhood of Holmlia with his children and his wife, who was the daughter of a Zimbabwean chieftain. Nobody remembered that anonymous boy from Skøyen with the thin voice and indistinct face until somebody phoned Dekor and said: 'That guy on the front page of the papers, it's the guy who used to write "Morg"!'

'It was a strange time back then,' Dekor said.

> I don't know if there are as many gangs or as much theft and conflict now. When the police wanted to question me, I wasn't sure to begin with, as I don't know anything about what Anders did. But then I started to think that it was worth trying to find out when things went wrong for him, what made him snap, in which case maybe those days are important. As for the conflict with the immigrants, the police wondered about those rapes, and of course I remember there were

> loads of rumours, but I don't know any more than that. They also wondered about that story of a girl having her face cut, which Anders wrote about in his compendium, but the only thing I've heard of that's similar is what happened to an acquaintance of mine at Sognsvann. She got in the middle of a fight and got a bottle in her face.

Dekor's face tells the story of the life he chose. After they finished having parties in Tåsen, Dekor moved downtown, and his twenties eventually became one long after-party. He took the lessons he had learnt while at school to the bars of the city centre. Wherever Dekor was, there would be trouble.

The left side of his face is split in two by a thick and jagged vertical scar from a broken bottle. Dekor did not win every battle, let alone every war, and there were even bigger and crazier lads in town than him. Above his left temple is another large scar, almost bulging out. Dekor never saw who did it. He was sitting at a bar when someone grabbed his shoulder and, as he turned round, a crowbar hit him as hard as a rock on the left side of his forehead. If the blow had been a couple of centimetres further down and to the left, it could have been life-threatening.

After having spent considerable time in prison for assault, Dekor gave up fighting in 2007. His schooldays finally came to an end, as far as he was concerned. Now he is a yoga instructor, a community worker and public speaker.

Somewhere inside most adults there still resides a high-school pupil, vulnerable, insecure and energetic. Adolescence is like an orienteering course without a map, in which you set off fumbling and have to solve problems along the way about sexuality, identity and belonging. Most of us eventually find our niche and a group to belong to. Anders' short appearance in the Tåsen Gang followed his usual pattern: he never quite became a full part of the group culture, remained an obscure presence on the periphery and vanished without leaving a trace. His signature as Morg quickly faded on the concrete walls. Nobody remembered the face of the boy who wanted to be 'big' and 'really famous' for his tagging. He arrived empty-handed and left equally empty-handed.

Perhaps a crack appeared in Anders' façade with the Tåsen Gang that summer. He started playing truant. The autumn of 1997 saw one of his first breakdowns. Until then he had followed the usual path at school, but now he started falling behind. People who want to make it big and be famous are likely to have frequent periods when they feel equally small and forgotten. Perhaps his journey from tagging towards the youth wing of the Progress Party and petty financial crime was accompanied by depressive episodes of varying duration.

Perhaps Breivik also drew the reasonable conclusion that he was not gang material and no street fighter and that he should seek out new groups to join. He was good at school, after all, disciplined like few others and good at planning. Maybe he had a future in business, self-employed or even as an entrepreneur. And what about politics? Completing his upper secondary examinations would be a good start, but Anders left the Commerce School in December 1997, half a year before the end. He did not tell Tove.

None of the teachers there remember this pupil who attended the school for a year and a half before dropping out a couple of months before his nineteenth birthday.

6

The 'Mother of the Nation' Returns to Utøya

Wearing Bano Rashid's Wellies

When former Prime Minister Gro Harlem Brundtland stepped ashore from MS *Thorbjørn* onto the ferry landing at about ten o'clock on Friday morning, the island had already been alerted. Although she said that she had never been there in worse weather, Gro was in high spirits.

'Fun fact: we're the same height,' tweeted her fellow passenger Hadia Tajik, a young member of the Storting with a background as a political adviser to the minister of justice and the prime minister.[1]

Gro's bright-coloured clothes highlighted her tanned face (she has a home in France), and she had white trainers on her feet. Trainers! Perhaps the 'Mother of the Nation', as she is known, had forgotten the demands of a Nordic summer, but someone immediately came running down with a pair of tall wellies belonging to an AUF member from Akershus. It turned out that not only was Gro the same height as Hadia Tajik (1 m 62 cm), she also had the same shoe size as Bano Rashid. Wearing the boots and dressed in a bright-red rain jacket with the hood pulled well over her head, Gro stepped into the car that took her from the ferry landing, across the yard between the main building and the barn and up the steep gravel road beside the slope where AUF members would sit and listen to speeches or discussions, past the Norwegian Confederation of Trade Unions' barbecue huts on the crest of the hill and on to the square in front of the central complex, known as the Café Building. Eskil Pedersen and other central AUF members with and without umbrellas escorted her quickly across the yard and into the warm hub of the Café Building.

Any concerns that the young ones might let Gro down were completely unfounded. There was an excited atmosphere as soon as she came into the hallway and shook off the rain. She went through the door on the left to be welcomed by Bano and five hundred young AUF members. Gro rocked Utøya. Why?

'Why?! Because she's Gro!' a smiling and hoarse Bano explained afterwards. She was standing outside the tent she and her sister were sharing, her hair wet, with purple flip-flops on her otherwise bare feet. 'I feel that she's done everything for women. If this were a festival with headline acts, Gro would be first, then Jens [Stoltenberg, the current prime minister].'

Many of the young people on Utøya identified with Gro, who had once been practically the only top female politician in Norway and one of very few in Europe. She had made a stand for equal opportunities, and that was a struggle that Hadia and the eighteen-year-old Bano could relate to. It was not only their height and shoe size they shared with Gro. Many of the girls from immigrant backgrounds had to fight a battle on two fronts in their quest to advance in Norwegian society, against the prejudice of Norwegians and against the expectations of their parents' culture.

The AUF's anti-racist profile was one of the reasons that Hadia Tajik had become a member, but this stance against discrimination and racism did not just appeal to girls from immigrant families. Many central members of the AUF were gay, including the county branch leaders from Oslo and Hordaland, Håvard Vederhus and Tore Eikeland, who were both killed that day, as well as the overall leader of the AUF, Eskil Pedersen from Telemark. People joked that there were so many gay members of the AUF that they would need to institute minimum quotas for straight members of committees. Asked why 'homosexuality flourishes' in the organization, Pedersen answered that 'it is easy and safe to come out in the AUF'. The county branch leader for Oppland, Even Aleksander Hagen, said that 'young gay and lesbian people have personal experience of discrimination and injustice, so it's quite natural that they get involved'.[2]

The homophobia characteristic of much of Norwegian youth culture was nowhere to be found on Utøya. People there were nice, as Anzor said. It was easy to get the impression that the AUF was made up of well-heeled school swots, the youth elite, the cream of the crop – like the former AUF leader Jens Stoltenberg – tall, dark-haired aristocrats. In reality, though, perhaps it was precisely those who were not so well heeled or fortunate who needed the AUF: young gay people from rural areas and minority youth who wanted to rise up and make headway in Norwegian society. To some of the young

AUF members, Gro represented the dream of a Norway with no barriers, where everyone had equal opportunities. To other people, she represented a blast from the past, a figure from a time that seemed more serious, dramatic and black and white than the summer of 2011, when the news was dominated by naked celebrities and disease-carrying ticks.

Those in the audience picked up on different things from Gro's talk at Utøya that morning. 'Everything is connected to everything,' tweeted Hadia Tajik, citing one of Gro's most famous quotations. 'Now I've heard her say it LIVE!' Stine-Renate Håheim took note of Gro's point that it takes time to make changes. Results are not a function of good ideas but of time and passionate determination. Ida Spjelkavik was keeping warm under a blanket at the back of Storsalen [the Main Hall], listening attentively when Sam from the global group made a comment. The secretary general of the Uganda Young Democrats made the point that Gro and the Ugandan President Museveni came to power at around the same time, but that Museveni had never left power. He pointed out the contrast between Norway and Uganda to demonstrate how bad things were in his home country, but the underlying point of Sam's question was possibly that drama and history had a different place than in Norway, where things went more or less according to plan.

The class struggle, the struggle for women's liberation, the cultural struggle – on the surface it could seem as if all the struggles in Norwegian society had already been fought to a conclusion. The yellow blanket Ida had over her legs reminded her of the nineties for some reason, as she sat there interpreting the debate for members of the global group.

By the wall, a tall and smart boy stood alone, following the debate attentively. He had also put questions to Gro, and, just like the global group, he was interested in seeing the struggle for rights from an international perspective. Arshad Mubarak Ali originally came from Madla in Stavanger but was the leader of the AUF's Oslo delegation. Unlike many of the ethnically Norwegian AUF members, Arshad had not had an easy journey to Utøya. He had followed his own path, crossing desert sands and deep valleys, before arriving in this fellowship on a green island.

11 September 2001

Arshad's parents came to Norway from Sri Lanka in the eighties. His mother's relatives were from an Arab background, while his father's family were Malays from East Asia. In Sri Lanka, for the sake of simplicity, they had been characterized as Muslims, one of many minorities on the green island paradise off the tip of the Indian subcontinent. The Muslims were a small group on the island, where the Sinhalese dominated and the Tamil people formed the largest minority. The Sri Lankan civil war had brought a large number of Tamils to Norway as refugees, but Arshad's cosmopolitan family came to Rogaland county in south-western Norway as economic migrants.

Arshad's siblings all went through higher education in Norway, in business administration and economics or social pedagogy. One of his sisters had continued the family's westward migration and worked as an economist in Montreal. His brother was a trainee at the Norwegian Embassy in Riyadh, and his father often took part in missions abroad: with the UN in Iran and Aceh, with the EU in Afghanistan and Kazakhstan. Arshad was the youngest of four children, and the only one to be born in Norway.

At Hafrsfjord, near Stavanger, three enormous swords stand in the rocks by the shore to commemorate the unification of Norway as one kingdom by King Harald Fairhair. The tall, slender school pupil gazed with interest at the monument to the Battle of Hafrsfjord in 872 (or thereabouts). Arshad was good at school, when he wanted to be.

On Tuesday 11 September 2001, Arshad Mubarak Ali was thirteen years old, almost fourteen, and was in year nine at Gosen Lower Secondary School in Stavanger. Just like most other fourteen-year-olds, he had a great and burning desire not to stand out. He wanted to be like everyone else, that was all. Anonymous, left in peace. He was a little quiet at his desk but was one of the gang. When the ill-fated aircraft slammed into the twin towers that afternoon, the media shockwaves reached Stavanger too. Everyone was affected, and everyone had thoughts about the attack. Why do they hate us?

As part of processing their impressions, the pupils in Arshad's class were all asked to write what they thought about the tragedy in New York. One by one, the teenagers went up to the board. Finally it was Arshad's turn, the only Muslim in the class. The teacher sat like a kind of judge, tilting her head, waiting to hear what he had to say. Are you with us or with the terrorists?

The day before, he had just been Arshad, but now he noticed his classmates looked at him in a different light. It dawned on him that it was not clear who he was. 'It's a terrible attack. An attack on everyone,' Arshad told the class. 'A massacre of innocent people. Nobody has the right to do something like that.'

Arshad said what he thought, but it was not pleasant standing there. He did not feel like himself but a representative of something else, something unfamiliar. A Muslim in Stavanger. Was he really Norwegian? Who was Arshad Mubarak Ali? Who was he really? He shuffled back to his place.

'Thought you'd support them,' one of the boys said. The boy did not mean any harm and stared open-eyed at Arshad. Neither had the teacher meant any offence when she said that the Taliban in Afghanistan were an example of how Muslims did not respect women. What could he say? Arshad shook his head.

Hip-hop is for everyone, but perhaps especially for those who are a little different. If you were young and from an immigrant background in Norway in the nineties or the first decade of the new millennium, it was logical to turn a little 'ghetto', or at least to pretend. For a few years, hip-hop became the answer to the question of who Arshad was. In New York, the jihadists had brought that question to the fore, and Arshad answered by becoming part of a youth culture that was both edgy and mainstream, black and white at the same time.

Arshad pulled on his hoodie and got a tag. 'Son' was his name on the walls around Madla. His crew was called KAP. They graffiti-bombed the local pump house and the walls along the main road from Sandnes. The cars rushed past while the boys nonchalantly sprayed throwies on the concrete, their own tags and 'KAP', 'KAP'. One night, the lads were near the local organic farm. Someone had already painted a piece there, and Arshad felt worried. He felt as if someone was approaching in the darkness and whispered a warning to the boys as they painted. His voice was calm, but the boys took him seriously, put their cans in their bags and ran off. They were not all fast enough, and one of the crew was caught. He grassed on a couple of the other lads, but not on Arshad. It was as if Arshad had a special talent for disappearing, for blending into the walls. Arshad was not the craziest member of the crew, nor was he the one who shouted loudest, and he avoided being exposed, getting fines or having to do community service.

KAP's pieces were so-so. Their vandalism did not make a big name for them in Stavanger, nor did it bring any six-figure fines as there had been for taggers in Oslo a few years earlier. Things never became really serious for 'Son' or 'Kids Against the Police', and Arshad did not follow the path to the darker sides of Norwegian hip-hop: crime, fighting or drugs. He did not even like rap, but preferred techno and trance to start with, then Rage Against the Machine, before ending up with the eighties heroes The Cure and Joy Division. Arshad did not want fame either, but anonymity. Tagging was exciting, but Arshad did not feel he had to seek out the extremes or cross boundaries. Most of all, he wanted to be part of the crowd, someone who would not stand out.

At the same time, he followed his own path. Instead of writing a history essay about Mussolini, he wrote a poem. Instead of doing his Norwegian homework, he went to the library at Sølvberget, Stavanger's cultural centre, and read the diary of Robert Falcon Scott, the British officer who gave his life in the race to the South Pole, losing with style against the Norwegians on their skis. He read *The Lord of the Rings* in his bedroom, and sometimes he played games from the moment he came home until he went to bed: *Hitman*, *Quake* and *Wolfenstein*, in which his American avatar shot Nazis by the bucketload. Strategy games and shoot-'em-ups, just like all the other boys. Arshad did not stand out.

But pressure came to him not only from his surroundings. Migrant families like Arshad's know that, however much you travel, flee or move house, there is one thing you will never lose and that nobody can take away from you: your education. School was a main concern for the family. In addition, his father, Mubarak Ali, sat on the city council for the Labour Party and was an example of how people could find their place in the community in Norway even if they were born abroad. Arshad's big brother was in the Conservative Party. Weighing down on the teenage Arshad's shoulders were expectations that he had to do well at school, as his siblings had, and that he had to take responsibility in the community, repaying his debt to society.

'Son' was signed up by his father to the AUF. Now the way to Utøya was open, but would he follow it straight there? It was almost too obvious. Arshad started at St Olav Upper Secondary School in 2003 and chose to follow the International Baccalaureate curriculum from his second year. It was then that he slowly began to find the answer to who he was. One afternoon, he sat there staring at his history homework. He had a Norwegian assignment to do as well: his class had to write a role play. On impulse, he decided to solve his homework problem by writing a dialogue between King Oedipus and King Harald of Norway about democracy and dictatorship. His essay was meant as a joke, but Arshad was given top marks and suddenly realized that he had talent.

He began writing poems. Instead of tagging walls, Arshad wrote about 'The Girl Who Vanished'. In short sentences, he described infatuation and a first-person voice in the tension between being isolated 'behind the windows' and journeying to 'the Holy Land'. In his poems, large concepts could be boiled down to only a few words. His poems were a way of dealing with big questions of love, identity, faith and doubt. Problems that were too complicated or too personal to be expressed directly could be described with images. 'Butterflies lie too', Arshad wrote, 'as they fly about, radiating joy.'

The pretences around him, or perhaps within him, turned into letters on a white page. Arshad studied the poet Sigbjørn Obstfelder and his famous lines: 'I must have come to the wrong planet! / It is so strange here . . .'[3] He read Knut Hamsun's *Victoria*, about the miller's son Johannes. Why could Hamsun's wanderer not be an immigrant too? During his time at upper secondary, Arshad definitively left his isolation 'behind the windows'. In his second year, he became active in the AUF. His father's party had values he identified with: fellowship and a minimum of benefits for everybody, irrespective of who they were and where they came from. A unified Norway.

In his third year, Arshad joined the youth group at Rogaland Theatre. He played the role of the Prince in the club's production of *Snow White* – an elegant prince from Rogaland, dark-eyed, tall and smiling. Drama was training for politics; it had to do with presentation and timing. Drama was also a way in which Arshad could express the pressure he felt from all sides, being able to act out situations and conflicts that reminded him of the time he stood alone in front of his class and distanced himself from the attack on the World Trade Center.

Unfortunately, life does not follow a straight line, with each year marking an improvement on the last. In the spring of 2006, Arshad failed his IB exam, and the following year would be a brutal re-encounter with the question of who he was. It was like ending up in a basement with no exit. His bedroom became a prison cell. He worked for a few months at the OBS supermarket. Arshad would go from shelf to shelf in the enormous shop, making sure that all the products were there and panicking at the thought of having to stay there for a whole year, or five or ten years. He had to move on.

That was when the idea of a pilgrimage to Mecca began to take shape. Arshad had always been a believer, even though he had concealed it well as a teenager, but now the situation became urgent. He had to take a stand on the question of Islam.

Ideas That Kill

Life is tangled, and the world is dirty. People have always longed for purity, unity and order, but sometimes this yearning has taken a bad turn.

In July 1942, a number of respected Japanese academics and intellectuals gathered in the old imperial city of Kyoto. At that time,

Japanese troops were advancing through the Pacific region, in China and in South-East Asia. Their German allies were on the cusp of conquering the Caucasus. The reflection of the Temple of the Golden Pavilion could still be seen in the lake as an image of timeless beauty. Hayashi Yoken had not yet been admitted to the temple monastery. The theme of the conference was 'how to overcome the modern', and the actual war was barely mentioned by the assembled Japanese academics, who were certain of victory. Instead, the participants defined modernity as Western influence, an illness that had infected the Japanese spirit. Capitalism, science, modern technology and democracy had all contributed to breaking down the original unity that had existed in oriental culture, and especially Japanese culture. One participant characterized the struggle as a battle between Western intellect and Japanese blood. The participants painted a picture of the decadent West as cold, mechanical and soulless, the opposite of the spiritual Japan.

In their *Occidentalism: A Short History of Anti-Westernism*, Ian Buruma and Avishai Margalit use this conference as a starting point to study the history of antagonism towards the West, defined as liberalism, individualism, capitalism and secularism. Contrary to how it may appear, Occidentalism is not an ideology that developed outside Europe, in post-colonial contexts or in parts of the world that did not end up under Western domination, such as Japan. Hatred towards the West originated in the West. The authors trace the roots of Occidentalism to German Romanticism, showing how ideas that emerged as a reaction to the Enlightenment and French military dominance have travelled across the world, from the Slavophile reaction in Russia via Japan, China and Afghanistan and back to Europe. Buruma and Margalit show how Occidentalism had affected a wide spectrum of political thinkers, from the German cultural pessimist Oswald Spengler, who wrote about the downfall of the *Abendland* (the 'evening land', or the West), to the young Afghan jihadist who allegedly said that 'the Americans love Pepsi-Cola, we love death'.

Buruma and Margalit stress that modernity and the West can mean different things at different times. Even though both extreme Marxists and extreme right-wingers can agree in their criticisms of the West, there are other things that divide them. Occidentalist ideas have also existed in other, earlier historical periods – for example, in Roman authors' descriptions of the contrast between Rome's purportedly noble Republican past and the decadent and corrupt Imperial Age or in the Judeans' condemnation of the Whore of Babylon. Occidentalism is permeated by images of decline and the end of days: Babylon is wallowing in sin, while Rome is heading towards ruin. Nevertheless, it was during the period of industrialization following the French Revolution that Occidentalism took on its present form. In modern times, such eschatological notions are often accompanied by conspiracy theories, hostile images, the rhetoric of victimhood and descriptions of oneself and like-minded people as the chosen few: a chosen few who kill in self-defence. The occidentalist reaction has run like a dark vein throughout the history of modernity up to the present day, acting as a starting point for some of the most dramatic conflicts in, and attacks on, the West.

Buruma and Margalit's book was written against the background of the War on Terror. One of the book's aims is to portray how Islamist extremism, as construed by people such as Osama bin Laden and Sayyid Qutb (a former leading member of the Egyptian Muslim Brotherhood), was rooted in fascism and other Western reactionary ideologies. Instead of defining Occidentalism by accounting for its historical context, they define it through its fundamental ideas. According to the authors, the occidentalist 'hostility' towards modernity can best be understood as hostility towards an image of the West made up of four interrelated elements: the city, the bourgeois, reason and the infidel.

> [W]e have identified particular strands of Occidentalism that can be seen in all periods and all places where the phenomenon has occurred. These strands are linked, of course, to form a chain of hostility – hostility to the City, with its image of rootless, arrogant, greedy, decadent, frivolous cosmopolitanism; to the mind of the West, manifested in science and reason; to the settled bourgeois, whose existence is the antithesis of the self-sacrificing hero; and to the infidel, who must be crushed to make way for a world of pure faith.[4]

Occidentalists hate the city, with its soulless markets, mixture of races, feminized men and unheroic bourgeoisie with wallets instead of hearts. They hate the mechanical Western reason without depth or soul, and the secular rationality that implies parting not only with God, but also with time-honoured institutions such as the family and the nation-state. Opposed to the Western merchant is the hero whose duty it is to purge the infidel enemy in order to create a divine mystical kingdom on earth. These are not just the exotic thoughts of bitter people sitting in their cellars but effective ideas that can kill, as the nature of Occidentalism is such that it encourages and is easily translated into brutal actions.

In a speech in 2002, referring to the 9/11 attacks, Osama bin Laden put it like this: 'The values of this Western civilization under the leadership of America have been destroyed. Those awesome symbolic towers that speak of liberty, human rights, and humanity have been destroyed. They have gone up in smoke.'[5] Destroying symbolic buildings, such as the Temple of the Golden Pavilion in Kyoto, the twin towers in Manhattan or the H Block in Oslo's government district, can be an expression of narcissistic jealousy of the elites and those in power. It can also be an expression of occidentalist contempt for the city. Often it might be both.

Occidentalism, Norwegian Style

The phenomenon of Occidentalism has many local versions. There are some facts that point towards an occidentalist tradition in Norway too, even though it may not be particularly strong. Norwegian National Socialism was a relatively confined phenomenon. Wilfred 'Little Lord' Sagen, Johan Borgen's fictional West End character, was the exception, an outsider, and not a typical representative of Oslo's West End or of Norway as a whole. Although the thirties were a difficult time, the AUF members who fought against the paramilitaries of the fascist party Nasjonal Samling were still more representative of Norwegians. Even after the German occupation, when Nasjonal Samling was installed as a puppet regime in Norway with wide-ranging powers and was the only legal party, it never achieved genuine popular support.

The leader of the movement, Vidkun Quisling, was, like the Japanese intellectuals in Kyoto, concerned about the spiritual decline he perceived at the time. 'The most crass expression of this spiritual crisis has been in the predominant selfish materialism that is killing ideality, belief and the spirit of self-sacrifice, and is causing disquiet in society and in the human mind,' the 1934 party programme of Nasjonal Samling stated. 'Our country is not served well either by the class struggle and party tyranny of Marxism or the conservative parties' laissez-faire policies and concessions to Marxism. They are two sides of the same materialistic outlook on life.'[6] According to Nasjonal Samling, the financial and social crises of the thirties were primarily expressions of spiritual weakness.

Quisling's solution, as he articulated it while plotting a coup as defence minister under Bondepartiet [the Farmers' Party], involved 'destroying the imported and pernicious communistic revolutionary movement, which does not agree with Nordic uniqueness and which in itself is fundamentally false and evil'.[7] That way, Quisling planned to awaken Norway and 'get our people to understand that their life-giving foundations are their Nordic descent and character [. . .]. The Norwegian people must get to know their significance, their duty and their responsibility as some of the leading representatives of the most esteemed race in the world, the great Nordic race, which has been and remains the most important creator and supporter of world civilization.'

As a thinker and an author, on the one hand Quisling was woolly and academic with a penchant for unrealistic philosophizing, while on the other hand he was aggressive, conspiratorial and self-centred – not entirely unlike his occidentalist successor, the writer Anders Behring Breivik. The Norwegian people would remain a disappointment to Quisling. Even though they stopped laughing at him in the end, he did not manage to awaken them. Instead he was sentenced to death and executed at Akershus Fortress in October 1945, after a trial that was followed around the world.

A group that laid the groundwork for Nasjonal Samling and Quisling was Den norske rådgivende komité for rasehygiene [the Norwegian Advisory Board for Racial Hygiene], which was founded in 1908 and developed theories about the racial composition of Norway (finding out, among other things, that the superior 'long-skulled' population was in some places mixed with 'short-skulled' people – in other words, people of inferior genetic quality). Some of the eugenics theorists warned against the hereditary material of Jewish people, which they associated with monetary power, while the Germanic race was genetically linked to the soil. The eugenicists were also interested in migration but, since at that time Norway was a country of out-migration, the problem presented was the opposite of today's. A worried Jon Alfred Mjøen, the group's central figure, wrote: 'As the years go by, Norway is giving away its best sons and daughters to overseas countries, while at the same time accepting and even supporting foreign, often inferior elements. [. . .] In terms of quality, if one considers the difference between the stock of people leaving and entering the country, it can be appreciated how disastrous this must be for our country.'[8] Many of the eugenicists' ideas were generally accepted in the interwar period, but Mjøen and his supporters also encountered considerable criticism from scientific quarters. With the significant and aggressive exceptions of Quisling and sections of Nasjonal Samling, Occidentalism has remained a marginal phenomenon in Norway.

After the war, the legacy of Nasjonal Samling lived on at the periphery of Norwegian society, inspiring the neo-Nazi circles among which Jens Erik – the bomber from Ris – moved during the eighties, as well as extremist opponents of immigration in the nineties and Muslim-haters in the noughties. Occidentalism has not, however, been the exclusive domain of the political right wing.

The left's hatred of the bourgeoisie, the city and capitalism reached an ideological and rhetorical peak with the political awakening that struck the Norwegian universities together with the 1968 generation. The Maoists of the intellectually influential Arbeidernes Kommunistparti (marxist-leninistene) [Workers' Communist Party (Marxist-Leninists)] supported both Mao's Cultural Revolution and the Khmer Rouge's genocidal project in Cambodia, which in fact implied not only the annihilation of the bourgeoisie and 'capitalism' but also a war against the city as an idea and as a reality. In an attempt to create the ideal communist state, city-dwellers were deported to the countryside and subjected to forced labour, leading to hundreds of thousands of deaths.

After 9/11, attention was also drawn to Islamist extremism in Norway. The best-known examples were the statements of a Kurdish refugee from Iraq, Najmuddin Faraj Ahmad, known as Mullah Krekar. In Kurdistan, Krekar had led the paramilitary group Ansar al-Islam, a group that was suspected of executing prisoners of war and that the US authorities later placed on their list of terrorist groups. Krekar supported bin Laden's struggle against the West and commended the Jordanian terrorist Abu Musab al-Zarqawi, who was killed by the Americans in 2006. Al-Zarqawi was known for having masterminded suicide attacks and for having beheaded hostages personally. The films showing the executions were uploaded onto the Internet and were widely distributed. It was not only Islamists who watched them. Many people were fascinated by the extreme images of the powerless victims and the executioner al-Zarqawi. Al-Zarqawi was judge, jury and executioner, thereby having supreme command of life and death.

Throughout the first decade of the new millennium, Islamists were the focus of attention for the media, politicians and the intelligence community, and Krekar was not the only one in Norway to make extremist statements. In 2010, during a demonstration against the newspaper *Dagbladet* (which had reproduced one of the notorious Muhammad cartoons), a young Norwegian Muslim from an Iraqi background warned Norway about a potentially imminent 9/11, an Islamist terrorist attack on Norwegian soil. The man was called Mohyeldeen Mohammad, and in the newspapers he defended the death penalty for homosexuality. According to Mohyeldeen, while democracy by definition broke God's laws, the death penalty for homosexuality was in pursuance of sharia.

Among his radical supporters was Arfan Bhatti, a former criminal thug from the Young Guns gang who had found religion while in prison. At one point, Bhatti was infamous as Oslo's most dangerous enforcer, and he had been convicted of having shot at a synagogue in Oslo. Mohyeldeen Mohammad was a student at a conservative Islamic university in Medina. There were a couple of other Norwegian students at the university too. One of them was a city councillor from Stavanger by the name of Arshad Mubarak Ali.

Mecca

Instead of going to Utøya to find his place in his father's party and in Norwegian social democracy, it seemed as if Arshad was heading in the opposite direction. Over the New Year period of 2007–8, he went on the Hajj, the pilgrimage to Mecca that, in principle, Muslims should make once in their life. Over 2006 and 2007, Arshad had reflected on his own position under the conflicting pressure of the demands and culture of his parents, Norwegian society and Islam. It had taken many years for Arshad but, as with many European Muslims, 9/11 had eventually brought him closer to his faith. It dawned on him that he was Muslim not only by belonging to an ethnic group from Sri Lanka but also in the sense that he was actually religious. He needed to explore in earnest what Islam meant, so he travelled to Mecca together with a friend from Stavanger.

They landed at Jeddah in December and went almost immediately to Mecca, two twenty-year-old Norwegian boys among hundreds of thousands of mainly older men from across the large Muslim world. In the warmth and the dust, wrapped in the prescribed white clothing, Arshad walked out onto the plain to pray. Later he was one of the enormous crowd slowly walking seven times around the Kaaba, the cuboid building incorporating the Black Stone and shrouded in a black silk cloth. This ritual is called Tawaf and reminds Muslims of the unity among believers, the community of which they are part. Approximately 3 million pilgrims performed the Hajj that year.

It was an intense experience. In Mecca, Arshad was far away from Norway and his family. The unity of faith implied by the Tawaf seemed to relieve him of a sense of deprivation he had felt, as a descendant of migrant families that constituted a minority within a minority, at least since that day at lower secondary school after 9/11. At Medina, Arshad applied to the Islamic University. He was inspired by his pilgrimage and wanted to study Arabic. Admission was also free of charge for foreigners. Over the course of the four weeks he spent there, he discovered things that surprised him. When Arshad had his admission interview at the university in Medina, the man at the desk asked him where he came from.

'Norway,' Arshad answered.

'And your parents?'

'Sri Lanka,' he answered.

The man looked at him and wrote on his papers that Arshad was from Sri Lanka. Was he not Norwegian? All kinds of service and retail jobs in Saudi Arabia were carried out by foreigners from Asia. They were poorly paid and had no job security. It was almost slavery. The guest workers looked like Arshad, but, since he was from Europe, he was treated differently. Saudi society had a double nature. There were almost no women to be seen. It seemed as if the literal interpretations of the faith, as advocated by many of the Wahhabi Saudi imams, were keeping people apart rather than bringing them together. The sense of community around the Kaaba was in contrast to the walls, barriers and hierarchies he encountered elsewhere in Saudi Arabia.

Arshad travelled home to the Norwegian winter and sent his final application papers to Medina from Stavanger. His interest in Islam and desire to learn Arabic were still strong. Time passed, and he felt that some of the people he had got to know in Saudi Arabia had almost stopped thinking for themselves. Some of the other Western students apparently believed everything they heard, swallowing it hook, line and sinker. The last straw came when he argued that Norwegian imams should be brought up in Norway and should be familiar with the cultural context. Arshad singled out Saudi Arabia as a bad example. 'This country has to change,' said Arshad. 'It's no example to others.'

In reply, he was told that the Saudi society was Salafi, fundamental – perfect in its faith. Saudi Arabia was following the right path and had done so from the start. 'Uh-huh,' thought Arshad. If he would also start to reason like that if he went there, then forget about it.

He had no contact with Mohyeldeen Mohammad, but he gathered that Mohyeldeen also stood out there. After Mohyeldeen's notorious speech in Oslo, the university in Medina had an Arabic translation sent to them. The university apparently wanted to keep him on in order to try to change his mind, but the authorities were opposed to having such a controversial student in the country. As a result, Mohyeldeen's place at the university was withdrawn, followed by his residence permit. He was deported from Saudi Arabia in September 2011. Back in Norway, Arshad criticized Mohyeldeen, not only for his aggressive statements but also for what Arshad saw as a primitive view of theology. The Koran was a text that needed interpretation, Arshad thought. Islam was a set of principles, not a collection of immutable dogmas to be used in connection with all things at all times.

Mecca was a turning point for Arshad. Back home in Norway, he thought about the pressures that had made his teenage years difficult. He saw himself at the centre of a triangle made up of his parents' Sri Lankan heritage, Norwegian society and Islam. Being pulled in every direction, it was tempting for him to concentrate on just one side, choosing just one thing – to do things by the letter. At the same time, though, to do that was just as impossible as choosing between your head and your heart. Arshad depended on all three parts of the triangle to feel whole; not just one thing, but many. Mohyeldeen Mohammad's belief in absolute purity was a dangerous illusion.

Arshad never took up the place he was offered at the university in Medina. Not everybody picked up on that piece of information, or not everybody wanted to pick up on it. The possibility that an Islamic extremist was sitting on Stavanger City Council was perhaps so shocking, or alternatively so appealing, that not everybody looked into the details more closely. The editor of the right-wing website Document.no, Hans Rustad, wrote that the father and son pair

> drew notice to themselves in national political circles with their proposal to ban alcohol in the city centre of Stavanger. [. . .] The [Medina] university's list of accepted students for 2009/2010 shows that Arshad Ali Mubarak [*sic*] attends there together with Mohyeldeen Mohammad. Mohyeldeen Mohammad has been portrayed by the Norwegian media as something of a freak. But he is not alone after all. Ostensibly well-integrated city councillors from the Labour Party can become so religious that they start religious studies in Saudi Arabia. The enigma is bigger and closer to us than we like to think.[9]

The cryptic final sentence may suggest that Rustad saw a connection between Islamic extremism and the Labour Party.

Instead of taking up his place at the Islamic University of Medina, Arshad began studying history. He took a specialist undergraduate module in Norwegian Viking history and started the master's degree in Nordic Viking and Medieval Culture at the University of Oslo. His dissertation dealt with the unification of Norway – in other words, the Battle of Hafrsfjord and its aftermath – as it was portrayed and utilized during the national awakening of the nineteenth century. Today the sword sculptures stand embedded in the rocks at Hafrsfjord, but was Norway ever really unified? Sometimes, the differences between people briefly gaped open like chasms. Arshad published an anthology of poetry in 2008 and became the cultural editor of the student newspaper. He became active in the Oslo branch of the AUF in addition to sitting on the city council in Stavanger. He worked as a journalist for *Stavanger Aftenblad*, reporting from Sri Lanka. In the summer of 2011, he decided to take action about the problem of anti-Semitism in Oslo's schools, when a report indicated that Muslim pupils were often responsible. Arshad argued in favour of increasing awareness and knowledge of the Holocaust among Muslim pupils and involving influential Norwegian Muslims in discussions about anti-Semitism.

'If we succeed in wiping out anti-Semitism,' Arshad wrote in *Stavanger Aftenblad*, 'we can use the same means to combat prejudice towards other religious and cultural groups, including Muslims.'[10] Given Arshad's own background, perhaps it was not that strange that he identified with the small Jewish minority in Norway.

Arshad had fought both internal and external battles to reach where he was in the summer of 2011, on Utøya as the election campaign secretary and delegation leader for the Oslo branch of the AUF. Instead of sailing with activists to Gaza, his engagement in Middle East issues involved criticizing Saudi double standards towards

Arshad Mubarak Ali (photograph by Mohammed F. Basefer)

Muslim believers. After having put up washing rotas for his delegation, Arshad went to the Main Hall. When Gro had finished her address, it was Prableen Kaur's turn. She was the deputy leader of the Oslo AUF, Arshad's closest friend on the island, and he had helped her to formulate the question she was now putting to Gro.

'So I was three years old when you resigned as prime minister,' Prableen said from the speaker's platform. 'I've tried hard to think back to when I was that small, but it's not easy to remember much. All the same, I do remember well what my parents used to tell me about you: that you were an incredibly capable woman who, among other things, made it possible for my dad to be at home with me and my little sister too. He was very pleased about that.'

She then referred to the fact that women were central figures in the Arab Spring, for example in Yemen, and that the struggle for women's liberation in many countries concerned quite fundamental rights: paid work, education and political influence. 'What do you think about these similar yet also quite different struggles for equal rights?' Prableen asked in conclusion.

Times change, and new generations were entering the social-democratic family. Arshad and Prableen could have been Gro's grandchildren, as could Bano and Hadia, but the struggle for equality and recognition continued in many ways as it had done before. When Gro left the island and headed back towards land, Arshad and Prableen went to Arshad's room in the downstairs back wing of the large Café Building. Together they took a short break before the afternoon's programme. It was still raining.

7

Andrew Berwick and Avatar Syndrome

The Entrepreneur

He wanted to be big, he wanted to be famous – and that required money. Breivik was finished with hip-hop, and the nineties were coming to an end. It was 1998, and now he had to conquer the adult world.

While he attended the Commerce School, he worked booking meetings for the company Acta Dialog. He made lots of phone calls and not much money. From 1997 to 2003, he worked for the telemarketing company Direkte Respons-Senteret (DRS), first as a telemarketer and later as a team leader in the DRS technical support department's customer service unit. He was earning money and had responsibility. Rather than being a salesman, though, Anders wanted to be an entrepreneur and self-made businessman like Kjell Inge Røkke, the former co-owner of Wimbledon Football Club, or the property investor Petter Stordalen.

He founded his first company in the cellar of his home in Konventveien at the age of eighteen. Together with a friend, he was going to sell cheap phone call packages to people in Oslo from minority backgrounds. The same idea was about to make a Norwegian businessman of Sri Lankan origins into a millionaire with the Lebara Group telecommunications company, but Anders and his friend ended up quarrelling and their company folded at a loss one year later.

Breivik's next idea concerned making money out of the knowledge he had acquired of Oslo's walls during the years he had written on them. The company Media Group was founded in September 1999 with an office in Nedre Slottsgate, in the city centre. Anders shared a canteen with the lawyer Geir Lippestad, the man who defended Ole Nicolai Kvisler, one of the neo-Nazis who was convicted for the murder of Benjamin Hermansen in 2001. Media Group was intended to sell spaces on walls to companies that used billboard advertising, but this plan did not go very well either, and the company was wound up in 2001 without having made any money for Breivik.

In April 2002, Breivik travelled via Ivory Coast to Liberia, which was ravaged by civil war. The twenty-three-year-old was still a restless wanderer and a dreamer. Liberia's so-called blood diamonds combined elements of violence and money and had a dark, sadistic appeal that had made headlines all the way to Oslo.

In 2001, American authorities banned imports of diamonds from Liberia, since President Charles Taylor was using the diamond trade to finance warfare in neighbouring countries. Accounts came from Sierra Leone of slavery, rape and the massacre of thousands of people. The following year, Breivik told his best friend that he was going to travel to Liberia to smuggle blood diamonds and gave him a letter to his mother in case he did not return. His friend could not resist opening the letter, which said that his mother should not feel sorry for him and that Anders had only gone there to seek his fortune.

It was a slightly riskier plan than going to Copenhagen to buy spray cans, but Breivik followed his dramatizing modus operandi with a cover name, cover stories and a somewhat exaggerated air of mystery. 'My name's Benson, Henry Benson,' Breivik introduced himself to the fixers who waited for him in Monrovia.

The Liberians drove him in a BMW through the small, ruined capital to the Metropolitan Hotel. The fixers saw a polite young businessman from Norway. The war was looming ever closer at that time, with rebel forces supported by neighbouring countries advancing in northern Liberia. The rebel leaders had names like Cobra and Dragon Master. Mercenaries were fighting on all sides in the conflict. Charles Taylor's government army was about to lose control of the diamond mines, so there were fewer diamonds on sale in Monrovia. War profiteers from all corners of the world, journalists, mercenaries and people from humanitarian organizations gathered in the bars of Monrovia to drink and tell stories. Was it true that the rebels were now only 40 kilometres from Monrovia? Did you know that in Sierra Leone Taylor's people were cutting off arms and legs, noses and ears? Soviet weapons and helicopters were coming in from Central Asia, and veterans of wars in Congo and the Balkans were looking for work in the jungle of Western Africa. The setting could have been from a novel by Graham Greene.

Morg had been resurrected as Henry Benson, international man of mystery, perhaps a step on the way towards being Andrew Berwick, Justiciar Knight. Breivik did not buy any diamonds in Monrovia but did later send his fixers around 40,000 kroner from Norway, an astronomical sum in Liberia. Perhaps he was unusually generous, or perhaps he wanted diamonds but was swindled. According to Breivik's own account, he met a Serbian veteran in Monrovia by the name of 'the Dragon'. The Dragon included him in the network of militant European nationalists that he called the Knights Templar network.

It is more likely that the stories the boy from Skøyen had heard in the bar on the ground floor of the Metropolitan Hotel, rumours of Serbian mercenaries and rebel leaders with colourful *noms de guerre*, grew over the years into a fantasy story in which Breivik himself was the protagonist. It was allegedly in London, on his way home from Monrovia, that Breivik started on the path to becoming a knight. The Serb supposedly sent him to a meeting there in early May 2002. The real story was less exciting. On the way from Monrovia to London, Breivik bought an expensive souvenir, a Montblanc Meisterstück pen. He stayed the night at the St George's Hotel in London before going home to Oslo.

While he was trying his luck as a businessman, Breivik also tried out politics. In 1997, at around the same time he had to leave the Tåsen Gang, he turned up as a newly fledged member of Fremskrittspartiets ungdom [the Progress Party's Youth; FpU] – a new group with new opportunities. There was a certain class logic in the fact that a boy from Ris School who belonged to neither the financial nor the cultural elites of the West End would end up in the Progress Party, a party of angry shopkeepers. He was in favour of a restrictive immigration policy, but not especially critical of Islam at that time. In his 231 posts on the FpU online forum, he wrote mainly about economic policy, as it was money that interested him most.

Breivik joined the mother party, the Progress Party, in 1999 and spent March and April of that year on the Party's course for aspiring politicians, at the same time as the eyes of Europe were on Kosovo and Serbia, with NATO bombing and Serbian forces carrying out ethnic cleansing of the Albanian population. He was given some minor local duties in both the youth wing and its mother party, including being deputy leader of FpU for the West End of Oslo. In spite of his extensive activity on the online forum and his ambitious idea to establish a centre-right youth platform consisting of the youth wings of Venstre [the Liberal Party], Høyre [the Conservative Party] and Kristelig Folkeparti [the Christian Democratic Party], as well as FpU, he did not succeed in being nominated to the party's list of candidates in the local elections of 2003. Breivik's strategic proposal of a centre-right youth platform was a new, expanded version of his notion of being the glue holding the taggers together, not a figurehead but the organizer behind the scenes. Breivik was thinking bigger and bigger, but little came of it. He left the Progress Party and the FpU in 2004.

During his trial, he said that he had kept his radical views on Islam, multiculturalism and the ongoing European Civil War hidden during his time in FpU, and that he was only interested in having something to put on his CV and advancing in the party. *Taqiyya*. He thought that conformism and politeness would take him to the top. His friends also thought that the most important thing for him was not politics but climbing through the party ranks. People from the tagging community called him socially overambitious, always wanting to be in charge. For Breivik, apparently the main thing was being seen. Beyond that, he tried to fit in with the rest of the pack.

Breivik remained a lone wolf, but perhaps he did not leave the Progress Party and the FpU with a heavy heart, as it was at the same time he left politics that he first began to make real money. In 2001, he established a third company, City Group, and in 2002 his turnover started to pick up. Breivik sold fake diplomas, including various degree and exam certificates. In 2003, he claimed to have made his first million kroner. Over the course of the three or four years the company existed, he made approximately 4 million kroner, according to himself. 3.6 million were transferred to the fourteen bank accounts he had in seven different countries, according to the police.[1] The earnings he buried in banks in Caribbean and Baltic states were not declared to the tax authorities.

Slowly and systematically, Breivik brought the money back home through cash withdrawals from foreign banks, withdrawals with foreign cards from Norwegian cash machines, and payments into his mother's bank account that she then transferred on to him. In such a way, his mother helped him to launder around 400,000 kroner. According to Breivik, the newspaper *Aftenposten* began to show interest in his company, which was in a legal grey area with its sales of false documents as well as money laundering and extensive tax evasion. He folded the company in 2006 because he was worried about media attention and potentially being investigated, he later claimed, and moved home to his mother, his partner in crime.

In the two safes in his bedroom there were hundreds of thousands of kroner. He had acquired experience in the production of false documents as well as in the use of the Internet for criminal purposes. The boy who wanted to be a big name made his first million at a younger age than other entrepreneurs such as Petter Stordalen or Kjell Inge Røkke, as he pointed out during his trial, but still he did not behave like a winner. He practically went into hiding. Throughout the decade, he stayed in touch with a group of friends from his time at the Commerce School, but, after 2006, they all described it as if Breivik went underground. Breivik was never without friends, but he spent the next few years in front of his computer screen.

Andersnordic, Conservatism and Conservative

Breivik was a keen gamer. He had always liked computer games, according to Tove. Back in his 'fart room', as he cryptically called it, in Hoffsveien, he now began a period of hardcore raiding in *World of Warcraft*, the biggest and most popular massively multiplayer online role-playing game.

Fantasy-based role-playing games emerged as a genre in the seventies, as a by-product of the cult surrounding Tolkien's *The Lord of the Rings*, and went online in the nineties. *World of Warcraft* entered the market in November 2004 and became the greatest commercial success in the genre. The game had 10 million subscribers by January 2008. The players are distributed over a number of servers (each with up to 20,000 subscribers), offering three different types of play: player vs. environment, player vs. player and role-playing.

For a period from 2006 to 2007, Anders was almost constantly logged on to *World of Warcraft*, carrying out quests such as killing monsters and finding treasure in a universe of wizards, castles, vampires and magical spaceships. Players control an avatar, and they can see that character either externally (in third-person view) or from its own viewpoint (first-person view) while they explore a whole world made up of several continents, medieval-style towns and other planets, as well as interacting with a number of non-player characters, fellow guild members and avatars from other guilds. The quests carried out by players include fighting with other players and slaying beasts.

World of Warcraft is largely about constructing an avatar. Breivik's avatars were called Andersnordic, Conservatism and Conservative. Andersnordic belonged to the 'mage' class, was male by gender and human by race, one of fifty-two possible types of avatar combination. On screen, Andersnordic looks quite robust and threatening, more of a warrior than a mage. Andersnordic was an avatar he mainly used early on, while Conservatism and Conservative were female avatars he developed later. Conservatism was a beautiful, blonde mage. In the compendium Anders was working on in parallel with his gaming, he mentioned that attractive women could help to increase the impact of messages. Perhaps that was why he created female avatars, because it is easier to receive help and tips from other players (who are approximately 85 per cent male in *World of Warcraft*) if they believe you are a woman.

The avatars in *World of Warcraft* have five different kinds of primary attributes, or stats, that affect characters' performance and are given as percentages: strength, intellect, stamina, spirit and agility. While playing, the player builds up these traits, so the avatar's strength, intellect and other attributes increase. As you carry out quests and gain experience, your avatar reaches higher levels. You rise up through the game's levels and achieve higher ranks, as in a Masonic lodge. An avatar is a player's representative in the game, his or her alias or alter ego. The avatar is not only present in the game but is also used when the players have discussions among themselves in chat rooms or forums. In February 2011, going by the name of Conservatism, Anders wrote on a gaming forum: 'Better hated than forgotten, or what?'[2]

In *World of Warcraft*, you can play alone, questing, or you can go raiding, which means carrying out larger missions together with other players. The missions can vary from fetching an object from an unexplored area to killing the biggest monsters on the server, so-called raid bosses. *World of Warcraft* is not really a difficult game, but it takes a lot of effort. Faltin Karlsen, a game researcher, stresses that the missions in *World of Warcraft* require players to plan and to be systematic: 'The quests are not so much intellectual challenges as logistical ones.'[3] The game requires a lot of time. While you progress quickly through the levels to start with, it takes a long play time to go from one level to the next when you get further towards the top of the ladder, perhaps as much as twenty hours. If you want to join in raiding, you will only be allowed if you are on one of the higher levels.

To go raiding, the players organize themselves into guilds made up of avatars with various complementary attributes, in a similar way to how taggers in a crew might have different tasks and specialities. In order for a raiding guild to work optimally, its players' avatars need not only to be at top levels but also to be equipped with the best weapons, magic spells and healing abilities. In *World of Warcraft*, hardcore raiders are in a kind of top-level sport. You could also say that the highest-ranked guilds were the gaming world's equivalent to the B Gang, Oslo's toughest criminals. Raiding has a social dynamic that forces the players to spend enormous amounts of time playing. If you do not play enough, you can become a burden for the guild, a weak link. If you are not logged on enough, you might risk being thrown out by the guild leader.

Anders' avatars reached the highest levels. Level 70 was as far as you could get in early 2007, and he later reached level 85 with Conservatism, the highest level when the game was expanded the following year. With Andersnordic, he became the leader of a guild called Virtue, which raided on the Nordrassil server. Having such a role in a guild of hardcore raiders (hardcore guilds seek to be the first on their server to kill the raid bosses) is very demanding. According to Breivik, Virtue was the highest-ranked guild on the Nordrassil server. This was high-level logistics, which required the guild leader to spend almost all his time on the game. Such a person has to keep making sure that the other players have the necessary equipment for the mission at hand and organize them in order to be able to carry out their difficult tasks and acquire 'epic' loot, while also listening to the other players' thoughts and complaints, as *World of Warcraft* is a social game in which the chat logs are a central part.

In the Virtue guild's discussion threads, the other players remembered Andersnordic both as a good leader – 'businesslike, organised and good tactically' – and as 'arrogant and a bully', kicking other players out of the guild when they were logged off and offending or irritating the other players.[4] Several people remember long discussions with him, some of them personal. Offler, one of his guildmates from Virtue, thought that for Andersnordic *World of Warcraft* 'was like a tonic to his depression'.[5] Another of Breivik's guild colleagues who read the recollections of *World of Warcraft* in his compendium thought that Breivik exaggerated his role in the gaming world too:

> To clarify, the only guild that Breivik ever led was Virtue who were never close to being a rank 1 guild on Nordrassil EU. They were a social group who played the game in a social, non-competitive atmosphere. Breivik was able to gain influence in that guild and attempted (quite ruthlessly) to change the guild outlook to that of a competitive guild but ultimately failed with many members abandoning him. He joined Unit, the rank 1 guild, but was never in a position of leadership at any time during his membership.
>
> After the latter guild moved to Silvermoon EU, he left them to join a guild called Nevermore. He, again, never held any kind of leadership position with them (that guild still exists and is led by the same person who has led it throughout it's [*sic*] entire 6 year history).[6]

Breivik evidently ended up in the same situation in *World of Warcraft* as at Ris. 'Anders used to be a part of "the gang", but then he fell out with everyone,' as it said in the yearbook from 1995.

Many old raiders have an ambivalent relationship to their gaming achievements, with some describing them as a waste of time and flights of fantasy. The gaming world consumes a lot of time but also gives a lot back. With a couple of keystrokes you can construct a new identity; another couple of keystrokes and you can join a new gang. In the gaming world, you overcome difficult situations, complete demanding missions and make friends with the other players. You feel happy when their avatars appear, and you are proud of your own avatar. What a guild we make! Once you have spent maybe a year or more in front of the screen, real life, or RL, becomes just one of many parallel worlds, another window on the screen – a window that might not be especially tempting to click on and open.

Anders also went on playing *World of Warcraft* after his most intense period in 2006 and 2007, when he would play for up to sixteen hours a day. At the same time, he was active on a number of other websites and blogs, as Anders communicated with the world even though, in a way, he had gone underground. According to the police, he operated around twenty different e-mail addresses and thirty different nicknames or nicks on around forty favourite websites and discussion forums, from the website of the tabloid newspaper *VG* to neo-Nazi websites such as Stormfront and Nordisk.nu.

Breivik preferred fantasy games, but in the last couple of years leading up to 2011 he also spent a lot of time playing *Call of Duty: Modern Warfare 2*. In his compendium, he wrote that the game made for excellent training. *Modern Warfare 2* is a first-person shooter game in which the player sees mainly through gun-sights and sneaks through Russian bases in Central Asia, Afghan towns, Brazilian favelas and the new airport in Moscow, where the player infiltrates a terrorist group and joins in a massacre of ordinary civilian passengers in transit. Dying civilians crawl along the floor, leaving trails of blood, while the terrorists run round executing them.

The airport level was controversial in many countries. It was discussed in the British House of Commons, while in Japan and Germany the game was modified so that players lost (and saw a 'game over' on-screen message) if they themselves were tempted to shoot civilians. Others thought that the game was made more realistic by introducing this aspect of moral ambiguity and not just being about killing baddies. While the heroes are American, the enemies are mainly Russian – a remnant of the Cold War perhaps, or because the game would have been accused of racism if the opponents were Chinese or

Arab. The game is set in a future in which an ultra-nationalist coup in Russia commanded by the game's villain (who for some unfathomable reason has a Chechen-style Muslim name, Imran Zakhaev) leads to a Russian military attack on the USA.

The graphics make the game very realistic. You have to look for cover and good observation points all the time while also not getting lost in labyrinthine open-plan offices and confusing outdoor settings. The game is frustratingly difficult for a beginner, who will get killed all the time, but proficient gamers can obtain a number of so-called perks – for example, becoming a 'one-man army', or OMA, after having killed a certain number of people. The advantage of being a one-man army is that players can quickly switch characters. The disadvantage of doing so is that players lose their secondary weapons and are left with only their primary weapons. Whether you are a complete beginner or a shrewd gamer, you will eventually get shot, but this is not especially realistic in the game, as you immediately 'respawn' and continue your journey, which ends with saving the USA from the Russian invasion.

The former tagger and petty-criminal businessman had always been keen on cover stories. Computer-game addiction was one of Breivik's recommended cover stories during this period. The stigma associated with computer-game addiction would stop people from asking questions about any peculiar behaviour, he wrote. But gaming also had other functions. Breivik claimed that he played *World of Warcraft* to make a break with his old life. Inspiration and lingo from the games permeated the compendium on which he was working.

He constructed ingenious rankings and military and civilian orders to reward various achievements, such as eliminating buildings and traitors or writing political works, almost in the same way that players are rewarded for carrying out missions in games. Gaming terms such as primary weapon, secondary weapon and one-man army made their way into his compendium. Breivik consistently quantified everything, from strength and agility, through his preferred cocktail of steroids, ephedrine and aspirin, to how 'hostile' countries were with percentages, almost in the same way as statistics and probabilities of success are shown on screen in computer games, such as a health level in *World of Warcraft* or a kill/death ratio in *Modern Warfare*. He describes terrorist scenarios with the same kind of percentages as a gamer would use discussing a raid in *World of Warcraft*:

> I know there is a [*sic*] 80%+ chance I am going to die during the operation as I have no intention to surrender to them until I have completed all three primary objectives AND the bonus mission. When

> I initiate (providing I haven't been apprehended before then), there is a 70% chance that I will complete the first objective, 40% for the second, 20% for the third and less than 5% chance that I will be able to complete the bonus mission.[7]

*****

When Breivik took 'a year off' to play *World of Warcraft*, he was a less atypical twenty-seven-year-old than might be imagined. As previously mentioned, the game had 10 million users in 2008, many of whom spent several hours daily playing the game for periods that might last for years. Breivik played a lot, but not to an exceptional degree, and computer-game addiction is a concept that is difficult to define. Extensive gaming that has an effect on players' social, professional and family lives is not necessarily a result of addiction as such. Excessive gaming can also be a symptom of withdrawal, depression or other problems, whether these are situational or fundamental, social or mental problems. To say that Breivik became isolated at this time is also slightly inaccurate, since he played *World of Warcraft* in an essentially social way.

Gaming is an interactive and often social culture that is especially appealing to boys. In *Modern Warfare*, you choose an avatar, a weapon and operational tactics, and you control your own movements. Should you shoot or duck? Your enemies fall in front of you, sometimes in piles. Should you run or wait? The choice is yours. In reality, players are of course subject to a number of rules and restrictions and move about in a landscape that other people have designed and produced for them, but the experience of being an individual acting independently is one of the game's attractions. If real life interferes in the form of your mother suggesting that you are a passive consumer – both of popular culture and of the food she makes – and that you should get out in the sunshine and get an education, a job and a love life, then it is tempting to shut the door. What has RL really got to offer that games cannot do better?

As recently as 2010, the thirty-one-year-old Anders Behring Breivik played computer games for an average of seven hours a day. Perhaps his work on the compendium, which he told many people about, was also a cover story over those years. His work putting together the compendium and preparing the 'event of the year' could in a way serve to camouflage his gaming, while also justifying it as 'training' and as a method of breaking away from 'the game' – in other words, his former reality. Games and cover stories were Breivik's world: layer upon layer of false identities, secret accounts, white lies and black lies. Beneath all those layers was one single burning desire: to be big, to be famous.

Avatar Syndrome

James Cameron's 2009 film *Avatar* became the highest-grossing film of all time and was ground-breaking in its use of technology and visual effects. Audiences gasped from behind their 3D glasses. How realistic, how close; what incredible scenery! True enough, *Avatar* was closer to the three-dimensional aesthetic of computer games than to any landscape on earth or in space, but still, imagine if such a world really existed . . .

The story takes place in the mid-twenty-second century on the planet Pandora. Owing to a lack of resources on the planet Earth, humans are trying to colonize Pandora. The problem is that the planet is inhabited by a humanoid indigenous population, the Na'vi, who must either move of their own accord or be cleared by force. In order to communicate with them, the film's hero, the disabled former soldier Jake, is linked up to a Na'vi–human hybrid, an avatar. Among humans, Jake is a neglected cripple with no future, but his avatar is fully mobile, falls in love with the Na'vi princess, carries out incredible feats and eventually saves the entire planet of Pandora. Jake turns out to be the chosen one, the saviour who turns against his masters.

While the humans live in tired space stations, the planet Pandora is like a collage of *National Geographic*'s top-ten list of natural wonders. Mountains float in the sky like clouds, while the landscape combines the vivid colours of untouched coral reefs with lush rainforests. Strange organisms float past that could have been fished from the bottom of the sea, and Jake whirls around the skies on the back of enormous dragon-like birds. He is no longer underestimated or overlooked.

'I *see* you,' the Na'vi princess tells Jake.

The film ends with Jake leaving his human body for good and being resurrected in the form of his blue avatar.

The film *Avatar* was controversial in places such as China, where some people saw it as an anti-colonialist film with reference to China's policy on Tibet. Others saw it as an epic for the environmental generation: a warning against tampering with nature. One day, Gaia will strike back. But, beyond the political analogies, the film also tells another story, or rather it describes a cultural concept. *Avatar* expresses the dream of a generation of gamers longing to become their avatars.

On some level, most of us can identify with wheelchair-bound Jake being resurrected as a blue giant. You can log on and assume an avatar too. Perhaps it is especially male gamers who fantasize about going from a demanding and complicated human culture back to a beautiful, simple and honourable idea of nature. While reality is made up of homework, demands, everyday work and complicated rules, the game world is simple, elegant and heroic. People who work hard at school or in the office are reborn as superheroes in online games. Which would you rather be, an unskilled worker on benefits or a wizard on level 70? Even though there are arguments and conflicts in the game world too, it is at the same time sanitized, without beetles, creepy-crawlies, smells, infections or ironic comments, without any bodies and without any other expressions than smilies and LOLs. Not only do the women on the Internet look good, they are also easier to relate to. Online, being a man is cool. There is room for all kinds of sexual preferences and all kinds of fantasies. Anything goes. Al-Qaeda's execution videos in which the helpless hostages' heads are cut off for real are only a click away.

As a teenager, Anders searched on the streets for a name and a gang. After five years on the Internet, he had found 'friends and contacts' in England. He had a European network, he thought. He was no longer Morg from RTM and the Tåsen Gang, to the extent that he ever had been. Neither was he the Progress Party's delegated member on the board of directors of Majorstua Retirement Home, one of the duties he had taken on as a member of the party's youth wing. In his compendium, he was resurrected as 'Andrew Berwick, Justiciar Knight Commander, Knights Templar Europe'.[8] The world was in crisis. Only a hero could save European civilization from destruction. Enter Andrew Berwick, a knight with spurs, an intellectual mage and part-militant Tauren. In a way, Breivik underwent the same transformation as Jake in *Avatar*. When he left his 'fart room' in Hoffsveien, he stepped into his own avatar.

The Counter-Jihadist Avatar

The Justiciar Knight Andrew Berwick came into being in the years between 2006 and 2011, at the intersecting point between tagging, freemasonry, Tolkienesque fantasy, sales techniques, first-person shooter games and apocalyptic notions from websites critical of Islam. This avatar was not created by joining human and Na'vi genes; it was stitched together using the cut-and-paste method. The noughties were a decade marked by sharp contrasts, fear and war, but it was hardly Occidentalism alone that made Breivik's knight so exceptionally brutal. Neither was it *Modern Warfare* 2. His murderous impulse may already have been there, and perhaps the blueprint was to be found in the fantasy executioner Morg. All the other elements – the European Civil War, jihad in Oslo, hatred towards modernity, the idea of a network of Knights Templar and the cultural Marxist enemy – were props and background material found by shopping around online.

As mentioned above, Breivik was not really isolated either in the years from 2006 to 2011. He sought out a lot of information on the Internet, particularly from the English version of Wikipedia. He also wrote on many online forums and political blogs. He no longer concentrated on FpU's website but on much more right-wing and in some cases extremist websites. He abandoned Norwegian websites to seek out international bloggers. For Breivik, Norway was small and uninteresting in the bigger picture and, besides, nobody had ever managed to become a prophet in their own land.

In the Document.no comment section, Breivik listed his favourite political websites: 'The pan-European/US community around Robert Spencer, Fjordman, Atlas, Analekta + 50 other EU/US bloggers (and Facebook groups) are the epicentre of political analysis [. . .].' These are central points of reference in what is known as the counter-jihadist community. These websites, together with some other blogs such as the racist Stormfront.org, made up Breivik's ideological superstructure and were where he collected the largest portion of the material for his compendium. Among other things, Breivik cited heavily from Wikipedia and plagiarized the ultra-conservative American historian William S. Lind's pamphlet *Political Correctness: A Short History of an Ideology*. Breivik probably picked up the term 'cultural Marxist' from Lind.[9]

Most of us respond to the anti-Islamic blogosphere by shaking our heads and clicking away to another page when extremism seeps into the comment sections of online newspapers or appears in the form of fanatical readers' letters to the editor. Few newspaper editorial staff paid much attention to what was regarded as a marginal extreme right-wing phenomenon, with weak empirical data surpassed only by its lack of democratic sentiment and the awkwardness of its language. When the media did show interest in extremism in the noughties, this was primarily in terms of radical Islam.

While the media and the general public trailed Islamist cleric Mullah Krekar from his flat in the Grønland neighbourhood of Oslo to various bizarre websites, the 'epicentre' described by Breivik was an isolated phenomenon that few people cared about, even if ideas did seep out from there to the wider public. Pamela Geller from AtlasShrugs.com, for example, is a frequent guest on Fox News in the USA, while some Norwegian politicians have stated that the Labour Party is guilty of 'sneaking Islamization' and cultural treachery. 'Do we want to help the Labour Party to replace Norwegian culture with "multiculture"? Never! Do we want to contribute to their cultural betrayal? Not even at gunpoint! Will we ever feel "multicultural"? Not on your life!' wrote Kent Andersen and Christian Tybring-Gjedde of the Progress Party in *Aftenposten* in 2010.[10] The Russian President Vladimir Putin said that France was in the process of being colonized by its former colonies. In Serbia, nationalist leaders discussed the conspiracy of the EU, USA and Muslims against the Serbs. The anti-Islamic blogosphere was largely left alone and was able to grow and develop in peace over many years. Like most sects, it was to some extent a self-sufficient machine that read itself, cited itself and eventually congratulated itself for its insightful contributions.

The paradox of the informational revolution is that misconceptions survive even if people have access to more information. In Europe and the USA, people are seeking out news as never before, not least thanks to the Internet. It might therefore be imagined that poor information would disappear as a result of natural selection, but the belief that Barack Obama is really a Muslim and a foreigner is still alive and kicking among many Americans who should know better. In Norway, the organization Stopp islamiseringen av Norge [Stop the Islamization of Norway; SIAN] claims that there will be a Muslim majority in Oslo by 2026, in spite of the statistics produced by Statistisk sentralbyrå [Statistics Norway] and objections from the Human Rights Service website Rights.no, which SIAN gave as its source. An explanation can be found in a phenomenon called audience fragmentation. People will look at news sources that are on the same political wavelength as they are (whether these are TV sources, newspapers or websites). As a result, parallel news niches develop, parallel media realities.

With informational self-pollination in these niches, people are split up into political tribes: the Fox News tribe, the *Huffington Post* tribe, or the Document.no tribe, to cite an example close to Breivik. Left to themselves and full of mutual admiration, members of such a tribe breed a whole variety of notions, extending what Breivik called an 'epicentre of political analysis'. SIAN is not exactly a huge popular movement, but its website still has quite high traffic, with often around a hundred comments on each article published.

It is not a group that should be written off as entirely marginal or uninteresting.

These ideological, religious and political niche communities exist online almost like isolated rainforest tribes, hidden from one another and from the societies of which they are part. The dynamics of these online written cultures, often anglophone, may be reminiscent of subcultures such as the neo-Nazi group Jens Erik joined in the eighties or isolated religious sects, but the difference is that they are far-flung and international. Such communities are sometimes described as electronic tribes, thought ghettos or echo chambers. Informational inbreeding can lead to extremism by increasing hostility towards those with different beliefs.

Extremism is perhaps best defined as a drastic approach to brush aside those who disagree with you. In the USA, where the political fronts are often uncompromising, media scholars consider online echo chambers to be one of the major new challenges for democracy. In the early twentieth century, the Scandinavian social democracies bridged deep class divides through the creation of institutions and arenas for negotiation and debate, thereby steering their way through times of economic crisis without ending up in the ditch of fascism. What kind of institutions or arenas can tackle this new form of tribalization in which people are isolated in their own media and information reserves? The phenomenon of online radicalization, which in the last decade has been linked to the growth of a generation of European jihadists, brought this question to the fore.

The Online Prophets of Doom

Breivik's great hero, Fjordman, was the anti-Islamic niche public's articulate golden boy, known as 'the dark prophet of Norway'. Fjordman was also a kind of avatar: bleak, fierce and learned – an eerie prehistoric Norse sorcerer resurrected online. Who was hiding behind his username? It was claimed that he had hundreds of thousands of readers. The mystical Fjordman was a sensation in the second half of the last decade.

Fjordman had published essays on the blogs *Gates of Vienna* and *The Brussels Journal* since 2005; he was a central figure in the international counter-jihadist online community and was distinguished by his extreme scepticism towards Islam. Fjordman belongs to almost the same generation as Breivik and cites 9/11 as a key landmark in his political development. He blogged in English, using some of the same references to popular culture as Breivik – for example, referring to the film *The Matrix* and claiming that Muslims are like orcs, the repulsive creatures from *The Lord of the Rings*. Tolkien's Manichaean universe, in which beautiful elves come up against hideous orcs, did not only give rise to the fantasy industry but also has offshoots in the counter-jihadist community.[11] Breivik's compendium contained forty-five essays by Fjordman,[12] and the compendium's subtitle, *A European Declaration of Independence*, was drawn from Fjordman.

For Breivik, Fjordman appeared as a kind of intellectual big brother, the man who tells it as it is. For outsiders, Fjordman's dead seriousness is the most striking aspect of his online reality. He exhibits no doubt, no irony and no attempt to seek out other perspectives. No nuance, just clear answers. A Tolkien-inspired, flat reality in which good comes up against evil, Muslims against Christians, black against white, doom and gloom in abundance. Perhaps this was Fjordman's forte.

In his 'European Declaration of Independence', Fjordman demands on behalf of European citizens that the EU should be dismantled, that the 'Eurabian' policy must cease and that those responsible for it should stand trial, that support for the Palestinians should be given to Israel instead, that the multicultural hate ideology must be weeded out of the state and schooling, and that Muslim immigration must be stopped, as Europe is being subjected to Islamic colonization. Fjordman often adopts a belligerent tone. 'We are being subject to a foreign invasion, and aiding and abetting a foreign invasion in any way constitutes treason,' he states. 'If non-Europeans have the right to resist colonization and desire self-determination then Europeans have that right, too. And we intend to exercise it [. . .] and take the appropriate measures to protect our own security and ensure our national survival.'[13]

Fjordman states strictly that the 'enemy number one' is not Muslims but traitors among his own people, 'those who fed us with false information, flooded our countries with enemies and forced us to live with them. They constitute enemy number one. We should never forget that.'[14] In his compendium, Breivik sounded like an echo of Fjordman when he asked: 'When the pipe in your bathroom springs a leak and the water is flooding the room, what do you do?'[15] Should you fix the leak or mop up the water? First you must fix the leak, Breivik concluded, before going further than Fjordman by saying that all actions should be directed against traitors – in other words, the cultural Marxist elites. Not only did Breivik endorse Fjordman's analysis or appropriate it, his own texts also adopted the same imaginary 'we' used by Fjordman.

The counter-jihadist 'we' included not only counter-jihadists themselves but also European citizens who had not yet woken up and realized the seriousness of the situation. Fjordman's 'we' is slightly reminiscent of how the revolutionary minority among Russian socialists called themselves Bolsheviks, meaning the majority faction, inflating themselves like an animal does when it wishes to appear more fearsome than it is. Breivik's corresponding use of 'we' appears as partly revolutionary stratagem and partly wishful thinking. If most people do not realize how serious things are, somebody has to take the lead and wake them up. In the compendium, Breivik's 'we' is a cover for 'I', while 'I' is a cover for a question mark, as who was the real Anders Behring Breivik?

The uncompromising attitude of Fjordman's texts is clearly expressed in his view of Islam and Muslims: 'Are Islamic teachings inherently violent? Yes. Can Islam be reformed? No. Can Islam be reconciled with our way of life? No. Is there such a thing as a moderate Islam? No. Can we continue to allow Muslims to settle in our countries? No.'[16] It also emerges in his description of Breivik, whom he considered 'as boring as a vacuum cleaner salesman'.[17] Fjordman's apocalyptic notions are based on a simplification of the world into a few manageable quantities: Islam is only one thing, while co-existence of races and religions is impossible. Full stop. For Fjordman, history is flat and two-dimensional, like a plain on which a single great battle is continuously being fought. Europe today is in the midst of the same conflict as when Charles Martel fought against the Saracens near Poitiers in 732.

The fundamental premise of Fjordman's analysis is the conspiracy theory of Eurabia, which is linked to the Egyptian-born Jewish writer Bat Ye'or, also known as Gisèle Littman. With her book *Eurabia: The Euro-Arab Axis*, Ye'or intends to document the existence of an agreement between Arab states and the EU to undermine Israel while also Islamizing Europe, so that the original population is reduced to a second-class citizenry, so-called *dhimmi*, who will live in fear and under oppression. For evidence, she refers to the ongoing dialogue between the EU and the Arab League, as well as a number of other initiatives for dialogue and co-operation across the Mediterranean, including the Euro-Mediterranean Partnership, or Barcelona Process, which started in 1995.

While Ye'or's conspiracy theory is based on a grain of truth, as these dialogue frameworks do exist, it also serves to blow things completely out of proportion. The EU's neighbourhood policies towards the Middle East can be accused of being ineffective and full of empty rhetoric (as many who have been involved in the Barcelona

Process will be able to confirm), but to accuse them of being the opposite, of being an effective cover for an ongoing Arab colonization of Europe, is far-fetched. It is almost like claiming that the Channel Tunnel is an attempt to carry out a second Norman invasion of England, or that the intention behind the ferries plying between Norway and Denmark is to restore the absolutist royal state as it was governed from Copenhagen in 1660.

Nonetheless, among the adherents of counter-jihadism the Eurabia theory is a central concept and a decisive factor for interpreting everyday phenomena large and small. In the light of this theory, even minuscule matters can achieve great significance, skewing proportions in a way that can appear quite comical to an outsider. Among the Eurabian niche public, as in Alice's Wonderland, things can assume tremendous new proportions. Matters that seem trivial to most people become loaded evidence for the initiated that Europeans are being turned into slaves in their own countries.

Critics of Islam and Their Norwegian Godfather[18]

The other Norwegian blogger Breivik looked up to was Hans Rustad, the man behind Document.no. Rustad would never dismiss Muslims as orcs. Document.no is an intellectually orientated website dealing with international politics and matters of integration and immigration. Rustad is critical of Islam but also critical of the militant rhetoric of counter-jihadists, of what Rustad describes as Bat Ye'or's 'conspiracy', and of right-wing sectarianism. While the website is critical of Ye'or, Document.no interviewed her in March 2011 about the Arab Spring (she used the opportunity to warn about the Muslim Brotherhood's intentions in Egypt). On the website's homepage, a pensive Pallas Athena rests her forehead on her spear, but otherwise the blog is free of pictures, video clips and sound files. No flippant nonsense. There is no fantasy silliness, no crusader kitsch or Viking symbols here. The aesthetic of Document.no is intended to turn the spotlight on the texts and on the thoughts therein.

Hans Rustad belongs to the same generation as Breivik's parents and is a kind of eternal dissident in Norwegian public life. He is an elegant and articulate man in his early sixties, resident at Eidsvoll, the birthplace of Norwegian democracy, where the constitution was signed in 1814. It can never be predicted whether he will turn up in Oslo wearing a suit and tie, an artist-like linen suit, or a fleece jacket, mountain boots and a traditional broad-brimmed felt navvy's hat. There are many people who refer to Document.no and many people who look up to Hans Rustad. In November 2011, the website had 52,000 individual users: a considerable number of readers for a Norwegian online publication.

Rustad has had a long journey as a public intellectual and media entrepreneur. A former journalist with Norsk Telegrambyrå [the Norwegian News Agency; NTB], he was one of few Norwegians involved in the Bosnian War of the early nineties. While trend-setting media outlets and significant elements of the Norwegian political elite described the armed conflicts in the former Yugoslavia as a civil war that required neutrality, Hans Rustad agreed with the French New Philosophers who viewed events in Bosnia as a moral cause. In his spare time, Rustad published books and printed Primo Levi's memoir of Auschwitz, *If This Is a Man*, a key text in post-war European humanism. There was a close link between Rustad's publication of books about the Holocaust and the activist attitude he took on in connection with the conflicts in the Balkans. He argued that the West could not sit by and watch while Serbian and some Croatian leaders led a fascist genocide against multicultural Bosnia and its Muslim majority.

For many intellectuals in Europe and the USA, Bosnia became a political and moral issue in a similar way to the Spanish Civil War almost sixty years earlier, a confrontation against fascism in our own time and against the compliance of Western democracies. For large sections of the European left – for example, the Greens in Germany – the situation in Bosnia changed their views of power, the use of military force, NATO and the USA. When the pacifist NATO opponents of the eighties moved from opposition to taking part in government, they ended up in the late nineties arguing for humanitarian intervention in Kosovo, Liberia and East Timor. The British-American journalist Christopher Hitchens represented the Bosnia generation when he said: 'That war in the early 1990s changed a lot for me. I never thought I would see, in Europe, a full-dress reprise of internment camps, the mass murder of civilians, the [reinstitution of] torture and rape as acts of policy. And I didn't expect so many of my comrades to be indifferent – or even take the side of the fascists.'[19]

Although he was not a Norwegian Hitchens, Hans Rustad stood for the same view. It was not a normal or straightforward position to adopt in Norway. The left was used to using the USA as a moral and political compass: whatever the USA favoured doing was bound to be wrong. In the Balkans, the Americans stood for the interventionist and 'idealist' line, while the Europeans (including the former Norwegian foreign minister Thorvald Stoltenberg, in a central role as the UN peace negotiator) attempted to resolve the war with 'realistic' negotiations.

Bosnia never became a campaigning issue in Norway; the left and the political elite shared the same view, while the right barely had a view at all. The conflict did not fit into the parameters of the Cold War. It was difficult to understand. As a result, there was no real political engagement until the USA and NATO became seriously involved by bombing Serbia in 1999 during the Kosovo War. At that time large sections of the Norwegian left protested against Norwegian participation in the US war, in some people's eyes accepting the genocidal Serbian policy that led to the Srebrenica massacre and the deportation of almost a million Kosovo Albanians. Rustad was one of very few Norwegians who were concerned about the Bosniaks and Kosovo Albanians (both mainly Muslim groups) being subjected to systematic acts of tyranny. How could it come to pass that Bosnia's advocate from the nineties became the godfather of critics of Islam in the following decade and a role model for Anders Behring Breivik, who claimed in his compendium that the bombing of Christian Serbia was what 'tipped the scales' for him?

In the autumn of 2009, Breivik was active on Document.no, writing a number of comments in which he criticized the MSM ('mainstream media') for not covering crime committed by Muslims. He suggested that multiculturalism was an ideology of hate along the same lines as Nazism, communism and Islam, and stated that the stigmatization of 'cultural conservatives' like himself was 'just as bad as the persecution of the Jews in the thirties or during the Inquisition'. He went on to state that '98 per cent of all Norwegian journalists' were 'cultural Marxists' with no credibility or legitimacy. Breivik then presented a comprehensive plan for how Document.no could be developed into a culturally conservative printed newspaper, collaborating with the Progress Party and becoming a right-wing political actor.[20]

While Rustad reacted negatively to Breivik's suggestion of establishing a Norwegian counterpart to the English Defence League in order to have a response on the street when Islamic extremists and 'Marxists' were harassing cultural conservatives, there was little else about Breivik that made any particular impact. At Document.no there was a high level of tolerance for what most people would perceive as paranoid, alarmist or ridiculous assertions ('just as bad as the persecution of the Jews in the thirties or during the Inquisition'). Breivik was one of many young men who were sceptical of Islam and the Norwegian authorities and who looked up to Hans Rustad as a kind of intellectual father figure. There was nothing extraordinary about that. Breivik also mentioned that he was working to finish a compendium in which even Fjordman would find something of interest. 'Incredibly well written, Hans :),' Breivik wrote in a comment on one of Rustad's posts. It was unclear whether this praise was coming from an admiring disciple or a slick salesman. Breivik characterized himself quite ceremoniously as a 'cultural conservative intellectual' and asked the other participants in the comment threads, especially Rustad, a number of questions about how a 'coup' had taken place in *Aftenposten* in 1972, causing it to move from being culturally conservative to becoming a 'cultural Marxist politically correct rag'.

Rustad is a product of the sixties counter-culture and also belongs to the Norwegian 1968 generation. He began his cultural formation by listening to 'The Times They Are a-Changin' and 'Nowhere Man' on the pirate stations that broadcast uncensored radio from ships in the North Sea. At the end of the sixties he took part in the youth camps organized by Sosialistisk Ungdomsforbund [the Socialist Youth League; SUF]. The summer, swimming, youth and politics were a winning combination back in 1968 too. In 1969, the SUF broke away from its mother party, Sosialistisk Folkeparti [the Socialist People's Party], taking a turn towards communism and becoming Sosialistisk Ungdomsforbund (marxist-leninistene) [the Socialist Youth League (Marxist-Leninists), SUF (m-l)]. When Stalin was brought on board, Rustad got off the SUF (m-l) train. He was critical and anti-authoritarian. In the seventies, he admired the anarchist author Kaj Skagen, who handed out leaflets at the 1 May procession saying that the communists had more blood on their hands than the right did.

'The Marxist-Leninists were furious,' Rustad recalled, 'but historical facts have a corrosive effect over time, eating into shining models.'

The Marxist-Leninists changed course over the seventies, eighties and nineties, quietly and calmly disappearing into Norwegian academia, journalism and politics. Rustad was left outside. Publishing his own books, and eventually his own website, he continued where Skagen left off, like a kind of pirate radio ship on the high seas of the media, sending out uncensored ideas and uncomfortable truths to the politically correct mainland. He saw how criticism of the authoritarian aspects of the 1968 generation and of the authoritarian inheritance of the Labour Party came up against a brick wall. Anybody who wanted to discuss such things did not get a chance. The Norwegian elite have a collectivist attitude. They confine and conceal difficult issues such as the Chinese attack on Vietnam in 1979, the Bosnian War in the nineties and the rights of immigrant women today. There was a connection between the left's lukewarm support of Salman Rushdie in the eighties and the Labour government's weakness in the caricature controversy.

'Foreign Minister Jonas Gahr Støre is trying to square the circle by launching the "new Norwegian we" concept,' Rustad said.

> The truth is that a number of immigrants do not want to be part of the community. If integration is as successful as the official statistics suggest, why are ethnic Norwegians moving out of eastern Oslo? This mishmash of good intentions cannot conceal real problems such as Muslims bullying Jews in schools in Oslo. And when Støre said that the right was to blame for all terrorism on Norwegian soil, he was lying. What about the Workers' Communist Party plans to wage war in Norway in the seventies?

Rustad thought that things had been swept under the carpet, and that the left's failure to confront the glorification of violence was the direct cause of erratic moral relativism. If such things were not brought to light, Norway would become like Germany was in the ten years from 1968 to 1978. After the war, the West Germans did not speak about their connections with the Nazi state. This silence made the youth rebellion there especially bitter. In the vacuum that emerged, in the silent lack of any coming to terms with history, the German 1968 generation constructed a monster. They claimed that the Federal Republic was Nazi Germany, and the Red Army Faction began its shootings and bombings. Silence, suppression and weakness provided a breeding ground for violence.

'This is where the connection between the bombing of the government district in Oslo and the silence about the 1968 generation's background emerges,' Rustad reflected. 'Breivik came out of the vacuum the '68ers left behind. That's why there is a historical logic in Breivik citing Ulrike Meinhof in his manifesto.'

The parallel between the Federal Republic of Germany in 1968 and Norway in 2011 might not be immediately clear to everyone. There is a difference between having a German father who was a concentration camp guard during the war and having a Norwegian mother who visited Enver Hoxha's Albania in the seventies. Furthermore, involvement in the Third Reich was a widespread experience in Germany, while the Norwegian Maoists were a niche group, a political sect without any real significance or influence beyond the fact that many resourceful people later rose up from the Maoist hole they had dug for themselves to reach the top of Norwegian society as artists, media executives, academics and leaders of organizations. Breivik must have identified with the criticism of the '68ers, however, and with Rustad's views of rape in Oslo. In Rustad's opinion, rape is a matter not of criminal behaviour but of war. In his article 'Sex som våpen' [Sex as a weapon] from December 2009, Rustad writes:

> Sex is the most transcultural currency of all [. . .].
>
> Women were the greatest challenge for Muslims when they started living among secular Europeans. How could they avoid losing them to modernity? [. . .] The hijab was the answer, because with it the woman marks her contempt for Western emancipation and establishes that she is not available [. . .] to non-Muslims. [. . .]
>
> The other side of using sex as a weapon [. . .] concerns Muslim men's views towards and treatment of Western women. [. . .] Why do Muslim men rape Western women? Is it because they are unable to control themselves? People often turn to this old sexist cliché, which conceals the aggressive nature of Muslim men's treatment of Western women [. . .].
>
> This is not a matter of cultural differences. It is a matter of warfare [. . .].
>
> It is a classic pincer movement in which rights and women's freedom are being crushed from both sides, and Western men are being subjected to a slow castration.[21]

Rustad's use of imagery is interesting. Sex is a 'currency' on a market in which it may seem as if he would like to see quota arrangements to save Western men from a 'slow castration'. Here, Muslims are treated as a monolithic entity, as with Fjordman, and as the opposite of 'Westerners', which means that a 'Western Muslim' would be a contradiction in terms. Is this the same Rustad who, in the nineties, defended Bosnia, with its many intermarriages between Muslims and Christians? Women are described in quite an objectifying manner as a 'challenge', and the female body is a battleground in the Muslims' 'pincer movement'.

Rustad constantly used military images and concepts in his article about sex. Sex and sexualized violence are lifted above the personal onto a group level. As for the notion that 'Western men are being subjected to a slow castration', it is unclear how that comes as a result of the war he describes before that. Can Western men no longer have sex because Muslim men are not showing respect for women? Can they no longer have children? Has their sperm count been weakened? The article illustrates a kind of underlying sadomasochistic tendency that exists in some anti-Islamic discourse. The encounter between Islam and the West is violent, but also erotic. The conflict Rustad describes between Muslims and the West has a strangely sexual element in which the combination of sexual denial and rape constitutes a pincer castrating Western men.

'Incredibly well written, Hans :),' Breivik wrote about the series of articles incorporating this one. He drew inspiration from the site Document.no and was interested in the idea of sex as warfare and the image of castration. Breivik also saw the female body as a battleground in the struggle between Islam and the West. In his compendium, he wanted to punish the 'traitor whores' who had relations with the Muslim enemy. Rumours of the rape of Norwegian girls in the West End of Oslo in the nineties reappeared in an inflated format. Rape became religious warfare and proof that co-existence was impossible. Rustad referred to the Canadian author and critic of Islam, Mark Steyn, when he asked the question: 'If Muslims, making up 3–4 per cent of the population, are creating problems today, how big will the problems be when their share becomes 13–14 per cent, or 30–40 per cent?'

'I don't want to live in a country where I'm forced to take my children out of school because of religion,' Rustad said. 'Look what happened in Bosnia!'

While, in the nineties, Rustad had defended the Bosnian government's multicultural project against the nationalists, now Bosnia has become the symbol that co-existence is impossible. He seems to have performed an intellectual and moral back-flip, from a humanistic focus on individuals to collective thinking. In so doing, Rustad represented a broader tendency. The great political awakening of the last twenty years did not happen with the war in Bosnia, but on 11 September 2001 in New York. The media revolution of the nineties, in the form of satellite news channels such as CNN International and BBC World Service Television, coincided with the end of the Cold War, creating a new international political paradigm, in which stories from human rights groups suddenly went straight on the front page, forcing political and occasionally military action that would have been unthinkable a few years previously. The nineties were the decade that shed light on the victim's story. But that light was switched off when George W. Bush moved into the White House and the twin towers came down. After 9/11, the focus shifted from the victim to the terrorist's bearded face.

The following years became a decade of fear driven by the War on Terror. The West is under attack! They hate our freedom! Liberal interventionists from the nineties occasionally allowed themselves to get carried away by these tempting generalizations. Bernard-Henri Lévy wrote gloomily about Islamic fury in Pakistan, and Christopher Hitchens ended up supporting the Iraq War, which many saw as a betrayal of the ideals he had earlier upheld. War without a UN sanction against a tyrant can possibly be justified by ongoing serious violations of human rights and in order to prevent mass murder, but can it be justified based on weakly grounded allegations concerning weapons of mass destruction? Is it morally defensible to carry out 'preventive warfare'? The focus on Islamic fascism was in itself commendable, but it led to turning a blind eye towards abuse at Guantánamo and Western extradition of prisoners for torture in Syria and Egypt. Other conflicts also disappeared completely from the radar screen or were used as proof of the conflict between Islam and the West, even when that factor was less significant.

It was at that time that warblogs appeared in the USA and Europe, blogs focusing on terrorism and the conflict between Islam and the West. In Norway, these blogs were closely concerned with the fact that the authorities were willing neither to take the problem seriously nor to do anything about it. Document.no emerged in 2003 at almost the same time as the US occupation of Iraq. The Norwegian blogger Bjørn Stærk wrote about how this phenomenon in turn gave birth to the counter-jihadist websites that appeared between 2004 and 2006, at the same time as the major terrorist attacks in London and Madrid and the beginning of the caricature controversy.[22] It may appear inexplicable that Rustad's defence of Bosnia has become a struggle against Islam in which Bosnia serves as an example that co-existence is impossible, but there is coherence in his project. He always situates himself where he can generate as much opposition as possible against the 'compact liberal majority', to use Ibsen's term from *An Enemy of the People*.

The struggle against the 1968 generation is the leitmotif of Rustad's journey via Bosnia to his more recent fight against the elites' deception of ordinary people with their integration policies. In the nineties, Rustad was opposed to Radovan Karadžić's Serbian ethno-fascism, and in the noughties he was opposed to bin Laden's Islamist fascism, but all that time – and most of all – he has fought against the 1968 generation's fuzzy hegemony.

In December 2009, Breivik turned up in person at a meeting about Israel held by 'Documents venner' [Friends of Document.no]. The thirty-year-old Breivik was one of the very youngest at this gathering. Rustad led the discussion, and Breivik wanted to talk about his plans to transform Document.no into the cultural conservatives' answer to *Aftenposten*. Breivik had introduced himself online as a 'cultural conservative intellectual' and a 'martyr ideologue', but he did not make an especially good impression on the others at the meeting. One participant described him as a 'meeting hog [. . .] like the little boy at the dinner table who is neither heard nor taken entirely seriously when he speaks and from whom people keep a distance'.[23] Rustad did not take him seriously either. 'He took the floor and had a lot to say, practically no holds barred,' Rustad said. 'You felt as if there were some inhibitions missing in his head.'[24]

There were not many occasions during this period when Breivik sought out new groups or met people at all. In a way, this meeting was his last attempt to be the glue holding the conservative gang together, the strategist organizing a raid against the Labour bosses. If he had gone to the meeting to make his name as an intellectual or to make new friends, he failed. Again. Rustad, the Document.no group, the Progress Party: none of them were turned on by his idea for a newspaper to take on *Aftenposten*. Apparently he also failed to find sponsors through his contacts in the Masonic lodge, a club that actually wanted to have him as a member. Breivik contributed more and more infrequently to the debates on Document.no. The weeks passed and 2010 came. Breivik wrote his last regular post on Document.no in October 2010. He was far from an extreme online debater, but a change can be seen over the course of the year he wrote comments on the website.

Having initially taken up a lot of space to describe his vision of a broad 'cultural conservative' alliance including newly established organizations, investors and the Progress Party, with a newspaper edited by Hans Rustad as the jewel in the crown, he later spent more time describing the impossibility of penetrating media society. The difficult climate for 'cultural conservative' social criticism meant that direct and 'honest' ways of confronting the 'cultural Marxist' hegemony were impossible. 'We were honest once, but Marx and Muhammad have forced us to become more like them, unfortunately,' Breivik wrote.[25] The circumstances forced Breivik into lies and double-dealing, which occupied more and more of his time. Cover stories. 'War is deceit,' as he quoted Muhammad.[26]

One of Breivik's keywords is *taqiyya*, an Islamic concept implying that Muslims can hide their real intentions and religious convictions if the circumstances force them to do so. The concept has been important to, among others, Shia Muslims, who have been subjected to extensive persecution throughout history. For Breivik, this was a form of institutionalized lying that meant that you could never trust Muslims. At the same time, *taqiyya* also signified for him a world of hidden motives and double-dealing in which cultural Marxists, the 'Stoltenbergjugend' (not the AUF, but various radical and state-subsidized youth groups) and *Aftenposten* joined forces with Islam to finish off cultural conservatives and the nation-state.

Taqiyya isolated Breivik in his own world of ideas: since society was full of lies, he had nothing to learn from it. Since he himself was playing a double game, he never allowed for any dissenting views. Breivik excelled in making up cover stories in his compendium and felt that the rest of the world was also hiding its true face.

Breivik sounded like an echo of Fjordman when he likened Islam to 'hate ideologies' such as communism, Nazism and multiculturalism, the aim of which was the 'complete destruction of Western civilization' and the creation of 'a Marxist superstate (EUSSR)'. He tersely brushed aside the established church as 'priests in jeans who march for Palestine, and churches that look like minimalist shopping centres'.[27] His posts on Document.no appear in part as an attempt to camouflage his criminal plans behind a modest political goal of 'strengthening the Progress Party and the Conservative Party' and partly as an attempt to gain the recognition and respect of his father figure Rustad, almost thirty years his senior. This development from hoping to create a common platform to a resigned belief in lying coincided with the development of his terrorist plans.

Breivik made his first equipment purchases during this period – 'the acquisition phase', as he calls it, using lingo from *World of Warcraft*. Just as he used to go to Copenhagen looking for art supplies, in the autumn of 2010 he travelled to Prague to buy weapons and fake police badges. Back home in Hoffsveien, Breivik pondered over why his suggestion to Document.no was not leading anywhere, in spite of all the volunteer work he had done for them in an attempt to transform the website into the new *Aftenposten*.

> Hans Rustad, the leader of Document.no, seems like an odd fellow. I'm usually excellent in psychoanalyzing people but I haven't figured him out at all. I know he has a Marxist background and I believe he is in fact something of a rarity – an actual national Bolshevik, and thus not a real nationalist. He likes to criticise the multiculturalist media hegemony in Norway but is completely unwilling to contribute to create any form of [alternative] political platform or consolidation. He seems extremely paranoid and suspect of most people and he likes to attempt to ridicule and mock Fjordman, every time he writes a comment.[28]

Breivik's psychoanalytic diagnosis of Rustad is characterized partly by disappointment and partly by strange terms: 'an actual national Bolshevik'. Does that mean Rustad's orientation is neither nationalist nor communist? The terms 'extremely paranoid and suspect' may be descriptive more of his own inner world than that of Hans Rustad. Breivik is always on the watch for attempts to ridicule him, but also to ridicule his adopted intellectual big brother Fjordman. At the same time, he captures some of Rustad's stance as the eternal dissident of

Norwegian public life. Breivik was enthralled by his father figure Rustad, but, just as with his real father, the interest was not mutual.

Home to Mother

But Anders always had his mother. They lived apart only for a few short years. In 2001, when his mother moved out from Konventveien and into a modest flat in Hoffsveien, the twenty-two-year-old Breivik went in the opposite direction, towards the city centre. He started sharing a flat in Majorstua, without making any particular impression on his flatmates. 'Reserved, but nice,' one of them said about him.[29]

Then Breivik rented his own flat in Tidemands Gate, in the Frogner area. His friends noticed that he would not always answer the telephone or return calls. They described a bachelor's den dominated by two large computers surrounded by pizza boxes and empty cans. Sometimes he sat down to play while they were visiting. He played or worked at night and slept into the morning. His mother came to do his washing. This was at the time he was making money. When his mother and her partner broke up in 2004, Breivik took care of her. He bought three presents for his mother: a trip to Malta together, a dog and a 'joke gift'.

2006 was a year to be remembered. Breivik's friends described how he isolated himself and disappeared 'into his cave'.[30] Breivik moved back in with his mother. Why? He said that he wanted to save money and play computer games. His mother explained that she was the one who had asked him to move in and that this had to do with the difficulties he was having with his last company, E-Commerce Group AS. 'Nothing worked out for him,' she told the court-appointed psychiatrists.[31] Breivik had lost a considerable amount of money on the stock market, and most of the money he had made was disappearing. He had also speculated unsuccessfully before, perhaps because he was 'risk perverse', as he later put it, someone who loved to gamble.

Anders spent that year 'almost entirely in his room', according to his mother.[32] E-Commerce Group was eventually liquidated in 2008, and an official receiver turned up in Hoffsveien to speak with Anders. The receiver reported him for violating not only the Taxation Act but also the Limited Liability Companies Act, the Accounting Act, the Auditors Act and the regulations on employers' contributions. From Breivik's tagging, via the blood diamond fiasco and his business activities, up to his more recent years of fraud with false payslips to get credit, he had always considered himself to be above the laws and rules that applied to the general public. According to the receiver, in 2007 he took funds and a BMW belonging to the company. The case was dropped by the police, apparently due to limited capacity. Anders continued dealing in shares but failing to make it big. Between 2003 and 2010 he reportedly lost over 350,000 kroner.

On the evening of 13 February 2007, Breivik's friends stood outside the door of the flat in Hoffsveien. It was a grey Tuesday with light snow falling. The frost the city had been experiencing over the previous sparklingly clear days had abated, and the snow came with the milder air. Breivik was turning twenty-eight years old that day, and his friends wanted to take the birthday boy out for a beer. They came to fetch him physically so that he could not dodge them again. They peered through the windows and saw that the lights were on. They rang the doorbell, and Breivik's mother let them into the flat. She went into his room. When she came back out, she said that Anders was too busy to go out. His mother was a peculiar gatekeeper, an eccentric lady, known in the area for her strange and often caustic remarks. In the end, all the friends could do was leave.

Breivik's closest friend, 'Paul' (who, like Rafik, was from an immigrant background, the son of Eastern European refugees), was affected by his friend's withdrawal. He felt sad and gradually became worried. To begin with, he thought Anders was 'kind and considerate', but also 'very, very stubborn'.[33] Now he had obviously decided not to meet people any more. His friends did get hold of him a couple of times in 2007, though, and they thought he had changed. He had become thin and pale, spoke less than before and was less intense. They described something that resembled depression, not unlike Breivik's guildmate Offler from Virtue, who said that *World of Warcraft* was like an anti-depressant for Andersnordic.

Paul and his girlfriend thought that Anders needed help. Paul got in touch with Anders' mother and told her that she was not doing her son any favours by letting him stay at home. She reportedly answered that she was happy to have him living with her and did not see anything unusual about the situation. From the USA, Anders' sister also reacted negatively to her brother's situation and tried to get her mother to do something: 'It's not normal you know, Mum!!'[34] Although Breivik's mother had sought help on several occasions during his childhood, she had more often rejected external interference. Now the small family in Hoffsveien put up a united front against the outside world.

Behind the brick-wall façade, however, it was not all joy and happiness, if we are to believe Breivik's mother, but even though she is the only witness apart from Breivik himself, it is uncertain whether we should believe her. In conversation with the court-appointed psychiatrists she spoke about her life with Breivik, but in a conspicuously imprecise way. She said that there was no history of mental illness in her family, which was false. She said that there were 'no particular concerns about her son's childhood development',[35] which was false. She claimed their stay at the SSBU in 1983 was a result of the custody case that his father initiated, while it was actually the other way round. She said that her son was caught for tagging once, but the truth is that he was caught three times (including once at Oslo Central Station), and she generally embellished both his childhood and his adolescence. She could not remember her son having gone to Nissen Upper Secondary School and thought that he had paid tax on the earnings from his company. It is a little unclear whether she knew about his crimes, but she generally had a relaxed attitude towards the moral aspects of selling fake diplomas. She called the business 'a great idea'.[36]

Her forgetfulness and misunderstandings may be partly due to a period of illness in the mid-nineties, which she also mentioned to the psychiatrists, but Breivik's mother generally emerges as not especially reliable.[37] She was unreliable in 1983 and again in 2011. When she said in 2011 that she thought it was 'awful' and that she 'panicked' when Breivik wanted to take 'a few years off' in 2006,[38] this might be something she arrived at later. In any case, Paul apparently thought that 'she would not accept' that Breivik had problems and needed help during the year he played *World of Warcraft*.[39] Even if she spoke convincingly and concretely about her son's peculiar behaviour more recently, it could be thought that her account was coloured by a desire that his actions were due to madness, that he was therefore insane and not responsible, and that she would not be blamed either.

In the meantime, things ran their course at home in Hoffsveien. Breivik's mother claimed that she would 'drag him out of bed',[40] but her son rarely made it any further than the office chair in front of his computer screen. He never made it as far as the local job centre anyway. Anders' mother remembered him from earlier years being 'incredibly kind and caring', and only moderately interested in politics.[41] Behind his bedroom door, however, something was happening. The years went by. Anders was writing a book, he proclaimed, about 'the world picture'.[42] He spoke about Christian IV, king of Denmark–Norway from 1588 to 1648, his mother mentioned. He was considering having more plastic surgery, perhaps something to do with his teeth, and grumbled about not being handsome any more. In the autumn of 2009, there was a general election.

'You're a petty Marxist', he told his mother harshly, 'a feminist.'

He accused her of supporting the Labour Party, even though she voted for the Progress Party, 'with his persuasion'.[43] Perhaps he saw her as a part of the 1968 generation Hans Rustad cursed on his website. The Labour Party and its red–green coalition won again, in spite of Fjordman's bleak predictions and the school election result at Ris, where the Conservative Party received 43.9 per cent of the vote and the Progress Party 19.4 per cent. Anders could get unreasonably angry when his mother knocked on the door. She said that small things irritated him. He ate dinner in his room, with his eyes glued to the screen.

The man who finally emerged from the room in 2010 was a different person. According to his friend, he showed up in town more often and was more like the old Anders. By this time, his flirtation with Document.no was practically over. His compendium was about to be completed, and his avatar would soon be ready for use. Breivik complained about his food and became unpleasantly intense when he spoke about politics. Strange things started appearing in the flat. A big, black trunk stood in the corridor, apparently bullet-proof. Anders explained it was needed to prevent his car from being broken into. He had a shotgun in his room. 'The Civil War is coming,' said Anders in a loud, intense voice.

In the autumn of 2010, he announced that his book was finished and that he was going to a book fair in Germany. He went away for a few days, and his mother thought no more about it. He had often run off before. This time he was not going to Copenhagen shopping for spray cans, but to the Czech Republic to buy an AK-47, a Kalashnikov assault rifle, which he did not succeed in doing. Instead he ordered a hunting rifle, a semi-automatic Ruger Mini-14, which is a legal weapon in Norway. He had licences for all his firearms, and the bedroom general decided to make most of his preparations legally.

Just before Christmas, Anders was receiving one parcel after another, filling up the cellar storage rooms with all kinds of strange things. Breivik hoped that the customs officials would not check parcels that came at Christmas. Heavy objects in black plastic bags disappeared into dark storage rooms. His needlework classes at Smestad Primary School came into their own when he had to design, develop and sew together his knight's body armour, made from Kevlar and ceramic plates, which he called 'Loki's Armour', after the Norse god of deception.[44] A weaponsmith, an artist and a knight: the project freed his talents. In the New Year, a large, black pistol appeared.

Then one evening he came out of his room dressed in a stately red uniform, covered with badges. His surprised and perplexed mother witnessed Andrew Berwick's birth and first tender steps. The Knight of the Ill-Favoured Face. The badger in his sett had become a copy-and-paste peacock.

Anders had become 'completely out of it and believed all the rubbish he said', his mother thought.[45] In the winter of 2010–11, he began to work out again, he ate nutritional supplements and his mother thought he was exaggerating and had gone 'all Rambo'.[46] He went to the fitness centre but otherwise did not spend much time outside the house.

Breivik's mother claimed that life together in the small family felt 'unsafe' and 'as if I no longer knew him'.[47] Anders also became 'so strangely moralistic', his mother said, with 'various ideas about how there should not be sex outside marriage and so on'.[48] During his last year at home, she also thought that he was not able to keep an appropriate distance from her, either not wanting to come out of his room or sitting right up next to her on the sofa, and once he kissed her.

After his sister disappeared, the small family eventually consisted of just mother and son. The two strangers on planet Earth only really had each other. Nobody else understood them, and they did not understand anybody else.

'Seriously,' Anders said to his mother, 'get a hobby.'

'You're my hobby,' his mother answered.[49]

In 1983, the SSBU observed how Anders' mother pulled him towards her and then pushed him away, but they also described the relationship between them as 'symbiotic'. It was as if they were one body.

Throughout his thirty-two years, Anders had never been in a long-term relationship. The question of Breivik's sexuality is a difficult one to answer. His friends confirmed that he had few relationships with girls, and none over his last few years at home. It was a standing joke among them that Anders was really gay. His best friend did not believe that and thought that Anders was just 'metrosexual'.[50] Anders' own statements were contradictory. He told the police that he had not had sex since 2001, since he saw his body as 'a temple'. In his compendium, on the other hand, he wrote about relations with women as recently as in Prague in the autumn of 2010. Perhaps he felt that Justiciar Knight Andrew Berwick also needed some women on his record, even though he was supposed to live an ascetic life. It was practically required for an international man of mystery like him. He was insistent towards the women at the Palace Grill one evening, but it was a little unclear whether he was really trying to chat them up.

According to the court-appointed psychiatrists, in police interviews some people had independently confirmed having had 'homosexual contact' with Breivik.[51] At the same time, Breivik liked Pamela Anderson and wrote messages on Facebook to the Norwegian glamour model Monica Hansen. He emerges as ambiguous on a sexual level too, 'metrosexual', capable of going in various directions, but without any major inner motivation to choose any particular way or without the ability to establish sexual relationships. The compendium he was working on contained what appear to be sadistic fantasies. There are not many grounds to describe the young Breivik as a sadist, but one of his friends said that Anders had told him that as a child he had put mustard in a cat's anus. In the spring of 2011, Breivik was planning to behead prisoners and purchased the equipment he would need. His inspiration came from al-Qaeda's execution videos, which he had probably watched in his bedroom in Hoffsveien. Those videos are among the most shocking things to be found on the Internet and would be difficult for most people to watch, entirely in another league compared to *Modern Warfare 2*. His sadistic side was something that he was able largely to hide from others but that, left to himself without any corrections from the rest of the world, he could still develop freely. In his compendium he appears completely without any filter. As his mother put it, he was 'completely out of it and believed all the rubbish he said', and she was unable to help or correct her son.

What was the reason for his cryptic withdrawal in 2006? One of the riddles behind Breivik's construction of an avatar and the execution of his gigantic project is why he moved back in with his mother. While his mother thought this was down to his setbacks as an entrepreneur, Paul's girlfriend spoke in a police interview about an incident in 2005. That spring, Breivik flew to Minsk to visit a young woman with whom he had come into contact through a dating website. The Belarusian girl later came to visit Breivik in Tidemands Gate. She was blonde and beautiful, just like his mother, his sister, Pamela and the girl he went after at the Palace Grill. But nothing came of it. The girl ostensibly thought that the well-dressed Norwegian was a male chauvinist who did not take her seriously.

Paul's girlfriend thought that Breivik's withdrawal from the world stemmed from this incident. The fact that the twenty-seven-year-old Breivik went as far as to travel to Minsk, as well as to pay for the girl to come to Oslo, suggested that he was extremely motivated and hoped that things would work out. When he was rejected again and failed to establish a relationship even with a mail-order bride, things went downhill for him, and his bedroom in Hoff was the end of the line. Perhaps there was a parallel here to his departure from the Tåsen Gang. When his relationship with Elin came to an end in the autumn of 1997, there followed a period in which Breivik was often absent from school and eventually dropped out.

Breivik reacted strongly to being rejected by women. He threatened women at the Palace Grill, and his mother made him cry when she criticized him, but it is difficult to establish any causal connection. He allegedly explained to Paul that he retreated in 2006 because he was tired of 'the rat race' in which 'people went out on the town and had to make as much money as possible', and perhaps in a way it really was that simple. He was tired of putting on airs, of conforming to rules he did not really understand. For years Breivik had tried to fit in, but he did not. He was a stranger on planet Earth, and perhaps this knowledge occasionally caught up with him.

While the Justiciar Knight Andrew Berwick intended to save the European people from the Asian hordes, Anders Behring Breivik was an empty shell eternally running away from self-knowledge that could crush him. On the screen he must have occasionally seen his own reflection. *World of Warcraft* was not enough. The compendium was his last resort. In it, he could re-create himself and the world as he saw it. He isolated himself in order to escape the rest of the world's correcting functions. Far away from the ironic Oslo smirk he had lived under for almost thirty years, he put on uniforms, looked in the mirror, posed and took photographs of himself with white gloves and combed hair.

'It's Going to Be the Event of the Year'

The winter of 2010–11 was long, cold, clear and snowy in the capital. The frost on dark branches and the snow crystals on the pavements glistened in the sun, while the inhabitants of Oslo trudged along, wrapped up well in their scarves, hats and big coats, with their breath hanging in the air. It seemed as if an old-fashioned winter from the fifties or sixties had overslept and ended up at the back of the queue with the slushy, mild winters that had been seen in eastern Norway over the previous twenty years. But by the middle of March it was over. Over the course of a few warm days, the winter wonderland came tumbling down like a house of cards. The thin layer of snow had remained constant throughout five months of freezing temperatures, but it was neither compact nor robust.

At the same time that the snow was disappearing from the city, a man came walking up a hill a few hundred metres from the Palace Grill and Oslo Commerce School. The grit on the pavement was wet, and the afternoon sun warmed the walls of the buildings. Streams of meltwater ran down the street where the tram clattered past on its way towards Frogner Plass. The man was carrying a large, flat cardboard box smelling of pizza. The man was Anders Behring Breivik. He was going to visit Tove in her studio flat in Frogner. Many years had passed since their Easter holiday in Cyprus, but Tove and Anders had stayed in touch not only after the divorce, but also after Breivik was no longer in touch with his father.

'I've given up now,' Anders told her. He had eventually realized that his father did not want to meet him. Tove did not see Anders often, but she was glad when he contacted her. She still had the pictures of him as a child: his white skin and white hair framed his wide grin as he sat on her lap. She also had the pictures from his time at lower secondary: a good-looking boy, pale-skinned and blond, posing in a blue shirt and with a slightly artificial smile.

For a few years it had seemed as if Anders were following a normal route to adult life. He moved out from home after school, sharing a flat to begin with and then living in his own flat. Even though it was a little unusual that he did not continue his education, it did not appear that he was lazing around or lacking money. His business ideas were a little odd, but life is all about trial and error. Every time Tove asked him about girlfriends, he brushed the question aside with a smile, saying that he did not have time for things like that. A few years before, he had suddenly moved back in with his mother in Hoffsveien, and now he was thirty-two years old. He was back at the start. What had he been doing in his room over the past few years?

Tove did not want to dwell on any difficult questions. She was not his mother, and besides it was not unusual for people of Anders' age to take a few years to settle down. It seemed as if people were taking longer to grow up with each generation that passed. It was like that joke about the young people of today being like Jesus: they live at home until they are thirty, and if they do something it is a miracle.

Tove had laid the small table in front of the window looking out to the back, and she put the pizza in the middle. Her flat was on the third floor, and from where Anders was sitting on the low sofa bed he could see the white verandas and the roofs on the other side of the backyard and the black branches of the large maple tree outside. The low sunlight shone in his eyes. Anders moved away from the light and into the corner of the sofa. 'Click': Tove took a picture of him. An elegant man, his hair thinning but well dressed and with a confident colour sense. On top of his lime-green shirt he was wearing a matching striped Lacoste jumper with orange, yellow, brown and mint-green horizontal stripes. His trousers were dark beige. Anders moved back into the sunlight when the camera came out, posing seriously for the last picture. He straightened his torso, put his hand on his knee and put his face in semi-profile. His eyes disappeared in the shadow. Tove put the camera aside. Another two moments in the story of their good relationship were recorded on the memory card. Tove noticed that the boy, or the man as he now was, seemed in high spirits, optimistic, even happy. He told her that his book was almost finished and that he had written it in English because he had contacts and lots of friends in England. It was important to reach as many people as possible with his message.

She would have to hear about the book's contents this time too. Tove tried to wriggle out of it. She had just been to a lecture about Saladin, the poor Kurdish boy from Tikrit who would become the crusaders' nemesis and the superior of Richard the Lionheart. If it were to be discussed which out of Saladin's Muslim soldiers or Richard's Christian knights were the most barbaric, Tove thought that it was not at all certain that the Muslims would come out worst. King Richard executed over 2,000 Muslim prisoners after his first battle in the Holy Land.

'But don't you see it's the same war that's still going on?' Anders asked. He preferred to ask questions when he wanted to persuade someone. He thought that the best arguments are often questions,[52] an idea that was perhaps based on his many years as a telemarketer and online debater. At the same time, his questions often became a little rhetorical and know-it-all.

'Imagine what will happen when the Muslims take over,' he continued. 'What will we do?'

'I won't answer hypothetical questions,' Tove said, dismissing his remark. She wondered whether the boy was making fun of her. It was uncomfortable when he set off on his tirades. Tove's attitude, which she did little to hide and of which he was perfectly aware, had always been that adult life was about getting an education and a job. Every time he started lecturing about politics and Islam, she would interrupt him. Just as she would interrupt him with a short 'Yeah, yeah' when he used to tell her a few years before about his plans to become a millionaire – selling advertising online or importing mobile phone covers. He always took it in his stride, as he apparently did this time too. He was impressed by her knowledge of the crusades in the late twelfth century. In his compendium, he described Tove as a former director of Utlendingsdirektoratet [the Norwegian Directorate of Immigration], which she never was. Perhaps he wanted to highlight his own successful background, or perhaps he was expressing how significant and important Tove was in his eyes.

Like a kind of human larva, Anders had ensconced himself in his cocoon since 2006 and moved away from the sunlight. Now he would soon break his shell. His self-imposed isolation was coming to an end and his book launch was imminent. Anders did not mention anything about the fact he would be moving out of his room in a couple of months and into a farm at Åsta, near Rena in Hedmark county. When they had finished the pizza, Anders put on his jacket and his shoes. They had known each other for twenty-eight years and, in a way, Tove had been his third parent – in a way, perhaps his only parent. Tove thought she knew Anders, and he thought that he was fond of her. Breivik wrote many nice things about Tove in his compendium, but he also wrote that he would not criticize his brothers in the Knights Templar if they executed her as a 'category B traitor', a supporter of the multiculturalist regime.[53] The hatred that had been simmering under the surface all those years was about to take shape. Execution was the fundamental image of his compendium, and perhaps especially the execution of women.

'It's going to be the event of the year,' said Breivik. 'Believe you me.'

'Oh really,' said Tove.

8

The Safest Place in Norway

Shock

'Oh no,' thought Arshad.

Prableen Kaur and Arshad Ali looked at each other. The boy who had told them the news had already gone out the door. They heard him knocking on the next door and shouting the news: 'A bomb's gone off in the government district.' There followed the sound of many feet trampling around and anxious voices repeating the same questions again and again: 'What's happened? Why? Who?'

Arshad grabbed his mobile and phoned his mother first, then his father. It was almost four o'clock. It was Friday prayer at home in Stavanger, and neither of his parents answered the telephone. Arshad made some other calls and eventually got hold of a friend from Ås, a short distance to the east of Oslo.

'Oh no,' Arshad thought again, as his friend described broken glass, fire and people bleeding in the centre of Oslo. Many people must have died. He frowned as the consequences sank in. Now it had happened here. He had travelled a long way to get to Utøya, and now it was as if a large wave flooded the island, carrying him back in time to that day many years ago when he stood alone in front of the class with his back to the board, with all the blue eyes of his classmates staring at him.

The cloudburst from that morning had turned into colourless drizzle. The rain struck the roof and walls of the large Café Building with an almost inaudible whisper. It would be impossible to be any further removed from the dust and sand of Mecca than this summer day on the Tyrifjord. The rain ran down the roofing felt, gathered in the gutters and poured out of the downpipes at the corners of the building. The water level of the inland fjord was rising. The waves lapped over the stones at the tip of Nakenodden [Naked Point], a part of the island that was usually above water. Prableen was busy on her phone. Somebody shouted that there was going to be an emergency meeting in the Main Hall. Arshad went towards the window. It was probably Muslims who were behind the bomb. On the slope down from the Café Building towards the rocky shores and the pump house on the western side of the island, the leafy trees were almost fluorescent green against the leaden sky.

Arshad phoned a friend who worked for the newspaper *VG*, with its offices right next to the explosion. His friend was unhurt but told him there was chaos and death in the centre of Oslo. Together with Prableen, Arshad went out of the downstairs back wing, up the concrete steps to Lillesalen [the Little Hall], and on through the corridor to the Main Hall and the information meeting that had been announced. He wondered whether it had all been useless. If there had been an Islamic terrorist attack on Oslo, would it ever again be possible to be both Muslim and Norwegian?

Planet Youngstorget

People came surging up the street towards Hadia Tajik in Møllergata as she walked towards the square in Youngstorget. Chaos. Confusion. Nobody really knew what had happened, but their instincts told them that if there had been one explosion, there could be others. Tajik walked against the current of people as she headed towards the centre. She had left Utøya together with three friends from the Party's central office about an hour before and had heard while in the car a sound that she thought was thunder. They had parked the car in a side street and phoned their colleagues as soon as they realized what had happened in the government district. They were told that nobody was hurt but that it was difficult to get a full overview of the situation. The people who were coming away from the centre were calm, but their wide-eyed faces showed surprise and fear.

Tajik was still wearing her fun red rose earrings and the red boots she had put on in honour of Gro Harlem Brundtland's arrival on Utøya. It was as if she were wandering into a different country, another world, as she approached her office in Folkets Hus. She felt that it was good to be wearing boots, as the asphalt was covered with glass from broken windows.

In Youngstorget, the extent of the situation dawned on her. The 200 metres across the square seemed like an infinite distance. It felt as if she were walking through custard, as if things were happening in slow motion. Together with her friends, she stepped warily over the paving stones. People wandered about while speaking intensely on their mobiles. The sound of alarms from buildings and cars was drowned out by the sirens of ambulances and police cars starting to appear in the city-centre streets.

It was only when she went past Internasjonalen, the café in Folkets Hus, that Tajik turned her head and looked up at the H Block. She had worked there as a political adviser first in the Office of the Prime Minister and later in the Ministry of Justice. For a short while, she felt lost for words. A journalist recognized her, but she waved him away. Outside Café Mono she met her colleagues from the Labour Party offices who had gathered on the pavement after having evacuated the premises in Folkets Hus.

Tajik took out her phone to find out if her friends in the government district were injured, while at the same time her brain slowly began the task of interpreting all the destruction. Was it a bomb? It looked like it. Who did it? If it was an immigrant, it was strange that the government district was targeted; an immigrant would have chosen the Storting, which was a more familiar symbol of power in Norway. On the other hand, if it was not an immigrant, then who else could it be? It had to be immigrants behind this. And who in Oslo would be thinking anything else that afternoon? In filthy-rich Norway, up in the top corner of a Europe experiencing what were historically positive and peaceful times, immigration and Islam were the only issues that could make temperatures rise and bring out doomsday scenarios.

As a well-known Labour politician from a Pakistani background, Tajik knew better than most what kind of attitudes could be found in Norway beyond Utøya. The messages that came from the dark mainland to her website, Twitter account and parliamentary e-mail inbox took many forms, but Tajik tried to answer most of them. The messages were influenced by current events, and there had been an increase in anti-Islamic messages in the period after Mohyeldeen Mohammad's infamous speech in Universitetsplassen in the winter of 2010. 'You have a completely exaggerated belief that the culture you appear to represent (read: Muslim) is sustainable or popular here. We are even being regarded as impure and inferior! Who are the real racists?!' wrote one angry person in the summer of 2010, suggesting that Tajik should take along 'like minds' with her, go back to Pakistan and enlighten people a little. He also thought that immigrants such as Tajik needed to learn about freedom of speech, democracy and equality. 'I'm not in Norway to learn about freedom of speech, democracy or equality. I'm here because I'm Norwegian,' Tajik replied.

North Along the E18

The rain hammered against the windscreen. Several of the leading members of the Labour Party were on their way into Oslo. Through the fan of the windscreen wipers, Foreign Minister Jonas Gahr Støre could just glimpse the winding road from the jetty, past small patches of fields and wooded knolls on his way towards the main E18 road. The time was shortly after four o'clock. It normally took four hours to drive back to the city, but the foreign minister ignored his officials' advice that it was 'inadvisable' to break the Road Traffic Act and accelerated as he headed towards the capital.

He was kept updated by his colleagues from the Ministry of Foreign Affairs, had the radio on and spoke briefly with the prime minister a couple of times to arrange where they would meet. They agreed that the government should avoid making any hasty statements based on unsound facts. A foreign number appeared on the display. The first one. It was from Ramallah.

'I can feel your pain,' said President Mahmoud Abbas.

In between telephone calls, Støre tried to sum up the situation. What do we know about the explosion? What are the probable explanations and what are our options? Since the chances were that it was a bomb, there was also a possibility of further attacks. At the Serena Hotel in Kabul, the terrorist in the lobby was dressed as a policeman. What might be the next target on the potential terrorists' possible list? And what would the consequences be for Norway?

Støre had launched the concept of the 'new Norwegian we' in a book in 2009 and in an opinion piece in *Aftenposten*. It was the foreign minister who had directed integration policy in Norway in the noughties. In this notion of a new Norwegian identity, including not only ethnically Norwegian nationals but also the immigrant population, there was an echo of Støre's French education and his one-time rebellion against conformity and uniformity that had taken him from Ris School to Berg Upper Secondary School. The idea behind the French Revolution was equal rights for all citizens irrespective of their background, race, sex or religion. At the same time, Støre had seen at Sciences Po how easily the idea could be watered down in reality. One of his fellow students, a girl, approached the professor. She had slightly poorer marks than the average and asked what she could do to keep up.

'You can get married,' the professor replied drily.

Støre's former boss Gro Harlem Brundtland had done her bit to shake up attitudes towards women, but the fact that it was still not evident that women and men had equal opportunities could perhaps be sensed in Hadia, Prableen and Bano's enthusiasm for Gro. Then there was the problem of conformism: even though all people should have equal opportunities, people do not have to be equal. The idea that variety is a strength was important to Støre, the idea that we are not just one thing but many. The 'new Norwegian we' was not only expansive enough to include people of different ethnic and cultural backgrounds; it also fitted in well with Støre's personal desire for freedom of choice and freedom to be different. It was this engagement, more than anything else, that had made Støre the AUF's ideological godfather.

Norwegian people generally agreed with Støre, if the figures from Statistisk sentralbyrå [Statistics Norway] are to be believed. In a survey that is repeated every year, 45 per cent of respondents in 2002 thought that immigrants contributed to insecurity in society, while 41 per cent thought that they did not. In 2011, the figures were 35 per cent and 52 per cent respectively. Attitudes towards immigrants were becoming more positive in line with increased contact with immigrants. In 2002, 66 per cent thought that immigrants made a useful contribution to Norwegian working life, while 19 per cent were sceptical. In 2011, the figures were 74 per cent and 13 per cent respectively.[1] The changes were not massive, but they were heading in the same direction.

In 2011, there were 500,500 immigrants in Norway, and 100,422 Norwegian-born children whose parents were both immigrants. These 600,922 people accounted for 12 per cent of the population.[2] In some parts of this new population segment there were low employment rates, especially among women, but otherwise immigrants' participation in working life and in society was generally high compared to the situation in other OECD countries. But there was another side to the statistics.

In spite of the figures above, half of Norwegians thought that integration was not working well in Norway.[3] In particular, the idea that Muslims were dangerous had spread considerably since 9/11. This was not merely a matter of attitudes among people with low education and income who were afraid of what immigrants might mean for their opportunities in the welfare state or in the labour market, or among people living in urban areas under strain who associated crime with immigration, and immigration with Islam. Neither was this a case of bitter male losers in their rooms or bedsits, venting their spleen on the Internet. That stereotype was too straightforward.

Støre remembered a party with some friends earlier that summer. It was a large outdoor party in a beautiful spot in southern Norway. People were coming and going. At one point, a peripheral acquaintance had sat down on the bench next to him. 'So, Jonas,' the man said, 'what are we going to do when the Muslims are in the majority then?'

Not 'if', but 'when', and implying that it would mean the end of Norwegian society. The man next to Støre was neither poor nor lonely but a highly educated man in the financial sector with a wife, children and a large home. He belonged to the elite of Norwegian wealth, with all the opportunities that entailed. The world was his and his family's oyster. Nevertheless, it was his fear talking.

A woman on the other side of the table had read the official Norwegian statistics and told the wealthy man that, while Muslims currently made up between 2 and 4 per cent of the Norwegian population, the number was projected to rise to between 4 and 6 per cent in 2030 and might possibly pass 10 per cent in 2060. However you chose to twist and turn the figures, a Muslim majority in Norway was only possible in the distant future.

'Which Muslims?' Støre added. 'They are a heterogeneous group, both in cultural and in religious terms.'

Bosnia, Somalia, Ghana and Indonesia all had Muslim populations. There were many people in Norway with backgrounds from those places, as well as from a wealth of other Muslim countries, including Arab and non-Arab lands. Some followers were Shi'ites, others were Sunni, and there were both Sufi and Ahmadi Muslims. There was great diversity, but the wealthy man from the West End of Oslo shook his head, apparently just as unimpressed by Støre's nuanced views as by the official statistics.

Even though the man represented widespread attitudes, Støre was still surprised that such attitudes were so openly expressed among privileged people from the West End of Oslo, among people similar to him. You would think that this man, practically an aristocrat with his wealth, would have very little to fear from Muslims or other immigrants. It seemed a dramatic question, but when a bomb had apparently killed many people and destroyed parts of the city centre it was bound to come up: if al-Qaeda or some similar Islamic group had bombed Oslo that Friday, would there ever be a chance for a 'new Norwegian we'? And what if Norwegian Muslims were involved?

As he rushed past Kragerø on his way towards Porsgrunn, Støre spoke with State Secretary Gry Larsen from the Ministry of Foreign Affairs, who was on holiday in Denmark. Larsen was a former leader of the AUF, and Støre told her what he knew about the explosion. He asked her to carry on with her holiday for the moment but to be prepared to come home and help if extra hands were needed to manage the emergency. Another foreign number appeared on the display. This time it was Defence Minister Ehud Barak calling from Tel Aviv to express his support as well as that of the Israeli government. Støre crossed the county border and drove on through Telemark. A dark Volvo making haste along the winding road.

The Information Meeting

The dark Café Building towers up on the plateau in the centre of the island and is not only by far the island's biggest building but also its social hub. Meals are held in the café at the northern end of the building, most of the events take place in the Main Hall or the Little Hall, which together can accommodate hundreds of people, while the rumour mill can be found where the camp newspaper *Planet Utøya* is produced in the room behind the Little Hall, at the western end of the building.

'*PU* is watching you!' the editor had warned the camp members the day before. 'If you've done something immoral and haven't read about it in the paper yet, that's not because we haven't noticed but because somebody else had done something even more newsworthy.' The kiosk can be found at the main entrance facing the yard on the eastern side of the building, forming a strategic business triangle in the centre of Utøya together with the waffle tent and the barbecue huts run by the Norwegian Confederation of Trade Unions.

When the information meeting began at about half past four, Anne-Berit Stavenes was standing by the entrance at the back of the Main Hall together with her colleague from Norwegian People's Aid, Hanne Fjalestad. The idea of Norwegian People's Aid was precisely to help people, and Hanne was comforting a young person out in the corridor. Many of the young people on the island were worried about family and friends in Oslo. Some had already heard that close relatives of theirs had been injured.

There was a strange atmosphere in the packed hall. Well over 500 young people had squeezed into the hall to hear a briefing about the situation in Oslo from the four leaders of the AUF and Monica Bøsei, the camp manager, known as 'Mother Utøya'. They stressed that it

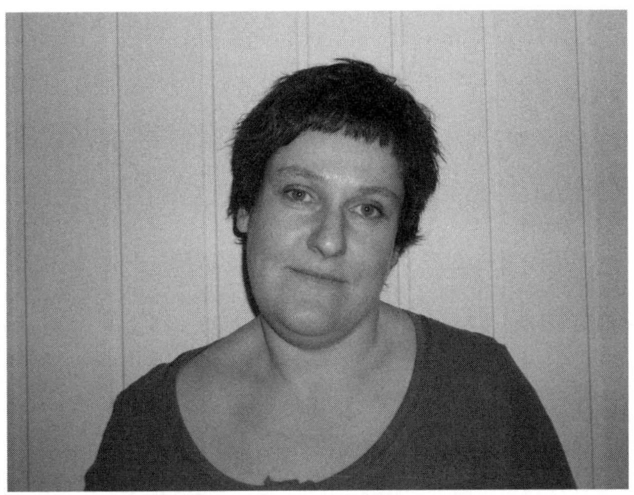

Anne-Berit Stavenes (personal photograph)

had not yet been confirmed that the explosion had been caused by a bomb and that it was therefore far too early to speculate about who was behind it and why it had happened.

A skinny boy with close-cropped hair and a hawk nose came strolling down the corridor a while after the meeting had begun. His shoes squelched with water. He stared in surprise at Hanne and Anne-Berit's fluorescent vests and sneaked in through the door with the others. Monica was talking about an explosion and Anzor frowned when he realized that the disco had been cancelled. That was the big event on the Friday evening. What a disappointment. Anne-Berit was wearing uniform trousers, a green fleece and a shell jacket beneath her orange safety vest. The stocky figure with her short, reddish-brown hair looked like the very definition of preparedness. It had been cold watching the football in the rain that morning and cold outside under the canvas too when Hanne was making waffles in the Norwegian People's Aid camp by the Schoolhouse. Now Anne-Berit was beginning to feel warm in the humid air. The young people there were wearing wet clothes and many of them had not left their shoes by the door as they usually did. It was too cramped for them to sit down, so everyone had to stay standing for the twenty-minute duration of the meeting.

Anne-Berit was wide awake now and studied the young ones closely from the door. She was in her early thirties, and worked as a nursery school manager. She led the Hadeland regional branch of

Norwegian People's Aid, which usually took part in search and rescue missions as well as carrying out educational work aimed at young people. On Utøya she sometimes felt as if she were back at the nursery. She had been on the night shift at the camp's first aid post all week and had been woken up at about six o'clock that morning. The casualty turned out to be a girl who had been bitten by a mosquito and said that it was itchy. Anne-Berit had shaken the sleepiness out of her head and had done her best to comfort the girl. It was not the most dramatic emergency situation to have to get up for, but that was what it was like to be a volunteer in Norway. Little sleep. Most of the times she was called out had to do with insects or jellyfish.

The Hadeland branch's role as first-aiders and emergency responders on Utøya dated back to the eighties. Over the course of the many years that Anne-Berit had been a volunteer at the AUF camp, she had not only given first aid to those who hurt themselves in the football and volleyball tournaments, or who were grazed on the cliffs when they went swimming, but had also comforted young AUF members who were away from home for the first time, afraid of the dark or missing their parents and teddy bears. Utøya was nevertheless one of the highlights of the year for the Hadeland branch. Volunteering there united them. The island was full of energy and a paradise when the sun was shining, and the newspaper *Planet Utøya* had joked the day before that the island's coolest after-party was to be found in the Norwegian People's Aid 'party tents'. 'With glow sticks and the island's only real source of music (a radio tuned in to NRK) they party long into the small hours,' claimed *PU*, stressing that the first-aiders on the island, which was kept free of alcohol or other intoxicants, were unfortunately quite sparing with painkillers, 'so bring your own drugs.'

Camping Life

The dark mainland across the water from the island at Utvika was at its busiest in late July. In addition to the long-term residents at the campsite, who generally turned up throughout the year except in the winter months, summer tourists from the rest of Norway and from abroad filled up the site's caravans, cabins and tent pitches. There were mainly older people at the campsite, together with a few children – a calm contrast to the shrieking, ball-game-playing, debating and tweeting young people on the island 600 metres away out on the fjord.

In spite of the catastrophic weather, there was a good atmosphere on the grassy field that stretched out along the small bay up towards the main road. After the worst of the rain had subsided around lunchtime, it was meet-and-greet day at the campsite, a day of activities, with air-rifle shooting, mystery walks along the nature trails and ball-throwing games for children. There was a smell of barbecued sausages and the clattering sound of empty fizzy drink bottles in boxes. At four o'clock, there was a prize-giving, and Allan Søndergaard Jensen was standing together with an excited grandson when a nearby mobile phone rang.

Allan was in his mid-forties, originally Danish but settled in Norway with a partner and a job. He was a self-employed carpenter. There was a great demand for carpenters in the Oslo area, an area that was growing in both wealth and population. New buildings were being put up, old ones were being renovated. Allan was a typical incomer to the capital: a craftsman from a neighbouring country. His own children were still in Denmark, but that Friday they had his partner Reidun's grandson visiting them, a nine-year-old boy.

The couple were normally resident in a flat in one of the tower blocks at Enerhaugen in Oslo's East End. From their flat there, Allan and Reidun had a panoramic view of the city centre, but they also had their caravan at Utvika. They had both grown up by the sea, and sitting with their morning coffee while looking out across the Tyrifjord was like paradise for Allan. He was shorter than the average, stocky and with close-cropped hair that was turning grey, making him look older than he was.

The news they heard seemed unreal. A bomb had gone off in Oslo. Allan drew his breath and glanced around. There was no reason to worry Reidun's grandson. As soon as the prize-giving was over and the boy had gone down to the caravan with his friends, Allan, Reidun and a couple of their friends went up to the ledge, to one of the cabins on the slope above the shore, where they could have a beer. They listened to the radio, checked on their mobile phones to see what the newspapers were reporting and discussed the news. What had happened in Oslo, and what would it mean? Nothing anybody could have prepared for, obviously. Still, perhaps it had been naïve to believe that something like that could not happen there. Both Norway and Denmark had been involved in wars around the world.

'Yeah, alright, maybe we have been naïve,' Allan said. 'But it's not wrong to see the best in people.'

It was well past five o'clock. There was a pause in the conversation. Allan and Reidun both looked pensively out across the grey

Allan Søndergaard Jensen (personal photograph)

fjord and the ferry landing on Utøya. Utvika itself was sheltered, with the wind blowing from the north. Low clouds drifted above the water and the mist was hanging down over the dark spruce-covered hillsides on the other side of the fjord. There would normally be many boats on the fjord now, but that day most boats had been left moored at the berths and pontoon jetties in the bay below the ledge.

The water was high, and small waves lapped at the grass by the shoreline. A road led up from the shore, past where the goats were kept and past the main farmhouse at Utvika. Above the red barn there was row upon row of tents, caravans and small red cabins. There were not many people outside now. Most people were probably crowding together in front of the television or standing over the pots and pans at their gas stoves. Reidun furrowed her brow. Her eyes followed the MS *Thorbjørn*, the ferry that plied the water back and forth to Utøya. The black and red boat with its characteristic white wheelhouse wavered strangely as it headed north, away from both the island and the ferry landing on the mainland. It looked as if it were heading in the direction of the larger island of Storøya, a few kilometres further up.

'Is he drunk or something?' Reidun wondered.

Faces

As soon as Anne-Berit realized the extent of the disaster in Oslo, she anticipated that it would be the task of the Norwegian People's Aid volunteers to comfort and assist those who might be worried or upset for whatever reason. The team from Hadeland was made up of seven people. The eighth person was on his way back to the ferry with extra supplies for the final weekend.

When the information meeting was finished, Anne-Berit walked across the dimly lit corridor and into the café, where a special meeting was taking place for the delegations from Oslo and Akershus county. She squinted against the rows of large windows along three of the four walls. The café was the brightest room in the building, and everyone who came in from the corridor would automatically squint. The message from the camp leaders was practically the same as it had been in the main meeting: Utøya was the safest place they could be, and travelling to Oslo now would be difficult. Some of them sat on the black, aluminium-framed chairs with their eyes fixed to the floor like obedient children.

Anne-Berit consoled a girl who had been told that her brother had been injured in the explosion. There were several other young people crying, and Anne-Berit feared that the rest of the camp could be affected and become nervous.

In consultation with Guttorm Skovly, who was the Norwegian People's Aid member in charge of emergency response, Anne-Berit decided to keep the ones who were directly affected apart from the others as much as possible, in order to comfort those who needed it and to avoid panicking the others. Skovly gave her the team's mobile phone and went off to make ready a room in the Schoolhouse, while Anne-Berit did a round of the campsite on the gently sloping field below the Café Building. The colourful campsite was in disarray. She met a boy who did not want to turn on his mobile because there would be so much stress with texts and calls if his family could get hold of him.

'Imagine if you were in their place,' said Anne-Berit. 'I think you should switch it on and let them know that you're OK.' The boy turned on his mobile.

She walked through the agitated crowd in front of the main entrance and back into the café. At the table where the coffee was, she recognized the dark purple dress and blonde hair of Ida Spjelkavik. Ida was in responsible mode, with a steady gaze and speaking in short, concise sentences. Her global group had taken the events calmly, but Ida had understood from the reactions of her colleagues abroad that the explosion in Oslo was major international news.

At the moment, Ida was concentrating on calming down the Norwegian participants at the camp. Where the Nord-Trøndelag county branch had their tents, at the top of the campsite, she had found a boy who was wondering where his brother was in Oslo. Ida had taken him back to the café to talk. The two women briefly discussed who needed help and support before Ida began pouring coffee for herself and the boy. Further out into the room among the rows of long tables was Stine Håheim. She had arrived late at her delegation's meeting.

After having made some calls from the media room behind the Little Hall, she had confirmed that everyone she knew in the Ministry of Justice had miraculously escaped unharmed from what appeared like Armageddon in the government district. In the café, Stine's usual pyrotechnic laughter had been exchanged for calm admonishment. Stine was another one of the more senior comforters on what had suddenly become an island of frightened children. On the wall by the corridor, a paper plate hung with the bottom part facing out above a steel canteen table where the boxes of plastic cutlery were. The catering team's motto and salute to Utøya was written on the plate, followed by six exclamation marks. 'YOU ARE FANTASTIC!!!!!!'

Ida, Anne-Berit and Stine suddenly heard some loud noises from outside. Somebody was screaming. Anne-Berit looked up. Outside the window, a group of teenagers came rushing across the yard, past the plaque commemorating the AUF members who were killed in Spain and past the large white tent at the end of the yard. Stine stood by the west-facing windows and watched the young people throwing themselves down among the trees and the scrub on the hillside that led steeply down from the northern side of the Café Building towards the beach by the pump house, which was hidden from where she stood.

Their expressions were unmistakeable. This was not for fun. This was not a joke. There was danger on the island. From their wide-eyed, stony faces, Ida realized that they were terrified, and that they were running for their lives.

9

The Book Launch

A Declaration of Independence

Anders Behring Breivik was running late. Tired. He only got up at eight o'clock. 'Today's the day I'm going to die,' he thought. 'Not that keen on dying, really.'[1]

He made himself a packed lunch of sandwiches and drank Red Bull for breakfast. Then it was time for the book launch. First Breivik installed a new modem on his computer. This took time. He uploaded the propaganda film accompanying the compendium and published it on two different websites. That took time too. The audio and video footage of fighting crusaders took up many megabytes. The upload slowly progressed towards 100 per cent.

He drove downtown only at about half past eleven, parking the Fiat Doblò at Hammersborg Torg just after midday. He walked past Einar Gerhardsens Plass, casting a discreet glance at the asphalted square in front of the H Block and disappearing down the street along Grubbegata. He hailed a taxi in the square at Stortorget. Back home in Hoffsveien, he sat down in front of his computer to edit out old cover stories from his compendium, the 'declaration of independence' that contained the justification for his 'mission'. Hidden in the enormous mass of text, which few would probably bother to read, was not only the description of how he constructed his avatar but also the key to his hate.

The premise of Breivik's compendium is that Western civilization is at stake and can only be saved through the heroic sacrifice of a group of revolutionary knights from the mystical organization

'Knights Templar Europe'. The extent of the 'KT' network is described in vague terms, and the impression given by the text is that the network may consist only of him, the consumer zombie who is transformed into 'Andrew Berwick, Knights Templar Norway'. The compendium is made up of three parts, or 'books', the first of which is a kind of historical description of the problems that have led Europe into the crisis in which it currently finds itself. The second part describes the stages of the ongoing 'European Civil War' from 1950 to 2083, when the war will come to an end and a new Europe will emerge. The third part is the longest, and is largely a kind of practical recipe for terrorism, the main elements of which are selecting a target and arming the terrorist. In addition to political targets, Breivik mentions literature festivals and the annual journalists' conference held in Tønsberg. A diary style takes over in the final third of this last section, which is in part strangely personal.

One peculiar addition is an interview Breivik conducts with himself, spanning sixty-four pages, in which he again accounts for his political convictions, while also telling about his background and family as well as listing his favourite drinks and favourite brands. This self-administered interview sums up the compendium and forms a sort of nucleus within its 1,518 pages. He answers many of the partly critical questions he asks himself with 'good question', apparently pleased that somebody is finally taking him seriously. The fundamental tone of self-love, immaturity and isolation that marks the whole compendium is strikingly expressed in Breivik's dialogue with himself. The knight rebelling against consumer society constantly defines himself through brands: Montblanc Meisterstück, Lacoste, Breitling Crosswind and Blizzard Entertainment.

The compendium is written in a style addressing the reader, but the second person used in the text often refers not to any external reader but to Breivik himself. Sticking to the world of Tolkien, it could be said that the interview with himself is reminiscent of Gollum's discussions with himself in *The Lord of the Rings*, a habit the old, spiteful Hobbit acquired after having lived deep in a cave below the mountains for hundreds of years with no company but that of the ring of power and his memories of having been banished from the society in which he grew up.

Behind the consistently optimistic tone, which Breivik stressed by peppering the text with smilies and LOLs, there is darkness. He ends the interview with himself by saying: 'Know that you are not alone [. . .]. It's really important that you focus on enjoying life and having fun in this process [the revolutionary, cultural conservative struggle]. Being a bitter old goat behind a computer will only drive you to depression, and defeat. Convert your frustration and anger to motivation and resolve. Be positive!'[2]

Lurking in the background of the whole story about Justiciar Knight Andrew Berwick are images of depression, anger and loneliness. 'Know that you are not alone,' he tries to convince himself. Breivik tries to repress his unpleasant feeling of loneliness with a message of positivity typical of self-help books. '[M]ake your favourite smoothie,' he suggests elsewhere in the interview with himself, when the threat of depression and isolation emerges.[3] A battle is being fought in the text between Breivik's two self-images: the 'Perfect Knight' vs. 'a bitter old goat behind a computer' plagued by 'depression, and defeat'.

Breivik accounts for his literary and political ambitions in something he calls a 'disclaimer', an attempt to avoid legal responsibility that acts as a preface to 'Book 3' of the compendium: 'the author, as a sci-fi enthusiast, wanted to bring and create a complete new writing style that has the potential to shock the reader with an incredibly credible fictional plot [. . .] describing a lead character (a fictional political activist who has decided to become a so-called "Justiciar Knight").'[4]

This disclaimer is an example of a characteristic found throughout the compendium, a kind of rational irrationality. Understandably enough, Breivik was afraid of being prosecuted for planning terrorist acts, but at the same time he was so far inside his own fantasy world that he believed, apparently in all seriousness, that he and his compendium could be spared criminal prosecution and censorship by stating that the compendium was a work of fiction. Breivik's faith in his lie is almost boundless, but at the same time he is not far off in describing the compendium as fiction, since it describes a past, present and future reality that few people will perceive as realistic or believable, and not only because his understanding of history is unfamiliar to those who do not share the counter-jihadist world-view.

It is not so clear, however, whether all the fictions he creates are delusions in a pathological sense or a form of revolutionary stratagem. Claiming to have a large and powerful network of like-minded warriors is in line with revolutionary tactics Breivik describes in his compendium when he cites Castro, who started his revolution with eighty-two men but would have preferred to do so with ten to fifteen dedicated revolutionaries.[5] It is not a question of how many you are, but of the impression you give. Lies are a narcissist's magic wand, his method of supporting his world-view. Since everybody lies, he can dismiss opposing views as propaganda and lies from the cultural Marxist elites. He waved his magic wand and, abracadabra, there was a war between religions in Oslo. Another wave and his childhood was stable and happy; one more wave and suddenly the bitter goat had been transformed into a knight in shining armour.

At the same time, the lies in the compendium undermine one another, making it unclear what are cover stories, what is genuinely meant and what is fiction. It must have been difficult for Breivik himself to keep track of which parts were lies and which were the truth. Was Justiciar Knight Andrew Berwick a cover story for a gaming-addicted and homosexual (or bisexual) Anders Behring Breivik, or was it the other way round? Knights Templar should be both poor (*pauperes*) and chaste, but a poor and chaste knight can also be a cover story for an unemployed, lonely man, a modern knight of an ill-favoured face, stuffed full of Tolkienesque fantasy and steroids.

Conspiracy and Castration

The rain was still bucketing down over Oslo in the early afternoon on 22 July 2011. In his room on Hoffsveien, Anders Behring Breivik sat in front of his computer. 'I believe this will be my last entry. It is now Fri July 22nd, 12.51.'[6] There were still a few things to do in the compendium. Some of the chapters were 'rough drafts', other chapters bore the text 'feel free to complete this essay', but it was taking too long to finish his masterpiece. Instead he started to send out the file as it was.

The time was shortly after two o'clock in the afternoon when Breivik pressed the send button. A simple click. Now there was no going back. His time spent in cellar storage rooms, chat rooms, *World of Warcraft* guilds and damp barns was over. Now he was heading out and into his avatar.

The Volkswagen Crafter was parked in a quiet side street. Since the fertilizer bomb smelt so strongly, he had put a piece of paper behind the windscreen reading 'AS Avløpsrens' [AS Drain Cleaning]. Breivik never managed to finish school or to finish his compendium, his companies went into liquidation and he lived with his mother, but when launching the event of the year there was little he did not think of.

But the minutes were ticking by and the error messages flooded into Outlook. It was as if everything was against him, and before long Breivik became 'extremely frustrated'.[7] Eventually he saw that some of the 8,000 messages he had planned to send were getting through. His 1,518 pages flew off through cyberspace to 1,002 selected addresses across Europe, to Finland, Norway, Belgium and the United Kingdom. The mailing list was made up of people who Breivik thought shared his views of the world, of his struggle and of history. The die was cast.

When Breivik sent off the massive chunk of text and pictures, he crossed the first of several boundaries that day. He swallowed a dose of a mixture of drugs he called an 'ECA stack', consisting of ephedrine and caffeine among other things. It had the effect of stimulating the central nervous system. He had been on anabolic steroids almost continuously for three months, since the end of April, which was twice as long as a normal steroid cycle. Now he had to leave. When he left his room, Outlook was still running.

If any of the addressees checked their e-mail that afternoon, they would read that the victims of the Eurabian conspiracy, according to Breivik, were white Western men. They are called racists or male chauvinists if they fight back or try to re-establish lost authority, while also ending up as sexual losers: 'we are the one group of men who are most demonised and attacked' – he cites Fjordman – 'whereas non-white men get treated with much greater respect. What white men see from this is that white Western women prefer men who treat them like crap, and disrespect men who treat them with respect.'[8] This brings us back to the sexual warfare depicted by Rustad, in which Western men are castrated in a slow pincer movement, and possibly in Breivik's own experiences as a beta male at the Palace Grill.

Castration also appears as a phenomenon and an image in the compendium, occasionally in unexpected contexts. In a discussion about the use of nuclear weapons and dirty bombs, Breivik pictures a potential collaboration between Islamist groups and Knights Templar, since the two opponents have the same enemy, namely the establishment. The problem is how the Islamists should distinguish Knights Templar from CIA agents. The difference between the 'system protectors' of democracies and nationalist freedom fighters is that the latter are willing to make sacrifices, including gladly sacrificing their own lives. As a result, '[t]he entity should demand that the alleged Justiciar Knight in question surgically remove his penis and testicles and/or execute a fixed number of civilian children. While this requirement seems morbid, absurd and unreasonable, it is perhaps the most effective method of confirming the intentions of an individual.'[9]

It is a little unclear whether 'the entity' refers to the Knights Templar or the Islamists, but the point remains that the Justiciar Knight Andrew Berwick is willing to castrate himself to collaborate with al-Qaeda, for 'the greater good of our cause'. He is also willing to execute 'civilian children', a term that might suggest there are children who are not 'civilian' but military or other legitimate targets in the struggle against the multiculturalist regime.

In his strange fantasy of being al-Qaeda's eunuch, there is an echo of the 'security alliances' into which the white taggers entered with representatives of the immigrant gangs in Oslo during the nineties. While Morg admired the alpha males in the B Gang, Andrew Berwick was interested in al-Qaeda and wanted to base the Knights Templar on them,[10] more or less in the same way that the Tåsen Gang were an ethnically Norwegian answer to the Young Guns from Bjølsen. Local situations in Oslo were blown up to the scale of geopolitics, world history or civilization, because the Justiciar Knight Andrew Berwick did not tag in the tunnels under Oslo's Ring 3 ring road. He had 'contacts and many friends in England' and acted on an international level, but it was still important to show the toughest boys in town that you were good enough, so the way to do that was through the surgical removal of the penis and testicles of the man in question.

Although this refers to co-operation between terrorist groups, al-Qaeda is not expected to undergo castration or to make sacrifices in other ways. The Islamists appear as an authority, while the Templar Knight has to prove his worth. It is like the relationship between a veteran and a new recruit, or between father and son. It may seem as if Breivik is fantasizing about a form of symbolic submission. By castrating the Templar Knight – in other words, himself – in order to gain respect and nuclear weapons from al-Qaeda, he is subjecting himself to an idea of brutal masculine authority. A psychoanalyst might say that Breivik's absent father returns in this paragraph in a fantasy of a terrorist patriarchy. He had once wanted Jens Breivik to be proud of him, whereas now he was seeking the recognition of al-Qaeda.

Perhaps the compendium's cover-story principle is in effect here too: the fact that Berwick is willing to sacrifice his ability to reproduce is, on one level, also a cover story for a sexual loser with no prospects of continuing his line. Desire and angst are closely linked. If the idea of executing 'civilian children' is placed on equal terms with castration, as two variants of the Justiciar Knights' ordeal by fire, it is an example of how sadistic fantasies are consistently closely related to thoughts of self-mutilation or suicide.

At the same time, this repressed and inhibited Western man is the hero of the war described by Breivik. The hero, the Justiciar Knight, is at once a 'judge, jury and executioner'.[11] 'A Justiciar Knight is not only a valorous resistance fighter, a one-man army,' Breivik writes, 'he is a one-man marketing agency as well.'[12] He has to market and to sell his revolutionary product '[i]n order to wake up the masses'.[13] Both the term 'one-man army', which Breivik borrowed from his tagging and from *Modern Warfare* 2, and his background as a salesman and marketer take on central significance in his description of the hero, the personification of brutal masculine authority.

The ongoing war has four phases, according to Breivik. Many counter-jihadists and those who think like them put forward prophecies, often bleak ones, of imminent wars, collapses or disasters, but Breivik surpasses most of them by constructing a future for Europe in which events have been determined seventy years in advance. His historical determinism is shared with left-wing Marxist revolutionaries – for example, with the Norwegian Workers' Communist Party members in the seventies who 'knew' that a war would break out between NATO and the Soviet Union – but his story, with its meticulous details of how Russia will repulse a US naval invasion of France in 2040,[14] is more reminiscent of a game scenario from an alternative version of *Modern Warfare* 2.

Breivik's version of history begins in the past, specifically in the 1950s, which for him has the status of a kind of patriarchal and culturally conservative golden age (in spite of the fact that this was also the period when the Labour Party's 'one-party state' was in its heyday under Prime Minister Einar Gerhardsen). The years from 1955 to 1999 were a prelude to the war, the 'Phase of Dialogue', as Breivik calls it,[15] when the Eurabia policy was adopted by EU leaders and the Islamic colonization of Europe gained speed. Phase 1 of the European Civil War broke out in 1999, when NATO attacked Serbia and occupied Kosovo. Phase 1 lasts until 2030 and includes the early cultural conservative counter-attacks. Phase 2 of the Civil War takes place from 2030 to 2070 and is characterized by increased resistance activity and an acceleration of the Muslim colonization of Europe. During the final phase of the Civil War, from 2070 to 2083, cultural conservative coups d'état in Europe will be followed by the execution of all Marxist traitors as well as the deportation of Muslims and, possibly, bloody battles.

The villains of this story come in three varieties – category A, B and C traitors – determined by their position in the cultural Marxist elite. 'No mercy will be shown for category A, B and C traitors,'[16] Breivik writes, even though he later ponders whether it might be enough to execute 200,000 category A and B traitors, deporting the rest to Anatolia.[17] The estimates vary of how many traitors there actually are, demonstrating that the categories are fluid. Who will live and who will die is largely up to the individual Justiciar Knight's judgement. In 2083, precisely four centuries after the Battle of Vienna, the nations of Europe will finally be cleansed of Marxists and Muslims and united in a loose European federation. Democracies will be controlled by cultural conservative 'guardian councils', and the patriarchal family structure will be re-established in order to control unrestrained sexuality and divorce.

The absent father gets his historical revenge. In this connection, the 'single most important' change to the law will be to guarantee 'that the father will always get the custody of the child'.[18] Patriarchy will be reinstated. This means that the conclusion of Breivik's historical system – the culmination of the cultural conservative revolution – is legislation to prevent fathers from losing their children, and vice versa. Breivik said that he had forgotten his early childhood. A psychoanalyst might say that he had repressed it, blacked it out or denied it.

It is difficult not to view the compendium as a kind of massive, quasi-literary adaptation of Breivik's own childhood, with personal traumas and conflicts blown up to an enormous scale and transferred onto a broad canvas of civilization, in which their historical solutions can be arrived at with the help of the intervention and martyrdom of the Justiciar Knight.

The Suicide Note

Breivik went in the back of the large van and changed into what he called his uniform and armour – in other words, uniform-style trousers and a Skins-branded triathlon shirt (he had drawn with a black pen over the compression shirt's yellow seams). He was wearing black boots with Black & Decker countersink bits sticking out of the heels like spikes. He had drilled holes into the boot-soles and attached the tools so that they resembled some kind of spurs, allegedly because he wanted an extra weapon for close combat, or 'melee fighting' as it is called in *World of Warcraft*. One of the avatars he had used the most over the previous couple of years was Conservative, a creature from the Tauren race, which was the game's most effective and brutal melee unit. Perhaps Conservative had inspired him, because he referred to melee weapons and melee fighting techniques a number of times in the compendium:

> a Justiciar Knight is armed with not only a primary and secondary weapon but melee weapons as well [. . .].
>
> If I were to attempt to describe the martial art form of my specific operation it would resemble that of the extremely mobile juggernaut (deployable human tank). [. . .] As for information concerning the

> operatives in my cell, I cannot disclose anything that might indicate [the] number of individuals or their methods and/or tasks. [My own technique of] using light vehicles to get from one location to the other [. . .] can be described as a 'system protector flank buster' technique [. . .]. The spikes on the shield, neck, arms and boots, in addition to the bayonet would also be highly efficient against any civilians or system protectors trying to jump you from behind.[19]

Primary and secondary weapons are terms from *Modern Warfare 2*. The Juggernaut is a character from the Marvel comics, a muscle-bound hunk who would make even Morg look puny by comparison. The description of 'operatives' in his cell, with their own individual 'methods and/or tasks', is reminiscent of a discreet guild leader's description of the members of a raiding guild in *World of Warcraft*. The 'flank buster' technique is a term from the game *Warhammer*, another of the fantasy enthusiast Breivik's favourite games. The bayonet and boot spikes were the Justiciar Knight's melee weapons (he must have rejected the idea of spikes on his neck and arms, even though he provided models of these in the compendium). The juggernaut Andrew Berwick, weighed down by Loki's Armour and his 'level III helmet with visor', was a kind of real-life Tauren. All in all, Andrew Berwick was constructed by sampling comic-book and computer-game terms. When he was fully dressed and armoured as a Justiciar Knight, Breivik closed the back door and got into the driving seat. It was time to die.

The Juggernaut

What kind of person was trying to carry out one of the largest terrorist actions since the Second World War? In the diary section at the end of the compendium, called his 'Knights Templar Log', Breivik accounts first schematically and then in detail for his preparations over the years, from the alleged founding meeting of the Knights Templar in 2002 until sending out the compendium on 22 July 2011. In between its endless lists and instructions about how to make 'Loki's Armour' out of Kevlar and how to mix cocktails of drugs, the log is also a portrait of an unusually systematic person with somewhat compulsive behaviour. It is possible to recognize the 'mildly pedantic' and 'extremely neat' boy described by the SSBU in 1983. Breivik appears to depend on many fixed routines to get through the day and describes a number of phobias and fears. He chronicles what appear as excessively suspicious, genuinely paranoid reactions to strangers coming to the farm at Åsta in the last few months before he drives the bomb to Oslo, but on some level he is aware of his own fears.

Breivik writes that '[p]aranoia can be a good thing, or it can be a curse'.[20] Paranoia or fear can make the Justiciar Knight cautious, which is useful, but they can also be a hindrance if they are exaggerated or irrational. Breivik is afraid of insects in the woods where he buries his equipment; he hates the spiders in the barn where he makes the bomb and the creaking of the farmhouse at night. He is tremendously concerned about avoiding infection when his mother has the flu. The connection between women and infection/illness/impurity is one of the compendium's refrains and one of the problems to be solved in Breivik's future patriarchy.

The sociologist Zygmunt Bauman has described the gardening impulse as a driving force in modern totalitarian projects: the desire to weed out dirt, infection, shades of grey, chaos and all that is unfamiliar in order to create the perfect garden. Breivik's desire to cleanse Europe of Marxist influence and Islamic presence is a variant of the gardening impulse that, according to Bauman, is especially characteristic of the Third Reich, in which the Jews were described as vermin, carriers of infection, impure blood and polluted cosmopolitan ideas. Nazism was 'applied biology', according to Rudolf Hess, who saw the German people as a single organism, the *Volkskörper*. Politics and war concerned cleansing this body of waste (Jews and Slavs), while also securing *Lebensraum* for the future.

Breivik's ideas about an organization of modern Knights Templar, PCCTS, is characterized by a fascination with uniforms, mystical rituals and intricate rank scales and could have been modelled on the Nazi executioners' organization *par excellence*, the SS. It is not only aesthetics that Breivik has in common with the SS, his idolization of the dominant, aggressive and armed man, the ultimate executioner; he is also interested in racial theory. He claims that the Nordic race is superior to other races – referring to Pamela Anderson as an example of an almost purely Nordic person – and calls for cultural conservative breeding projects to preserve the Nordic race for the future. Otherwise, the race could vanish within 150 years.[21]

On the other hand, Breivik writes that he 'would not hesitate to sacrifice [his] own life for the English, Slavic, Jewish, Indian, Latin or French tribes in their fight against the EUSSR/US multiculturalist hegemony'.[22] He is unclear about where the biological boundaries lie and what the difference is between the 'tribes' he mentions. It could appear as if Breivik were striving to find out who 'the free Europeans' are – in other words, the 'we' of his political project. Should 'we' be defined in terms of politics, religion, or perhaps biology?

Even though Breivik criticizes Nazism (writing that he would have liked to have killed Hitler), there are actually many points of contact between the compendium and Nazi aesthetics, racial theory and perceptions of history. His distancing from Nazism in the compendium is linked to large parts of the extreme right wing in Europe having abandoned racist ideology (including anti-Semitism) after September 2001, finding an anti-Islamic platform instead. This also applied to his 'contacts and many friends in England'. With the definition of a new enemy, the old enemy Israel became a new ally in the fight against Islam, and the former heroes, the Nazis, were redefined as socialist villains.

Breivik is no ideologue or a fundamental thinker. He shops around. Just as there is a shift in his comments on Document.no from an optimistic wish for 'conservative' co-operation in 2009 to a dark focus on the necessity of lying in 2010, there is a shift in the compendium too. Breivik moves from aisle to aisle in the ideological supermarket, picking out things depending on where he thinks he might find friends or allies. Wolves seek out a pack. This became clear during his trial. He did not want to shoot Hitler any more but wanted to be seen as part of a crew with the Norwegian neo-Nazis Erik Blücher and Johnny Olsen as well as the Nationalsozialistischer Untergrund [National Socialist Underground, NSU], a German neo-Nazi group that has been killing people of foreign origin and police since 2000. While he attached great importance in the compendium to the Kosovo War in 1999, writing that NATO's attack on Serbia was the event that radicalized him, Breivik seemed completely uninterested when the prosecutor questioned him about this in court.[23]

While the ideological and political levels fall apart, the compendium can be read quite coherently as a grandiose suicide note. In contrast to the consumer zombie's short-sighted hedonism, the Justiciar Knight must 'embrace voluntary poverty and martyrdom'.[24] Martyrdom, the sacrifice of the Justiciar Knight's own life, is a central element of his shock attack, intended to wake up Europe from its slumber in the early phases of the Civil War. The third part of the compendium is permeated by what emerge as images of suicide, although it is often described with other terms: martyrdom, sacrifice or self-termination.

Throughout the compendium, Breivik portrays himself as a member of the living dead: first he was a 'zombie' in the hands of market forces and consumer culture, then he awakened to a political life as a Justiciar Knight, making it his task to wake up the masses. But even this 'living' political life features a conflict, as a Justiciar Knight is also dead. The difference is only that he has already accepted it: 'The core strength of a Justiciar Knight is that we accept the fact that we're already dead.'[25] This means that there is a common denominator for the consumer Anders Breivik and the Justiciar Knight Andrew Berwick in that they are both dead, at least figuratively. Even if a Justiciar Knight's death is, paradoxically, what will give him life as a martyr, the personal sections of the compendium are marked by a fascination with death.

Breivik sometimes drifts into emotionally charged fantasies of his own imminent death – for example in the following extract, in which he discusses the exhilarating effect during a potential mission of the theme music from the computer game *Age of Conan*, performed by the Norwegian singer Helene Bøksle:

> imagine fighting for your life against a pursuing pack of system protectors ([. . .] also referred to as the police). You try to avoid confrontation but they eventually manage to surround you. You hear this song as you push forward to annihilate one of their flanks, head-shotting [*sic*] two of your foes in bloody fervor trying to survive. [Bøksle's] angelic voice sings to you from the heavens, strengthening your resolve in a hopeless battle. Your last desperate thrust kills another two of your enemies. But it isn't enough as you are now completely surrounded; your time is now. This voice is all you hear as your light turns to darkness and you enter into the Kingdom of Heaven.[26]

Even though the moment of death, when 'your light turns to darkness', is reminiscent of how avatars die in first-person shooter games such as *Call of Duty*, this quotation is one of few that also allude directly to notions of Christian faith. Neither God nor heaven occupies any considerable space in the compendium, even though Andrew Berwick is a Christian knight from the outset.

Breivik normally portrays life after death as a question of fame: 'They may physically kill a Justiciar Knight, but your name will be remembered for centuries. [. . .] Your sacrifice will be a great source of inspiration for generations of Europeans to come. You will become a role model for hundreds, perhaps thousands of new emerging martyrs fighting the good fight, our fight.'[27] The Justiciar Knight's name will live on, according to Breivik, in a similar fashion to the thirty-four names carved into the memorial stone outside Ris School. Fallen resistance fighters become the role models of the future. Even though the prospects for the Justiciar Knight personally are poor, he knows that his sacrifice will contribute to final victory. Besides, a martyr is never alone. Through his death, a martyr becomes mystically united to his 'people' – in other words, the community for whom he sacrifices himself. In death, he makes a name for himself and becomes part of a group, or he gets an identity and a sense of belonging.

In macabre tandem with these images of suicide, the focus on execution flows through the compendium like an undercurrent. The words 'execute', 'execution' and 'executioner' can be found throughout, describing Justiciar Knight Andrew Berwick's main purpose. In that respect, he is an echo of Breivik's first avatar, Morg, who was known in the Marvel Universe as the executioner, the one who had butchered his own people. Perhaps there was also a component of sexual desire in this executioner fantasy: Morg, with his enormous, phallic double-headed axe, is the very image of aggression, control and total violence. The repeated focus on executions, on taking the lives of defenceless and captive people, including children, gives the compendium a sadistic tone.

When the Civil War comes to an end, writes Breivik, all category A and B traitors will be immediately arrested and executed in a comprehensive operation, but '[c]ertain category A and B traitors may be incarcerated during the operation (if there is sufficient capacity and manpower) with the intention for an official celebratory lynching at a later point (to boost moral[e] for our forces etc.).'[28] An execution is an extreme situation. The victim is completely powerless and the executioner all-powerful. When the executioner is also the judge and jury and operates alone, the person in question is the supreme master of life and death. It can appear as if executions are not only a political instrument for Breivik but an aim in themselves.

The 'official celebratory lynching' to strengthen morale takes place after the end of the Civil War, so it is neither a wartime measure nor a peacetime method of punishment but a form of social ritual in the future political society he envisages. Breivik's radiant future is a society with the character of a sadistic mass cult.

Hatred of Women

After having started the Crafter van and got it in gear (he had needed to phone the rental company, Viking, the week before because he was not able to get the van in reverse), Breivik drove down Hoffsveien towards Skøyen. In addition to his black uniform-like clothing, he was wearing a handgun holster and a bullet-proof vest. He had carved the name 'Mjolnir' onto the Glock in the holster with runic letters, after the name of the hammer of Thor in Norse mythology. The motorbike in the back of the van was called 'Sleipner', after Odin's eight-legged horse. His helmet was on the seat next to him. At Skøyen, policemen were standing next to a car that had come off the road. The Crafter drove past them on its way towards the city centre.

Breivik had made it so far partly because he acted alone, but his fantasies of collaborating with al-Qaeda are also an example of how the extremes meet. This is the key to the ideological tradition to which Breivik belongs, with one important exception. There is an occidentalist logic in Breivik's compendium containing many quotations, not all of which are credited, by a number of the Islamists and Marxists to whom he was so hostile from the outset. They all hate modernity.

There is also a revolutionary logic, because Breivik admires revolutionary terrorists of the past. He is citing Ulrike Meinhof when he writes that '[p]rotesting is saying that you disagree. Resistance is saying you will put a stop to this.'[29] Breivik mentions Muhammad, Fidel Castro and Mao in positive terms, and his critique of consumer society sounds like an echo of the Red Army Faction, which claimed that 'the system in the metropole reproduces itself through an ongoing offensive against the people's psyche [. . .] through the market'.[30] Breivik is anti-democratic, against globalization and in favour of a corporative state but, at the same time, he is not consistently fascist. For example, he would accept segregated liberal zones within the new Europe with their own more liberal laws on the freedom of expression, substance abuse and sexuality, in an idea he called 'a doctrine of "Las Vegasism"'.[31]

Professor of history Øystein Sørensen points to similarities between Breivik and Ayatollah Khomeini in Breivik's call for a conservative 'guardian council' to administer a new, totalitarian Europe. The totalitarian nature of Breivik's notions of Armageddon, revolution, mass murder and a future 'conservative' ideal society link him to other totalitarian ideologies, with red, brown and green (Islamist) tendencies. The gardening impulse emerges in his need to clean up and to control, his view of the contemporary age as an apocalyptic lake of fire, in his need to cleanse Europe with blood and his dream of a hygienic future.

Although Sørensen characterizes Breivik as a right-wing extremist or extreme right-wing authoritarian, he also writes that 'neither of these expressions totally makes sense of the elements of armed rebellion and revolutionary rupture to be found in his manifesto'.[32] This aggressive and sadistic impulse is the motor of the compendium, the force driving him from shelf to shelf in the extremism and totalitarian departments of the ideological shopping centre.

In ideological terms, not only does Breivik transcend categories such as right wing and left wing, he also mixes ideas from Orthodox, Catholic and Protestant traditions together with ideas from political Islam. It can appear as if he got lost in the religion department, but then he also writes that he is 'not an excessively religious man'.[33] In Breivik's contradictions there is still a coherence, some basic notions that are also characteristic of many other violent groups on the fringes of society, irrespective of their religious or political labels.

Breivik belongs to the occidentalist tradition: his hatred is directed towards the city (in court he said that Oslo is a 'multicultural hell'), the bourgeois (or the consumer zombie, the antithesis of the heroic knight) and politically correct reasoning (secularism, egalitarianism and social democracy). Regarding the lack of heroism in the bourgeois West, Breivik writes that '[t]he mass-democracy model of Western Europe [. . .] has cultivated the principle of mediocrity instead of continuing to pursue excellence.'[34] Regarding the West's soulless regimes of rationality, he writes that '[s]piritually bankrupt nations without civilizational visions are nothing more than devastated wastelands of meaningless noise and excessive consumerism.'[35]

Breivik's hatred of the city is not only directed towards Oslo. In his compendium, it is often translated into hatred towards supranational institutions such as the EU or the European Court of Human Rights, which is a 'racist and genocidal political entity'.[36] He is inspired by ideas of anti-globalization – for example, in his desire to nationalize global companies and to establish protectionist tariff barriers. Since global capital forces at a supranational level support the conspiracy between the 'cultural Marxist' elite and the aggressive

Muslim minority, 'capitalist globalists' are also on Breivik's list of traitors to be executed.

With his rose-tinted notion of mono-ethnic Japan, respect for Japanese kamikaze pilots and practice of Bushido meditation, Breivik could have been a fly on the wall at the conference in Kyoto in 1942 that Buruma and Margalit used as a starting point for their exploration of Occidentalism.

What distinguishes the compendium from other occidentalist texts is its focus on women. In the occidentalist tradition, modernity is often linked to women, and hatred towards women is part of the mixture, but for Breivik, feminism and Marxism constitute his main enemies. He was to some extent inspired by counter-jihadists such as Fjordman also with regard to his notion that women represent the threat of modernity to an even greater degree than the four symbols of the West brought up by Buruma and Margalit: the city, the bourgeois, reason and the infidel. Breivik's violent attack on feminism, his desire to re-establish patriarchy, his metaphors of rape and the underlying connection between women and infection concern more than ideology alone.

Breivik is worried about the feminization of society, claiming that 'the forced ordination of female priests ravaged the very fundament of the Church', and that 'women's emotionally unstable nature quickly [led] to the propagation of gay marriage, the ordination of gay priests, ignoring chastity, ignoring people's duties in relation to procreation, the support for mass-Muslim immigration and even the inter-religious dialogue with the Muslim community [which is] in fact no more than a formal discussion for the terms of total surrender'.[37] Not only are women unstable, they also contribute to regression in terms of reproduction. They open the door for homosexuality. They seem to be susceptible to treason, or at least 'total surrender' to the hostile, sexually aggressive and colonizing masculine Islam – the Islam with which Breivik, al-Qaeda's eunuch, identified on some level when he dreamt of collaborating with Islamists.

This thought leads us to Oslo in the nineties, to Breivik's background, where researchers found that Norwegian girls often preferred the immigrant boys, and to Rustad's notion of a pincer movement in which Western men end up as castrated sexual losers. Women and their bodies must be controlled, and not by women themselves.

Femininity is penetrating everywhere, and 'the feminisation of European culture is nearly completed'.[38] Europe is a woman who would prefer to 'be raped than to risk serious injuries while resisting', writes Breivik, quoting a German author and falling back on rape as an image once again.[39] Breivik himself was also feminized by his matriarchal upbringing, which was 'super-liberal' and without discipline: 'I do not approve of the super-liberal, matriarchal upbringing [. . .] as it completely lacked discipline and has contributed to feminise me to a certain degree.'[40] Perhaps he was worried because his friends saw him as vain and 'metrosexual', or perhaps he was ashamed of the incidents of 'homosexual contact' described in the court-appointed psychiatrists' report.

On one level, Breivik's construction of avatars appears as a wish to purge himself of female influence, just as his revolutionary struggle is largely a struggle against women. '60–70% of all cultural Marxists/multiculturalists are women,'[41] he writes, and traitors are to be executed. The struggle against women is both an external and an internal battle, as the female forces of chaos have penetrated not only Europe or Norway but also Breivik himself. For Breivik, the very symbol of decline in Norway is the former prime minister Gro Harlem Brundtland, whom he described on Document.no in January 2010 as 'the murderer of the nation', as opposed to her established nickname 'the Mother of the Nation'. She personified the Norwegian Labour Party state while Breivik was growing up in the eighties and nineties, and she was on Utøya on 22 July 2011. The occidentalist Breivik fundamentally saw the West as a woman and Norway as a vaginal state, to borrow an expression from the author Nils Rune Langeland, a kind of depraved Whore of Babylon and suffocating Freudian mother all in one.

The problem of women is to be tackled in several ways in Breivik's future state. With limits on the freedom of expression and women's rights, the state will take control of procreation and ensure that '*Sex and the City* lifestyles' do not gain ground.[42] Women are to return to the home and to leave working life and academia. But Breivik does not stop at that; he also fantasizes about removing women altogether, first by 'outsource breeding' – in other words, making use of available wombs in poorer countries.[43] By planting ready-fertilized eggs in the wombs of surrogate mothers, genetically Norwegian children can be carried by mothers in the Third World and taken home to an upbringing in which the state has full responsibility for care, providing quality-controlled foster parents, nursery schools and boarding homes. In such a way, Breivik would solve the problems of boundless female sexuality and 'super-liberal' upbringing by mothers.

He also envisages a society in which artificial wombs will eventually support reproduction.[44] In the end, he imagines a society in which women are practically non-existent, in which the sexual market is regulated by the state – in other words, by a cultural conservative guardian council, which appears to be a euphemism for himself. The mother/murderer coupling perhaps had a particular significance for Breivik, who in his compendium wants to remove mothers completely. Perhaps this is the central project of his declaration of independence.

In reality he struggled to free himself. Breivik moved back in with his mother, and he formulated the thoughts above while living with her. He called his mother his 'Achilles' heel', his weakness. 'She is the only one who can make me emotionally unstable,' as he told the court-appointed psychiatrists Husby and Sørheim.[45] To the second team of psychiatrists, Aspaas and Tørrissen, he recounted an incident in 2007 when he felt that his mother 'did not appreciate his capabilities'. He cried for several minutes afterwards, he explained.[46] When his mother makes him 'emotionally unstable', then in a way she also turns him into a woman, as to him the nature of women is precisely to be 'emotionally unstable'. His mother had infected him with femininity or, as he wrote, she had contributed to feminizing him.

Breivik's mother fixation had an aggressive dark side that also emerged over the years in their everyday life in Hoffsveien. In his mother's conversation with the court-appointed psychiatrists, she said: 'We had been so happy together, but now it was just politics and negativity towards me.'[47] In the diary section of the compendium, his aggression towards his mother is expressed in many ways, including accusing her of infecting him. 'On April 9th, I was inflicted with a virus by my mother and I came down with something that later appeared to be a very resilient throat infection. [. . .] It was the third time she had infected me the last two years and I was very pissed off and frustrated.'[48] This was the reason for his sporadic use of a face mask at home. He was afraid of being infected by his mother and perhaps also of being further feminized.

The narcissistic shame he felt about his own inadequacy, about the gulf between the 'bitter goat behind a computer' and the 'Perfect Knight', is apparently attributed by him to his feminine side. Had he not been feminized, he would have been perfect. Female influence had, in the same way, brought Europe to its knees if not even lower at the feet of the Muslim invader. Even though he claims that he cannot remember his own early childhood and that the rest of his upbringing was happy and harmonious, the most violent attack in his text is reserved for the women closest to him: his mother and his sister (whom one source described as his mother's ally in her conflicts with the young Anders).

As previously mentioned, Breivik condemns their sexual morality and behaviour in a detailed and violent tirade, concluding that they have brought shame on him. Sending the compendium out into the world with such accusations against them, even if this was not done consciously or deliberately (and perhaps rather out of emotional instability), carries a note of revenge. The avatar Andrew Berwick is the male avenger. The question that remains is perhaps what he needs to avenge so urgently: what did the deficit of care really amount to?

Revenge on women is a motif that can be found on many levels in the text. Women are purged from his utopian state. His closest family is exposed to criticism. The murder of female cultural Marxists is legitimized. There is a constant use of rape as a metaphor. The idea of revenge on women sometimes also bears traits of sadistic fantasy. Even though 'cultural conservatives' are more chivalrous than others, according to Breivik, they must also 'embrace and familiarise [themselves] with the concept of killing women, even very attractive women'.[49] The compendium is an unfinished patchwork, a rough draft, as he said in court,[50] full of cover stories, lies and contradictions.

If the text is seen through the lens of psychoanalysis, it is easier to find meaning in the chaos. In the compendium, Breivik exacts revenge upon his mother. His father is placed back on the throne, and he overpowers 'depression, and defeat' in both social and sexual fields. Last but not least, the compendium liberates him. It is a 'declaration of independence', as the title says; the compendium gives him the excuse he needs to live out his sadistic fantasies. Finally he can dedicate himself to his hate. Breivik prepared himself 'by looking at terrible pictures and trying to visualize what was going on'.[51] 'Killing women, even very attractive women', was not just something he wrote about and visualized. On 22 July 2011, he went out as his avatar into the real world to live out his fantasy.

Shortly after half past three, Breivik reappeared at the roundabout at Skøyen. This time he was driving a silver-grey Fiat Doblò. He left behind eight dead and dozens of casualties in the city centre. Breivik drove into Hoffsveien, turned left before the tramlines and carried on westwards along Harbitzalléen, heading in the direction of Vækerø and Lysaker.

At 15:56, the Doblò passed the city boundaries heading west. Seven minutes later, the car was in Sandvika.

At 16:05, the Oslo Police requested neighbouring districts to look out for a silver-grey Fiat Doblò. They gave the registration that the surprised man at Hammersborg Torg had the presence of mind to note down.

In the back of the Doblò was a Pelican case containing, among other things, wrist ties. The Ruger was also there, with a bayonet mounted. The rifle bore the inscription 'Gungnir', the name of the

Norse god Odin's spear.[52] Breivik had an iPhone with him that could be used both as a video camera and to upload video clips.

The plan was to capture Gro Harlem Brundtland on Utøya, cut off her head while he read a prepared text and post the video online. Al-Qaeda had been beheading people for years in order to instil fear. There was also a tradition of beheading in Norway. Why else would the lion in the badge of the Norwegian Police Service be holding an axe?[53] This lion also features in the coat of arms of Norway and was really just another version of Morg and his axe.

The question was whether he would get as far as to Utøya and whether he would be in time to kill 'the Mother of the Nation'. At 16:16, the Doblò passed Sollihøgda, the last village before Utøya.

10

Survivors

The Ferry Landing

First, Even was told that the ferry was cancelled. There had been an explosion in Oslo. Then he was told that it would be coming after all. The volunteers, youngsters wearing red wristbands, said that a policeman had arrived. He was heading over to the island, so MS *Thorbjørn* was coming to pick him up. The young ones on the stone pier lit up, as they had been wondering how they would get across. There was a disco that evening and the prime minister, Jens Stoltenberg, was coming on Saturday morning.

Even Kleppen walked a short distance away. He was the eighth member of the Hadeland branch of Norwegian People's Aid, a lorry driver, and he had been on the road all night. After a few hours' sleep, he had packed equipment and goods in his car and driven off to Utvika. His colleagues and a weekend on the island were waiting on the other side of the water. Even peered over at the ferry landing on Utøya, a strip of concrete below the sharp profile of the white main building, and saw the MS *Thorbjørn* moving away from land and slowly reversing out. The yellow glare from the lamp post on the pier shone brightly in the dark afternoon light. Next to the ferry, he glimpsed two gleaming white objects at the water's edge, which had to be the Norwegian People's Aid boat and the old ferry *Reiulf*.

The news on the car radio was turned up at high volume, and the youngsters gathered round. Had al-Qaeda struck in Oslo? Who could be interested in attacking the Norwegian government? A man stepped out of a silver-grey van that was parked in the small car park. As the man approached him in his black uniform, Even recognized him as a policeman. Everything he was wearing was dark: some kind of vest, a side arm, his ID card on a lanyard round his neck, white reflective bands around his legs and on his back. The policeman dragged a large black plastic case and a weapon out of the back of the van. Even did not say hello to him. If the policeman had something to say, Even would surely hear it on the island.

The camp manager, Monica Bøsei, known as 'Mother Utøya', walked ashore from the ferry's metal ramp to greet the policeman. On the way across the water, Even stood on his own, dark-haired and unassuming. The green deck was slippery with rainwater. The young ones stood in a huddle while Monica and the policeman spoke with each other. It was a quarter past five. In the white wheelhouse were the ferry captain – Monica's partner – and his first mate, a young AUF member. The short trip lasted a few minutes. The rumbling of the old engine and the rushing of the wind drowned out all other sounds. On grey days like this it was as if the fjord stretched out and its shores drew back. The steely grey water blended in with the mist and the woodland, dissolving all distances.

'I'll take the equipment to the camp,' Even told Monica as he stepped ashore on Utøya. 'Then we'll take it from there.'

He had still not introduced himself to the policeman. Even did not stick his nose into other people's business and reckoned that he would find out what he needed to know about the explosion in Oslo soon enough anyway. Even walked slowly up the steps to the main building, where his colleague Wenche was standing with the security officer on Utøya, a plain-clothes policeman. They said hello and exchanged a few words. The young ones walked past the main building, up the hill and towards the centre of the island. At the pier, the skipper helped the policeman with his case, which was obviously heavy.

Together with Wenche, Even sloped up across the volleyball court to the left of the main building and, without looking back, walked on along the gravel track leading to the Schoolhouse. As soon as he arrived at the camp, he put down his bag in one of the visitor tents. When he went out to the others, who were pottering about among the tents in their uniforms, he heard a crackling sound. It was coming from somewhere further towards the centre of the island. Even came to a halt. It sounded like a strip of firecrackers going off.

Ida Spjelkavik

The people Ida could see out in the yard were not running away from firecrackers or fireworks. 'Calm down!' somebody called from the Main Hall. 'We're just jittery because of what's going on in Oslo.'

Normally Ida would have been one of those urging people to stay calm, but this time she realized that it was serious. The eyes of the young people who were fleeing ignited with fear. No more questions or deliberations, no whys or hows or maybes. Time stood still. Some impressions were etched in permanently, while others vanished off into the darkness, perhaps disappearing forever or maybe becoming the stuff of nightmare and visions.

Her reflexes took over. Together with many of the other youngsters in the café, Ida ran towards the corridor in the centre at the back of the room, away from the yard where the people were fleeing. Away. Ida was already standing by the coffee machine and was one of the first out of the café. The crowd of people squeezed through the narrow passageway from the café, down the corridor to the right and into the Little Hall, which was the place furthest from the noises and the running, at the opposite end of the building.

At the end of the Little Hall was the exit, a door with large windows leading out to a concrete step and the gravel track down to the campsite. Ida could see a policeman down there, a dark, robotlike figure with white reflective bands around his lower legs. Robust. He was holding a large weapon in both hands, and it seemed as if he were moving towards the tents, away from the Café Building. People came rushing into the hall behind her, and Ida ran on into one of the group meeting rooms, the middle one of the three rooms at the back of the Little Hall.

This was where she had just been speaking with the global group. The window looked out towards the outdoor stage, the campsite and the wash house, while the woods were to the right. Shots could still be heard. Ida went to the window and looked towards the left, where she spotted the policeman again. A boy in a grey hoodie peeped out around the corner of the building. The policeman lifted his weapon and fired. Ida saw the boy being hit in the chest and collapsing right by the corner of the building. The policeman was the threat. They had to get away from him.

It looked as if the policeman was moving on towards the tents, so Ida thought about going back into the Little Hall. There were some boys with her in the meeting room. Through the window in the wall between the room and the hall outside, Ida suddenly saw people start to scream. They shouted, fell down and crowded together around the door out to the corridor leading to the café and the toilets. Shots. Panic. They wanted to get away. More firing.

Ida realized that the policeman was on his way up the concrete steps, that he was heading into the building. He shot his way in. Glass, thin plasterboard and an open door were all that stood between her and the Little Hall. She backed away. The boys had already opened the window behind her. One by one, they dropped down or jumped out. Ida climbed up onto the window ledge and leapt out.

It was about 5 metres from the window ledge down to the ground. A bluish belt of rough gravel ran around the building between the black walls and the green grass. Ida landed on the stones with her weight on her right foot. She heard a shattering sound. Her right ankle snapped, and the left was slightly fractured. Ida got up and ran off down the steep slope and in between the trees and bushes. She got out her mobile phone and called the emergency number 112, but could not get through. The twigs scratched her and she saw glimpses of other young people fleeing through the thickets. Under a spruce tree a short distance above the path, barely a hundred metres from the Café Building, she crept in among the branches. There were already several AUF members there.

Where you ran and where you hid were not choices or conscious actions. Ida felt as if she were acting on impulses, reflexes and reactions. Something could be right one moment but wrong the next. Chance, and where the sounds seemed to be coming from, determined whether it was time to flee or to stay put. She could still hear the continuous sound of shots. Ida drew her breath and tried to calm down. She was wearing dark clothes and black boots, but one of the boys under the spruce tree, one of the security guards, was wearing a reflective vest. 'Take it off,' said Ida.

The boy took off the vest and covered it with leaves and twigs. Other young people took off other coloured items of clothing. 'What's going on?' they asked each other, asked Ida or just asked thin air.

Many people were hiding in the piece of woodland behind the Café Building. Below them, the so-called Kjærlighetsstien [Love Path] wound from north to south along the steep western side of the island, with pine woods on one side and cliffs and stony beaches on the other. People wandered about between the trees, moving back and forth on the lookout for hiding places. Some people were chatting. More people came. The sound of constant shots kept coming. Ida felt that there were too many people. It did not feel safe any more.

'I'm going,' she said to the others, letting them decide for themselves whether they wanted to leave or stay.

Ida carried on downwards, away from the Café Building and towards the Love Path. Instead of following the more straightforward route to the right and down to the pump house, she took the path to the left and walked in the direction of the island's western tip, the area where the slope of cliffs down towards the Tyrifjord is at its wildest. On her way out towards the tip of the island, the bangs grew louder, as if they were coming closer.

Ida leapt once again and plunged down between the pine trees. She half-clambered and half-slid down the wet rocks along the side of the steep, 15-metre-high precipice. For a moment she clung on to a rotten tree trunk hanging down at an angle along the crag. Finally she tumbled down onto the stony beach. There was a clear view up towards the trees and the path. Not safe. The water was high and reached right up to the cliff face in many spots. Ida scrambled over the rock and through the water to the left until she found a large block of stone that had toppled half-way out into the water. Ida crept in under the overhang. There were many people around her. Some of them squeezed into the rock wall, while others hid below rocks or overhangs.

Ida saw a girl she knew right next to her. The two of them squeezed up close to each other beneath the rock, pulling the girl's dark green jacket over them. Ida took off her red leader's lanyard with her counsellor's card, which the organization's representatives wore on the island. It was quiet. Wet clothes, cold. The waves lapped against the stones. Ida stayed still for a long time. Shots could still be heard in the distance. She thought she heard the noise change. Different weapons. Was there more than one gunman? Ida texted her parents and her boyfriend. Why had nobody answered her emergency call? What did that mean? Did anybody know what was happening on the island? Were the police on their way? 'It's alright,' Ida whispered. 'We'll be fine.'

She was speaking to the girl next to her but just as much to herself. Her right ankle ached. Across from them was a boy speaking on his mobile phone – loudly, with his mother. Ida scraped up some pieces of green moss, rolled over onto her side and threw the moss at the boy. She pointed at his phone. The boy nodded and put the phone back in his pocket. Messages came through to Ida's mobile and were logged in the inbox. She read a text from her father.

Many shots rang out from not far away. Fifteen to twenty AUF members suddenly came running along the water's edge from the right, from the direction of the pump house. Some were swimming in the water, while others scrambled between the rocks.

'He'll shoot us in the water too,' someone shouted. 'He'll shoot down at us!'

They were exposed on the sides, leaving Ida visible. It was not safe. She crawled out from under the rock. Together with the other girl, Ida ran on towards the left, partly wading through the water, towards the tip of the island. Some of the AUF members started swimming straight out from the island. The shore on the other side of the fjord was 5 kilometres away and the water was cold. Ida was a swimming instructor but kept to the rocks along the shore. There was no way out through the water. Those who swam risked drowning.

At the tip of the island, the cliffs went straight into the water. Ida swam towards the promontory, heading south towards what was known as Nakenodden [Naked Point]. The cliffs rose into the air about 20 metres above her. It looked as if they stretched right up into the clouds. Some dark branches stuck out from the edge in certain spots, showing how close the path was above her on the island. A boy was drifting in the water. An AUF member from western Norway, a friend of Ida's, tried to bring him back to life, but he had no pulse. It was pointless. The shots came closer again. In the end they had to run away from the body. On the other side of the promontory, Ida ran into a girl from Swaziland, one of the members of her global group. The girl could not swim, so Ida pulled her along with her to one of the caves in the cliff face. It was half-filled with water, but about ten AUF members managed to squeeze in there, with Ida furthest out. There they were sheltered from shots coming from above, but Ida realized that at the same time they were even more exposed if they were attacked from the water.

Ida stood there with the water up to her waist. She kept on moving, trying to make sure that air came in for those behind her. Some of them wanted to go, but Ida said: 'We're staying here.'

Out in the water she could see AUF members swimming, who would surely drown. She heard the sound of a helicopter. Since the shots were still being fired and the helicopter showed no sign of saving the AUF members in the water, it had to be on the side of the attackers. She had seen people lowering themselves down from helicopters to save lives many times on television, as well as shooting people on the ground, but this helicopter was not saving those who were drowning, nor was it stopping the shooting. It just circled around the island, making it difficult to hear where the shots were coming from.

If the attackers had a helicopter, Ida thought, then they were certain to have a boat. Did they stand a chance if the attackers came around the island with a boat? Not from were they were standing now. 'It'll soon be over,' Ida said.

A stone came tumbling down, falling into the water outside the cave. Was somebody abseiling down the cliff? Then a boat appeared in the water. It came towards the island, with a man and a woman on board. Shots could be heard again. They came from close by, from just above Ida. There were two or three shots, then the boat made a sharp turn and disappeared.

It dawned on Ida that someone was trying to save them. They were not all on the side of the policeman with his gun. Since the boat had been shot at, however, there was little chance that it would come back. That was it. No way out. Ida was bruised and bleeding from having fallen. Her right ankle was broken, but she had run and climbed with it. Her left ankle was fractured and her neck hurt. She had no boots or jumper and was up to her waist in cold water, in a sleeveless dress with her tights torn and full of holes. 'It's alright,' she said. 'It'll soon be over now.'

But a boat was coming after all, from the north. It was picking up people in the water further out. Then the boat steered with its bow heading straight towards the cave. It was already packed with many AUF members. Ida recognized several of the faces in the boat. She was standing furthest out of the cave. When necessary, your body does what it has to: Ida waded one step out, grabbed onto the black gunwale and pulled herself up into the boat. She noticed that the boat immediately started drifting back out into the water. 'Get the others!' she screamed. 'There's a girl from Swaziland; she can't speak Norwegian!'

A woman with short dark hair answered calmly: 'He's been caught. It's safe now.' She explained that the boat could not take any more, but that others were coming. 'I promise we'll go straight back to the cave to get the rest,' she said, 'as soon as we've dropped you off at the jetty.' Her tone made Ida feel calmer.

Ida crawled slowly aft and slid down into the boat. She was in shock. No sound, and she could not open her mouth. Ida could not hear, she could not speak and she could not see. As soon as the boat driver's confident voice took over control, she collapsed and passed out cold.

Arshad Mubarak Ali

'Idiots,' thought Arshad. Fireworks? It had to be a bad joke. The sounds came from near the main door to the Café Building, and a crowd of people squeezed down through the corridor towards the Little Hall and the exit towards the campsite. Arshad followed the stream of people. He was in his stocking feet. He was dragged along almost against his will towards the Little Hall, as one of the last in the crowd. He stopped by the door and peered inside. Prableen vanished into one of the rooms at the back of the Little Hall. It was already full of people in there, packed.

Then the people suddenly began to rush back, away from the glass door and the exit. A man went past on the path outside, heading towards the outdoor stage. Blond hair and a police uniform. His face and torso were turned back. He shot at the Café Building with a pistol. Arshad froze. He was standing at the right-hand side of the door leading in from the corridor to the Little Hall. A dark-haired boy stood on the other side of the door. They were like sentries on each side. Arshad saw the policeman staring towards the Main Hall. Then he shot again.

Arshad took a step back. He was about to turn and run further up the corridor. In the split-second he was facing the dark-haired boy, Arshad saw him being hit. The boy fell down to the floor and shouted out. He must have been shot through the wall. Unlike Arshad, he could not see the policeman. Instead of escaping up through the corridor, Arshad vanished through the door to the left, which led into the washroom and the toilet area. The cubicles were already full, so Arshad squeezed in behind the wall together with another AUF member. He was not visible from the corridor, but if anybody stuck their head in, Arshad would be the first they would see. The sound of gunfire kept coming, shot after shot.

The boy who had been hit was in the corridor 1 metre away, on the other side of the plasterboard wall. He was calling for help, moaning. Arshad heard calm footsteps coming to a halt.

'I can't breathe,' the boy said. 'Please help me!'

Then there were three or four shots. The sound was so fierce that Arshad instinctively put his hands over his ears. The corridor fell silent, and the boy was not speaking any more. Arshad prayed. He knew that he was going to die. His life was over. Parents, friends . . . What an idiotic choice: the toilets were the most dangerous place of all. But then the calm footsteps continued, became fainter and disappeared. Where was he going? His awareness of imminent death vanished and was replaced by uncertainty. Shots could still be heard, but further away. A boy from Arshad's delegation opened a cubicle door. 'He's gone; we can run away,' he said.

Arshad gestured that he should go back inside. The boy came out anyway.

'No,' said Arshad. 'We've got to stay here.'

The boy disappeared into the corridor. Arshad called after him a few times, but the boy did not come back. Arshad and the AUF member next to him went into the cubicle instead. When Arshad went to close the door, he saw the body in the corridor. The dark-haired boy was sixteen years old.

'This can't be happening,' said Arshad.

The other AUF member shut the door but did not lock it. From now on, their world was made up of four tight walls, a hard floor, a toilet bowl and the sounds from outside. Arshad sank down to the floor, holding on tight to the hand of the other AUF survivor. They sat packed like sardines. The sound of creaking and whispering could be heard from the other cubicles, where other people were hidden. A sudden noise startled them. Who was outside? What was happening?

'I love you ma,' Arshad texted in English. 'There is a gun attack here. Some people are shot. I don't know what's happening.' It was not cold in the cubicle any more but clammy. Was he alive or was he dead? He was caught like Schrödinger's cat in a box. Neither living nor dead. What if the policeman set fire to the building? It would have been better to be down by the water. There were so many things he would miss out on, so many things he wanted to do in life. Arshad concentrated on keeping a cool head. Someone came running along the corridor. The footsteps came closer. They came into the toilets. Someone touched the door, which was not locked. Arshad prepared to die.

The other AUF member opened the door cautiously, and a girl squeezed in. She had been hiding by the tents. When the policeman went there, she had run towards the Café Building. He had shot at her, she said, but had not hit her. It fell silent. What if he followed her into the building? Would he find them this time? Time passed slowly, very slowly. While the other two whispered, Arshad stared at the floor. There was nothing to say, nothing to talk about. If they survived, they could talk afterwards. The three of them held one another's hands and checked the time on their mobile phones. Arshad texted his *VG* journalist friend. They had exchanged roles. Now it was the journalist who was worried. The dead boy's mobile phone kept on ringing. What was it like to lose someone? The people calling him would find out. Perhaps Arshad's own parents would too. Elsewhere in the building, he heard the shouts and moans of the wounded. Arshad had reconciled himself to death.

Thoughts raged through his mind in pieces, incomplete and fragmented. One year ago, he had sat by an aunt's deathbed reading the Koran to her as she died. That was in Sri Lanka. Now it was his turn, but there was nobody to read to him. He kept hearing shots, but they were still some distance away. Shrieks of pain could be heard in the Café Building. Not everybody had died yet. You cannot choose where you will meet your death: death could find you in your bed, at the cinema, or in a toilet cubicle. There were footsteps in the corridor.

'Police!' somebody shouted.

The perpetrator was a policeman, in uniform. The three of them stayed still and kept the door shut, but they heard other doors opening outside. People cautiously came out of the cubicles. Eventually, Arshad and the other two also went out.

Arshad immediately saw the glowing red eyes of laser sights in the corridor. The red dots drifted over them and carried on searching through the room with its five cubicles and sinks on the opposite side.

'Stop! Put your hands on your head!' a voice shouted in Stavanger dialect. 'Come slowly towards us. Who are you?'

Arshad was searched. He was allowed to sit down but had to keep his hands on his head. There were others sitting on the floor, and the police asked those who knew first aid to help the wounded.

Arshad managed to call home and tell them that he was unharmed. He phoned his brother. The wounded were eventually stretchered out of the Main Hall and the Little Hall. The bodies of the dead were just left there. There were large pools of blood outside the toilets, a chaos of muddy shoes at the top of the corridor in front of the door. What about Prableen? He had last seen her in one of the rooms at the end of the Little Hall. There were many dead there. Somebody checked Facebook on their mobile phone and called out the names of AUF members who were safe. Prableen's name was mentioned.

The police ordered everyone to get up and marched the survivors in single file down to the ferry to be evacuated. Arshad had no shoes on. He felt the gravel under his feet and soon got wet. His last impressions from Utøya were a body on the ground and several more dead bodies by the pier. As they got onto the ferry, they were told that they could take their hands off their heads. Arshad dropped his arms. The ferry backed out from the pier and turned its prow to the north, towards the mainland.

Stine Renate Håheim

Stine Renate Håheim stood among the crowd in the Little Hall, trying to calm down one of the unnerved youngsters. The girl had come running in from the yard outside. Her eyes were like black holes, and she was trying to say something. She was hyperventilating and repeated the same sentence: 'Bullet holes in the wall, bullet holes in the wall!'

'Calm down,' said Stine. 'Breathe calmly, take deep breaths.'

Stine had been caught up in the panic as people ran from the café to the Little Hall. She realized that the girl had seen something, but she was still most concerned with calming people down. Stine took hold of her, clutching her by the shoulders.

Then there was suddenly a bang right outside the door from the concrete steps a few metres away, and the room filled with screams and scrambling arms and legs. It was a shot. There was no doubt about it. Stine flung herself back through the door and into the corridor together with the others. She followed the surge of people past the toilets, up the corridor and into the narrow passageway leading from the main corridor to the dining hall. The AUF members in there were packed like sardines in a tin. Stine came to a halt. People pushed her.

'Somebody's shooting,' a boy shouted. 'Keep your heads down. Stay away from the windows; get down on the floor!'

He locked the door at the end of the corridor to stop anybody getting in that way. People lay down, some obeying the voice that had just been shouting, while others scrambled over each other in panic. Stine was carried along by the stream of people squeezing out of the dark corridor towards the light of the café, and she ended up back in the dining hall. Some people jumped out of the windows, but Stine had bad knees that were easily dislocated. The drop down outside the windows was too far on the western and northern sides. She needed her knees intact. There was a long queue to get through the door out to the yard. Stine thought about throwing a chair through one of the side windows so that she could climb out where it was not so far to the ground, but she dismissed the idea. It was a bit too drastic, in spite of everything. Instead she stood in the queue and waited her turn.

As soon as she was out of the door, Stine saw a crowd of young people running down into the woods to the side of the white tent at the northern end of the yard. Stine followed as quickly as she could. She did not want to be alone. The ground between the trees was wet, slippery and steep. While Stine jumped over roots and rocks, slipping and falling on her way down towards the shore, her mobile phone rang. She stared at the number. It was her father. 'I'm so glad that you're on Utøya,' he said. 'Have you heard about what's happening in Oslo?'

'Dad, it's come here,' Stine answered breathlessly. 'There's somebody shooting here!'

'OK,' her father said. 'But have you heard what's happening in Oslo?' It eventually dawned on her father that she was serious. He promised to call the police. 'You've got to hide, Stine!' he said.

'Good idea, Dad,' Stine grunted. 'Great advice.'

She laughed. Together with a number of other AUF members, Stine ended up on some cliffs by the shore between the pump house and the small cove named Bolsjevika [Bolshevik Cove]. What had really happened? What had people seen? Nobody really knew. To begin with, Stine thought that somebody could have come out to the island to take revenge for what had happened in Oslo. Then she thought that it could be a madman who had been triggered by the bombing in Oslo and started firing wild shots up by the Café Building. Something random, frenzied and sudden. It would probably soon be over, whatever it was that was really happening.

Out on the water they saw the MS *Thorbjørn* vanish towards the north and towards land. Was it over? Had he left? Silence fell for a while. Was it finished? Then there was more shooting, this time nearby, from the trees behind the cove at Bolsjevika. A boy from Lebanon, a member of Ida Spjelkavik's global group, gesticulated towards them and said they had to get away. Stine thought that if anybody could give real advice today, it had to be him. He was from the Middle East. They ran south, stumbling in panic on the steep rocks by the water's edge. They eventually reached a stony beach 30 or 40 metres below the pump house. There were many people there, down on the beach, by the pump house and further on along the rocks.

Some of them sitting there had swum out but turned back to the island. They were cold and exhausted. Stine gave her jumper to one of them and tried to warm up another by holding and rubbing her. Stine did not sit still; she did not try to find her bearings in terms of where she was or where the shooting was, focusing instead on those around her. Stine tried to comfort them, talking and talking . . . Eventually she sat down on a rock and started texting for dear life. She wanted to tell the world what was happening: 'There's shooting here,' she wrote. Gunfire. Somebody shouted up by the pump house.

'The police are here! We're safe.'

Stine put her arms round one of the boys there. Finally. For a couple of seconds she thought it was over. Then came more shots.

A man came out of the trees along the path with his weapon raised, walking down towards the pump house. He shot the young people in front of him quite coolly and calmly. It dawned on Stine that this was not a hasty act of revenge or the sudden whim of a madman. This man dressed in black was walking round the island systematically in order to kill. What they saw was hate coming towards them. He wanted to take them all, to kill them all. There were some young people sitting completely still by the pump house. Perhaps they were in shock, or resigned. The policeman went over and shot them down, calmly and systematically.

Stine jumped, turned and raced back over the rocks towards the cove at Bolsjevika. The others were in front of her and around her. The shore was made up of rocks, cliffs and overhangs. It was impossible to get through, but Stine made her way through anyway. She fell and slid but scrambled her way along. Hard rocks, sharp edges, slippery and black with rain. Stine fell in the water and had no energy left. She was breathless. 'I should've done more exercise,' she thought. She had no more strength left but was on open ground, visible from the dark woodland. After a couple of seconds, she carried on, pulling her way forward across the rocks in the water, swimming, crawling and wading in turn. Eventually Stine was at the cliffs at the end of Bolsjevika.

Most of the group she had met by the shore to start with after having escaped the café were still there. They could see the boats coming out on the fjord. After a brief deliberation, they decided to swim straight out and away from the island. Stine was just wearing a summer dress and swam out quickly. The cold water calmed her. After a while, she turned round and trod water. There was no sign of the perpetrator in the woods. Some of the AUF members around her were wearing clothes and shoes. 'Take them off,' Stine ordered them. 'Get off your shoes and boots. They're slowing you down.'

The group stayed together as they headed out, swimming as hard as they could. The boy from Lebanon had already been picked up by a boat. He shouted at Stine, who immediately splashed off towards the boat, swimming for all she was worth. She reached the boat, took hold of the side, and that was it. All her strength left her. Stine clung on to the boat, suddenly indifferent, like an extinguished bonfire. It took a long time to manoeuvre her in over the rail. Her feet were just a mass of cuts, with deep wounds under the soles. She apologized profusely for all the blood in the boat and thanked the boat driver politely for the lift as she limped ashore at the pier by the camping ground at Utvika.

She realized that there was a system in place at the campsite. The kind strangers were all working together, making one big effort. Some people gave her a jacket and some words of comfort, others organized onward transport to the hospital for the injured and to Sundvolden Hotel for the rest. Some people lent their mobile phones while others went back out onto the fjord in boats. A great and deep sense of emotion emerged as Stine was escorted through the efficient campsite and up towards a waiting car.

Anzor Djoukaev

Disco or no disco, keeping neat on Utøya was still important and yet a real challenge too. Mud, rain and long queues for the shower: Utøya was an eternal struggle against body odour, dirty trousers and wet shoes. Anzor was on the way to his tent to change his socks. There was a loud bang behind him. When you are in a daze of sleeplessness, things happen in glimpses and fragments. Sounds are like echoes. Another bang. Anzor was standing in the yard. He turned round and looked down towards the main building. More loud noises rang out. People ran on the gravel track and fell. Perhaps three or four youngsters fell to the ground. Shots? Anzor caught sight of a dark figure. The man had his weapon raised and was aiming at Anzor.

Anzor ran – away from the gravel, across the grass and in among the trees. He heard shots fly by, ricocheting off the branches and trunks above him, and rustling among the leaves and twigs. Bullets struck the trees. He ran on, turned round, and went to the right through the trees, past the tents and all the way to the western end of the island. On the edge of the cliff he thought about everybody who had called their families to ask if they were alright after the bomb. Now their families would have to call them back . . . He thought of the sins he had committed, and that now he would meet God. Anzor was not afraid of pain or of dying, but he was thinking about the moment after he had been shot dead – being held to account for his actions. He regretted things that had happened and pictured them in his mind: never again. Why could he never learn? Ever since he was little, he had been taking beatings. Still he had not learnt anything. Was it the same for other people, or just for him? Disgrace. Perhaps this was just what it was like being human. Struggling to learn, struggling to understand, struggling with language.

When he was a child, he had seen war. The towns in Chechnya were bombed, and many people died in Tsotsi-Yurt, the village where he grew up. Many of the young men went to war; few came back. Anzor's family survived, but the cemetery in his village looked like a pin cushion: the stakes marking the graves of the martyrs who had fallen in *Gazavat*, the holy war against Russia, were closely packed in the green grass. There was peace in Chechnya now. There were no longer any Russian soldiers in the village, and it was warm and peaceful when Anzor was in Tsotsi-Yurt on his summer holiday the week before he came to Utøya. The electricity had come back long ago, while the tanks and checkpoints had gone. But the stakes on the martyrs' graves told a story to everyone who passed the cemetery on the edge of Tsotsi-Yurt.

Shots could be heard further away. Violence is a language all people understand. Anzor used it too if he needed it. If warnings did not work, then in the end you had to strike. Even if you could not speak the language, if you lashed out, people knew where you stood. They knew what you meant. Then they would not mess with you. Still, it was as if he was unable to stop making the wrong decisions, in spite of all the beatings he had been given. And now he would have to answer for it, now he was going to die . . .

Utøya is shaped like a heraldic shield, and its tip is like an eagle's nest above steep cliffs. One of Anzor's friends appeared next to him: a tall, blond boy of the same age. There was gunfire on the island, single shots and salvos. A body lay next to them. The light-haired boy wanted to get away; he could not stand the sight of the dead body. The two seventeen-year-olds crept back in between the trees, from the edge of the cliffs, through the pine woods to the broad-leaved trees at the edge of the campsite.

'Over here,' said Anzor, 'come on!' He had found a hiding place and bent down to crawl into the narrow crevice. They lay there in the darkness underneath the wash house, between the wooden floorboards and the moist earth. It was so tight that Anzor was only barely able to turn over onto his side, and there was no other way out than the crack through which they had crawled in. Outside, Anzor could just see grass, parts of tents and the legs of a girl lying completely still. She was dead. If anybody came after them, there was nowhere to go. The shooting subsided now and then. Was he looking for them? Anzor could not see the sky. Thunder could be heard in the distance, as well as the water dripping off the trees and the rain slowly draining off the woodwork. Now and then the wind whispered through the trees.

A long silence. Most of the others were probably dead. Were they the only ones left alive? The boys filmed with their mobile phones. They filmed and whispered, 'We're the last survivors on Utøya.'

'We can hear shots all over the place,' his friend whispered. 'I'm afraid of everything.'

Anzor took the mobile again. 'Are you glad to be alive, man?' he asked, gasping with laughter.

They had seen the police come, legs running past wearing uniform, and had not heard any shots for a while. They were hesitant because the man who had been shooting was a policeman. But eventually the boys crawled out. The police were there in an instant.

'Hands up!'

They were searched and escorted to a room in the Café Building. Once inside they were allowed to lower their arms and sit down. What is the right reaction, the right answer, when you crawl out from your hiding place convinced that everybody is dead and afraid that the shooting might start again? Anzor was far away; it was as if the island had vanished into the distance. The policemen stared at Anzor. Eventually they handcuffed him.

He stayed sitting with the group of young people in the Café Building together with his friend from Hamar. On the floor between them lay a girl who had been shot in the back. She lay on her side and was stable but unable to breathe. Her face was blue. She said that she could not breathe and that she was dying. A policeman asked for a volunteer to carry her out into the car. Anzor's friend volunteered. While the policeman took hold of her upper body, the friend clutched her legs. When they lifted her up, she moaned one last time. She died on the way out to the vehicle.

While the other AUF members were evacuated to Sundvolden Hotel, Anzor was questioned on the island into the evening. The police asked him why he had socks in his pocket. 'Are you nuts?' Anzor asked. 'Do you think I've got something to do with this?'

Norwegian police at their best, Anzor thought to himself. Late that evening, he arrived at Hønefoss Police Station. They took his things and gave him a painter's overalls. 'That's all we've got,' the hefty policewoman explained.

Anzor ended up in a small cell with half the floor covered by a yellow mattress. He lay down and went out like a light. A skinny young jail-bird. He was only released the following morning. The policemen had asked him who he was, but none of them called his mother to inform her that he was alive at any point during the seventeen hours he was in custody.

11

Rescuers

Heroism on the Tyrifjord

Of the sixty-nine people who died in the Utøya massacre, sixty-five died on the island, two on the jetties across the water from the island, one at Ullevål Hospital in Oslo and one in the Tyrifjord. Almost all died of gunshot wounds. The boy Ida found in the water died of injuries he incurred when falling down the cliffs. Only one person drowned, a boy who had been weakened by an infection.

The air temperature that afternoon was 14–15°C. It was windy and raining. According to the camping ground staff at Utvika, the water temperature was 15–16°C. Cold water drains body warmth about thirty times faster than cold air. If the water is colder than 16°C, the body becomes cold relatively fast. Symptoms of hypothermia such as unconsciousness or total exhaustion will normally occur after one to two hours, but the body loses heat much more quickly when swimming or treading water. When the body exerts itself, blood is pumped out to its extremities – arms, hands, legs and feet – and cools quickly. For people swimming, in this case as fast as they can, the loss of heat will therefore be considerably greater, and hypothermia and exhaustion will set in faster. This is why it is difficult to swim long distances in cold water. Among the survivors from Utøya, many had swum fast straight out from the island. When they were out of range, they slowed down. Staying still in the water limits the loss of warmth and extends survivability. The disadvantage, of course, is having to depend on somebody coming to help before it is too late.

Both Ida and Stine were good swimmers, they were both among the oldest members of the AUF, and they both saw fleeing into the fjord as suicide. Stine started swimming only after having survived the massacre at the pump house, when she saw the boats in the water off the island. True, both Ida and Stine were at the back of the island, on the western shore. It was not as far to land from the eastern side of the island or from the northern and southern ends, but the distance even from the other sides was still at least 600 metres. For good swimmers, the Tyrifjord was a possible escape route, depending on where they swam from. The first swimmers reached the jetty at Utvika at around 17:35 or 17:40, after having swum for twenty minutes. They must have been fast swimmers. For many of the young people there, perhaps the majority, the cold fjord was extremely dangerous. Normally Ida would have been right that swimming away was tantamount to drowning. Anders Behring Breivik had planned that the fjord would be his 'weapon of mass destruction': he would kill the AUF members by chasing them into the water.

That did not happen. If Ida was mistaken, it was due to the spontaneous civilian rescue operation started by the residents of Hole and the campers from Utvika as soon as they realized what was happening on the island. Many lives were taken on Utøya. Perhaps just as many lives were saved in the Tyrifjord afterwards.

The people who had organized the meet-and-greet day at the camping ground at Utvika a few hours earlier redeployed at about six o'clock, becoming for a couple of hours a key part of one of the largest-scale rescues ever carried out in Norway. The rescue bore the hallmarks of their energy, speed and co-operation. Some of the boat drivers put themselves in danger. From her position at the entrance to one of the grottos, Ida saw one of the boats being shot at while it participated in the rescue operation.

Allan Søndergaard Jensen

Allan Søndergaard Jensen and his partner, Reidun, looked across at Utøya in bewilderment. The MS *Thorbjørn* had just vanished from sight, and now bangs could be heard coming from out on the island. Muffled thuds. A cloud of smoke rose up from the green trees like a reddish ghost, slowly drifting out towards the calm waters. 'That's silly of them to be shooting off fireworks now,' said Reidun.

The small boat from Utøya, *Reiulf*, was in the water. It was slowly gliding towards land to the south of the camping ground, with long oars sticking out on each side. Behind it, they glimpsed ripples in the water. There were people swimming from the island far out into the fjord. The cabin door suddenly opened and somebody yelled at them. 'You've got to come!'

There was one of the other residents standing in the doorway. 'They're calling for help,' she said.

Allan had a 17-foot Kegnæs plastic dinghy with a 30 hp outboard motor moored at the camping ground jetty. A nutshell of a boat with an echo sounder. He jumped into the boat at almost exactly the same moment as two of his neighbours from the camping ground. The German Marcel Gleffe was already on his way out in his little red Pioner dinghy. A boy stood dripping wet on the jetty, his flesh bare and bright. He had swum from the island and reached land some twenty minutes after the shooting had begun.

'They're saying that a policeman is shooting them out there,' one of the neighbours shouted. Firing could be heard from the island, as single shots and salvos: thud, thud, rat-tat-tat.

Perhaps acting more on instinct and impulse than with careful consideration, Allan started the outboard motor and swung the boat out into the Tyrifjord. The grey water looked like molten lead, and the sky came down over the fjord like a headache. In the gap between the water and the mist, the green July shades of the woods on the opposite shore were visible only as a distant dark shape. Utøya rose up in front of him like a cat arching its back as he approached it. What appeared flat and green from a distance turned out at closer range to be steep and multicoloured, difficult to describe in a single word.

The ripples in the water were pointing towards land. The pin-sized heads at the end of the ripples seemed motionless. They were as small as ducklings on a mountain lake. Allan steered towards the small dots, and it was as if the rest of the world disappeared. When Allan slowed down in front of the first head in the water, he saw that the boy was wearing a life jacket, presumably thrown out to him by Gleffe. Allan made the same judgement as the German and steered onwards. More dots in the water ahead of the bow. He turned towards the southern tip of the island. There were many people heading across the water from there in the wake of the *Reiulf*.

Two heads turned towards him in the water ahead of the prow. Their eyes were like black holes in their white faces. Their gazes became etched into Allan's mind. He knew that they had seen death at close range.

'Who are you?' one of them asked.

Allan explained that he wanted to help them. The AUF members stared at Allan and his boat distrustfully. Eventually one of them grabbed hold of the stern. It was as if the boys were paralysed as soon as they caught the railing. Allan had to haul them onto the boat. Two young men in their early twenties. They threw themselves down on the boat's deck. 'He's shooting!' they shouted. They wanted Allan to get down too.

Gasping, the boys told him about a policeman going round the island firing a gun. Allan did not know much about weapons, but he wondered whether it might be a shotgun the killer had. The wheel was in the middle of the boat, and the steering column also contained the echo sounder he used when fishing. If it was a shotgun, he thought, perhaps he could take cover behind that small veneer box if the policeman appeared on the shore. Allan knew that a shotgun was not particularly effective at long range. It was just that the salvos from the island did not sound as if they were coming from any shotgun.

Next, Allan picked up another two boys from the fjord. One of them sat like a zombie in the boat, speechless and looking blank. He took them back to the ferry landing at Utvika. A towering figure stood over them at the *Thorbjørn*'s pier, wearing a bullet-proof vest and a helmet with the visor up like a halo above his head. The policeman was fully armed. He gestured towards Allan. 'Go to Storøya,' he ordered him. 'The Delta Unit needs boats. Take more boats with you.'

Allan steered north along the shore. People obey the police, after all. By the jetty at the camping ground at Utvika, he stopped and called to one of his neighbours who was with his boat by the shore. Each in their own boat, they carried on together towards the island of Storøya, which is connected to land by a bridge. The wind hissed, and the rain lashed at Allan's face as he accelerated. Allan's neighbour had a more powerful motor, and his white boat pulled ahead. In a sinking inflatable boat ahead of him, Allan suddenly spotted a group of policemen wearing the black uniforms of the emergency response unit, Delta. Their red rubber boat was drifting slowly and helplessly towards land, with the policemen almost down in the water.

The neighbour's white boat passed the MS *Thorbjørn*, which had landed in a small cove, and reached the policemen first. Their rubber boat was now completely still. The policemen went over into the pleasure boat, took their equipment with them and set off about a minute later. The neighbour's boat lay low in the water and went more slowly after having taken nine policemen on board. As for Allan's neighbour, he was left floating in the police's red inflatable boat.

Allan steered his boat towards the end of the bridge on Storøya. Blue lights were flashing in the bushes that obscured the road above. Policemen dressed in black stood by the crash barrier. As he slowed down, he could hear the sirens of emergency vehicles on the roads, some quite near and others far away. The whole dark green ridge was rippling with sirens and blue lights, and a helicopter roared overhead. Had World War III started? Both the E16 road and the other main road were pulsating with activity. An enormous policeman jumped on board Allan's boat. Another immediately followed, and then another. Eventually there were six dark figures in the boat, with guns and bags. 'Out!' one of them said.

Allan clambered ashore and saw the boat head off. From a distance, the policemen looked like cormorants on a rock, stooping forward, concentrating, focusing on the island's distant silhouette ahead of them. Allan was left standing on the shore, suddenly helpless. He was out of the tunnel, suddenly on the other side, and the cold afternoon on the fjord re-emerged. Now and then the sirens fell quiet. A woodpecker carried on indefatigably hammering at a tree on Storøya. The willow warblers chirped but fell silent when the rain started again. The clouds drifted along the hillsides on both sides of the fjord.

Half-way out into the fjord, the police climbed out of his boat and into a faster one. A few minutes later, Allan's boat came chugging in towards the shore by the foot of the bridge. There was a woman at the wheel. Allan jumped back into the boat impatiently. He took his neighbour with him and quickly headed back to the rescue operation. The pin-sized heads were still in the water, but there were more boats in the fjord. The two campsite neighbours picked up three boys who were in the water to the north-west of the island and went back to the ferry landing. The neighbour got off there and Allan continued alone.

He filled his boat twice with young people from the water to the south of the island. The next time he was out on the fjord, he could not see any more people in the water, but there were many of them waving to him from the island. Allan went in by the cliffs to the rear of the island and fetched seven wet youngsters who had been hiding in caves and beneath overhanging rocks. The boat lay low in the water as it headed back towards land. His mobile phone vibrated. It was Allan's father calling from Denmark. 'What on earth is going on up there in Norway?'

Allan tried to explain that he could not talk very much just then. He hung up and lent his mobile to a girl and then to a boy.

'Does anybody else want to call home?' he asked, but the other young ones just sat motionless in the boat, like five statues.

When Allan arrived at the jetty by the camping ground, six of the youngsters went ashore. The seventh one was injured, and a policeman in a Pioner dinghy shouted to Allan that he should take the injured to the ambulances at Storøya. Then the boy began to scream. 'No fucking way!' he protested. 'I want to go ashore. Now!'

This was the third time the police had given Allan an order, but this time he did not obey. People on the pier helped Allan to haul the boy over onto the pontoon jetty.

Allan went back to the island again. He had little fuel left, he was cold and his clothes were soaking wet. There were many boats circling Utøya now, and there were no more heads to be seen struggling in the fjord. He steered slowly round the island. Young people stood along the shoreline waiting for transport. Some of them waved, but Allan did not stop. As he slipped around the southern tip of the island, he saw young people lying completely still on the rocks. Not piles of clothes, but people, some of them in strange, unnatural positions. Others were stretched out peacefully, like sleeping children. Many of them were barefoot.

There was a group of bodies on the flat stony beach at the southern end of the island and up towards Nakenodden. Some of them were down in the water; others had their upper bodies and heads hidden in the light green hazel bushes. Pale skin stood out brightly on the bodies of those who had got undressed to swim, but who either had not managed to get out into the Tyrifjord or had turned back to the island. His own children were fourteen, nineteen and twenty-three years old, the same ages as the dead bodies on the rocks.

Allan turned round the steep end of the island. There was a youngster drifting in the water under a rock wall, with his head down. He carried on past the tallest cliffs. Light-coloured crags gave way to dark coniferous forests. The pump house was a square of breeze blocks under a pitched roof of black tarred felt, in a small clearing among the lush woods. A few white birch trunks on each side lit up the dark, steep shore. A pipe led out of the building and down into the Tyrifjord. Along the wall on the side of the pump house facing Allan was a cluster of bodies. It looked as if they were leaning against one another, holding onto one another. Down towards the shore there were more of them. There was dark blood on the cliffs. Clothes were left among the rocks, red and blue spots against the dark stone like letters on the bare crags.

At the top of the island, at the rock called Stoltenberget, the bodies lay separately. A heavy-set young boy wearing jeans and a brown jacket sat a few metres above the waterline, leaning against the rock wall. A metre below his feet, a girl lay horizontally at the water's edge, her skinny legs in black trousers and her upper body partly hidden among the rocks. Five metres further out towards the tip of the island was another body. Then it was another 5 metres to the next body, and two more young people lay a couple of metres away and a little further up the cliff – one in a black jumper and one in a red jumper, together in death. Their faces were unseen and the boys were often indistinguishable from the girls. Allan thought he counted between twenty-five and thirty bodies at the back of the island, from the southern tip to the north.

Allan came ashore for the last time that evening at about half past eight. He had lifted thirteen or fourteen youngsters out of the water and picked up another seven from the caves. He did not have the strength to tie up the boat but made do by pulling a loop of rope from one of the jetties over the rowlock. Allan staggered across the steel-grey gravel on the jetty. He stopped on the steep slope up to the caravan on the ledge. He stood still and became aware that his legs would not carry him any further. Getting up the last few metres seemed impossible.

A small, stocky figure on the wet hillside. Something inexplicable had happened. Krokkleiva rose up above him like a green canopy, but its familiar red cliffs resembled bloody slates. Until that day this landscape had been Allan and Reidun's paradise in storm and wind, sun and clouds, but now it had been torn apart, leaving a scar. Allan and the other people with boats had picked up every single head they had seen swimming in the fjord, gathering in every single one, but they had not been able to stop something strange and unfamiliar being carved into the stones on the island. Something running from the island and seeping out into the grey waves of the fjord, rising up into the air like mist and casting a shadow over the surrounding blue hills.

Anne-Berit Stavenes

The rescue operation had started before the boats picked up the youngsters from the water and before the ambulances and helicopters transported the wounded to hospital. It had started on the island while the massacre was ongoing.

Anne-Berit Stavenes lay on her back in the ferns above the track leading from the pump house up to the clearing where the wash house was. She could not move. The grey windowless pump house was down by the water less than a hundred metres away, but Anne-Berit could not see anything apart from the branches of the trees, the ferns and the thick, dark blonde hair of a slender AUF girl lying on her stomach. A few hours earlier, this girl with pronounced dimples had been standing together with two of the other cooks on Utøya, saying 'You – are – fantastic' to everyone coming to eat lunch. The three cooks said one word each: 'You', 'are', 'fantastic', like Huey, Dewey and Louie. The essence of the Utøya spirit.

Now she was bleeding to death. A shot had gone through her jaw, from her left cheek to her throat beneath her chin. She had a graze shot to the chest and gunshot wounds to both arms. Anne-Berit thought the girl had been hit by at least three shots and assessed the wounds on her arms as the most serious. Her arteries were torn open and she was bleeding profusely from both arms. 'I can't feel my arms any more,' she whispered.

It was almost an hour since she had been shot, Anne-Berit reckoned. Her mobile phone showed that the time was ten past six. Anne-Berit used her mobile sparingly to call the police and her colleagues while saving the battery.

If the girl was to survive, she would have to get to hospital as quickly as possible. They were lying in the ferns and could not move. Anne-Berit had instructed the AUF members who had stretchered her out into the woods from the Café Building to bandage her arms and neck with a triangular neckerchief she had fished out of her pocket. They had collected stones to put pressure on the wounds. Eventually Anne-Berit pulled the girl on top of her, without thinking that this put her in a position from which she could not run away any more. The cold ground would kill the girl. She had to be kept warm. While Anne-Berit focused on the wounds to her face, the AUF members took care of her arms.

With Anne-Berit from Norwegian People's Aid below, the injured girl on top and four young AUF members putting pressure on her wounds on each side to stem the bleeding, they looked like a crystallized form of the human will to survive. They were in spontaneous formation, like a statue hidden in the bracken.

Anne-Berit could just hear and not see what was happening on the island around them. She had tried to stop the massacre in the Café Building but had not managed. Together with Ida Spjelkavik, Anne-Berit had been one of the first to reach the Little Hall when the shooting began in front of the main entrance. While Ida ran into the group meeting room, Anne-Berit had gone out the glass door and had stood at the top of the concrete steps leading down towards the campsite.

A policeman was walking calmly towards the tents on the gravel track below the steps with his gun raised. It looked as if he were clearing the area. A girl came towards him. Anne-Berit was about to shout to him and ask if everything was alright. The policeman came to a halt and shot at the girl. She collapsed and lay there. In the background, Anne-Berit saw a group of young people standing at the campsite gaping. Someone was at the door behind her.

'Wait,' Anne-Berit hissed. 'Don't come out here.'

'I want to get out!' shouted an angry voice.

'No!' Anne-Berit screamed. 'Go back in.'

Anne-Berit went back inside, ran into the Main Hall and called her colleague at the camp who was in charge of crisis management. They briefly summarized the situation: there was a policeman on the island, and he was shooting to kill. The shots picked up again and Anne-Berit realized that the policeman was not heading towards the tents after all, but had turned and was approaching the Café Building. She threw herself down on the floor and crawled out into the corridor to shout that they had to shut the doors, but it was too late. Amidst the screams and the panic, she heard shots already being fired indoors. The policeman was firing in the Little Hall.

'I can't feel my legs,' the girl whispered.

Anne-Berit reassured her that she would be alright and that the police were on their way. The shooting was moving around the island. A few minutes earlier, the shots had been coming from the north, from the area around the rock at Stoltenberget and the cove at Bolsjevika. Now it was quiet again. She heard people sneaking through the woods around her, a voice whispering that 'he' was on the football pitch. Everybody knew who 'he' was. There was just one of 'him' on the island. Anne-Berit finally got through to the emergency number 112, but one of the AUF members hushed her.

Calm footsteps were approaching from the woods. Somebody was coming along the footpath from the north. To start with it seemed as if the footsteps were coming in their direction, then they went further away and down towards the shore and the pump house.

'It's the police,' a voice said. 'The boat's come to help you. It's safe to come out.'

Some AUF members answered, but there was only one person walking calmly around Utøya that day. And then the gunfire started. Shot after shot, salvos and single shots as if it would never come to an end. Shouting. Dying screams. The smell of gunpowder came drifting through the wet bracken.

The shots continued. Anne-Berit lay motionless, unable to move. She could not run away and realized that she was going to die. 'That's as far as I'll get in life,' she thought. 'He's going to shoot me in the head, and then I'll die. Here. In the ferns.' The shots rang out down the hillside. On the phone she heard the voice of the police operator shouting to her colleagues.

'There's gunfire there now! [. . .] I don't think the caller's being shot at.'

It fell silent again. Perhaps he was reloading. Perhaps he was on his way through the grass. But then she heard the sound of feet running along the track from the pump house. He was not walking calmly now but running in her direction. The steps approached fast, passing just below them and running on up towards the clearing by the wash house. Anne-Berit heard the steps disappear towards the centre of the island. A few minutes later, shots rang out further away from the southern end.

The AUF members began to whisper again. Anne-Berit spoke to the girl lying on her stomach.

'Yes,' said the girl. She was still alive and still conscious. 'I know I'm going to die, because you're so afraid,' the girl whispered.

'No,' Anne-Berit replied in protest. 'You're going to live.'

A helicopter was circling over the island now, the loud roar of its engine drowning out all other sounds. Anne-Berit remembered the girl with the mosquito bite who had woken her at six o'clock that morning.

She only got through to the police again shortly after seven o'clock. They said that one perpetrator had been caught, but that they should not move because there might be more of them. Neither Anne-Berit nor the AUF members lying there thought there was more than one perpetrator, and when they heard boats down by the shore they got up. The way down to the water was steep and rocky. Tall flowers, northern wolfsbane, were waving to the right of the pump house. Using strength she did not know she possessed, Anne-Berit carried the girl down the slope towards the cove where the boat was waiting. She took no notice of the bodies in the grass around them and did not see the blood on the stones.

There was a seriously injured boy on board, lying with his legs half-way out of the heavily laden boat. Anne-Berit counted three wounds on his body and saw that he was pale with a distant look in his eyes. She took hold of him by the shoulders and spoke to him in an attempt to keep him conscious. They came ashore at the ferry landing. The girl with the dimples called for Anne-Berit one last time. She was lying on a stretcher and was about to be taken away. She wanted to say goodbye. Her face was pale, but there was still life in her eyes. She was not gone yet, and Anne-Berit took heart: perhaps she would live after all. The girl said she did not want to call her parents before knowing whether she would live.

Anne-Berit helped out at the ferry landing but was beginning to move slowly, like a sleep-walker. She took blankets for people who had already been taken on to hospital or to Sundvolden Hotel. Her reactions were slow, as if she were underwater, submerged. Some other volunteers from Norwegian People's Aid turned up on the gravel track and told her that her other colleagues on the island were alive and had saved themselves, as well as many youngsters, by barricading themselves in the Schoolhouse. They did not say that Hanne Fjalestad was missing.

Her fingers were dripping red. Anne-Berit washed her bloodstained hands, but they would not come clean. She washed them a second time. Her hands were immediately covered in blood again. It was her clothes that were dripping. Her fleece was drenched with the girl's blood after having spent almost two hours in the ferns. Anne-Berit washed herself yet again. She blinked, shook her head and stared down, but her hands were still just as red.

Erik Øvergaard

Unlike Allan, Erik Øvergaard did not have his wife or any grandchildren with him at the campsite. Instead Erik had all three of his children in the caravan. Two boys aged thirteen and eleven and a girl aged nine. The previous year he had become a permanent resident at Utvika and acquired a powerful sports boat to have something to play with when the children visited him at the weekends. Now he was standing on the jetty when he saw two girls swimming up from Utøya in nothing but their underwear. 'Are you going to shoot us?' one of them asked.

As soon as Erik realized what was going on, he ran up to the caravan. He fetched the children and took them to the caravan of a couple he knew. Erik sensed the children watching him as he jogged back to the pier. A black car with tinted windows came driving down towards the shore. It stopped, turned round quickly and accelerated back up towards the main road. One of Erik's neighbours was standing at the jetty staring out at the boats that were already rescuing people. 'Are you up for it?' Erik asked. The neighbour jumped into his boat, and Erik backed out from the jetty.

On his second trip out, Erik went to the northern side of the island. The grey cliffs at Stoltenberget rose up ahead of them, with large pine trees bristling in all directions at the top. Beyond it was the white strip of sand in the cove at Bolsjevika and a glimpse of grey sky above the track leading in towards the football pitch and the main building.

The banks of clouds hung low over the pine trees, but Erik was not looking at that. On the island there were ten to fifteen youngsters screaming and waving. Shots could be heard from the woods behind. They were close by now, not distant thuds but ear-splitting cracks nearby. The young people on the shore were desperate.

'We've got to head in,' the neighbour said. The young ones were right down by the water's edge, waving their arms and screaming in terror. The shots rang out again even closer.

'It's not safe,' Erik decided, steering the boat out. He headed south towards the heads swimming in the water on the western side of the island. 'Do you think I'm a coward?' asked Erik.

They threw all the life jackets they had to the people in the water and picked up a full boatload of seven people. When they went back, it was silent on the shore by Stoltenberget. The young people they had seen were lying on the stones now. Erik knew they were dead. When they took the children back to the camping ground, somebody said that they had seen the bullets landing in the water near the boat.

'They were shooting at you,' one of the campers said.

But Erik did not believe it. If he had been shooting at the boat, he would have hit it, but, if the gunman was up in the woods shooting down at the children on the rocks, the bullets that missed or that went straight through the children would reach some distance out across the fjord before penetrating the surface of the water. That could make it look as if the boat were being shot at, even if it was not what the gunman was aiming at.

For some reason or another, Erik was unable to imagine that somebody might shoot at him. Why would they want to do that? But, even if Erik had not seen the gunman among the trees at Stoltenberget, he realized that he had taken the boat to where people were being killed. Would he have been able to save any of the young ones by going in closer towards the island? There was no time to think about that question at that moment. Neither was there time to think about the moment of bitterness when a policeman in full emergency gear pushed his boat back out from the *Thorbjørn*'s pier, back towards the island, while the policeman himself stayed on the pier. By that point the shooting had stopped, but nobody knew whether there were more gunmen out there. While the strobe lights of Norwegian officialdom flashed all along the road at Krokkleiva, camping tourists and residents of Hole were out on the Tyrifjord, risking their lives for hundreds of young people.

A burly, blond boy was about to go under when they reached him. The other young ones in the water around him shouted to Erik to

Erik Øvergaard (personal photograph)

leave them and save the injured boy first. The boy had been shot in the legs and the groin during the massacre at the pump house but had managed to drag himself down to the water and then to swim just with his arms for almost a kilometre out from the back of the island. When Erik pulled him up into the boat, he was pale with blood loss and exhaustion, but the boy was still alive when they took him ashore. Erik and his neighbour filled up the blood-stained boat several more times before starting to fetch young people from the island.

Afterwards, Erik and his neighbour were unsure of how many children they had picked up, but Erik thought he had gone out six times and taken about thirty-five to forty people back to the shore. Most of these youngsters were picked up from the water. He remembered a few of them: a young boy from northern Norway the same age as his youngest son, a stout girl in a cook's apron who apologized for bleeding on the seats. Even if Erik could not remember every single one of those he had ferried back to the shore, he could not get the glimpses of their faces out of his mind. It was like a slide show in which the still pictures followed each other so quickly that you could barely take in one image before the next flickered across the screen. Girls in their late teens, soaking wet and with a look of something wild and unfamiliar on their faces.

12

What Is Happening in Norway?

Shooting in Progress

While the campers were rescuing the young people from the Tyrifjord, and Anzor, Arshad, Ida and Stine were fighting for their lives on Utøya, the rest of Norway, which was still hypnotized by the bomb in Oslo, was slowly beginning to see that something was wrong.

'There's shooting on Utøya,' one of Hadia's friends whispered, as she came back with bags full of fizzy drinks, pizza and crisps to the temporary party office they had set up in a flat in the Grønland area of Oslo. 'The kids are tweeting about it!'

Shooting? What does that mean?

As he sat in his Volvo heading towards Oslo, Foreign Minister Jonas Gahr Støre spotted a missed call on his phone. It was State Secretary Gry Larsen calling from her holiday in Denmark. Again? They had only just spoken. Støre called her back. Larsen told him to call the leader of the AUF, Eskil Pedersen. Pedersen had just reported that a desperado was shooting on Utøya. Larsen had spoken with him but said that she thought it was difficult to know what to make of it all. It was too unbelievable, and he had seemed worked up. Støre got through to Pedersen, who at that moment was on board the MS *Thorbjørn*. The ferry was escaping Utøya and heading north on the Tyrifjord in the direction of Storøya. The distance between Støre in his Volvo and Pedersen on the boat was not just geographical. Pedersen was in a different state altogether. From their short conversation, Støre made out that Monica Bøsei, 'Mother Utøya', had been shot and that somebody on the island was attacking them. The fleeing AUF members on the boat were terrified and very distressed.

The wing-beats from the panic on Utøya could be sensed in the car. The tweets and text messages from the island began to stir the attention of people right across the country. The foreign minister knew that it was serious. In spite of the unclear accounts of what was happening, the response was nonetheless to call out police and ambulances immediately. This was happening now. He called the minister of justice, Knut Storberget, who had already been informed and was able to report that the police were on their way.

At 17:51, the first two policemen from Northern Buskerud police district arrived at the *Thorbjørn*'s pier, half an hour after the first shots were fired. One of them was in full uniform, and the other was wearing a Kevlar vest on top of his civilian clothing. Both of them had submachine guns and helmets. The emergency response unit, Delta, was on its way from Oslo in six vehicles and was approaching when they passed Sollihøgda at 17:57. Other units were on their way from Hønefoss, but what could the two policemen do now?

They had a clear line of sight to the island across the water. There were sounds of gunfire out there; a shooting was in progress, which according to police regulations meant that all necessary measures should immediately be taken to protect citizens at risk. Smoke rose up behind the main building, orange and diffuse. There were boats by the pier at Utvika, boats in the water and people swimming, but, even though 600 metres is not far, it suddenly becomes a huge gap when it is a matter of 600 metres of water. The two officers stood on the pier while the questions of command responsibility, boat transport and where to land slowly put a damper on any immediate action. The initiative was lost, while every shot out on the island demonstrated that the killer's macabre meter was running.

Terror in Buskerud?

Norwegian journalists were also struggling to tear themselves away from the bomb in Oslo, like fascinated onlookers at a car accident not noticing a hand tapping them on the shoulder. They were watching out for another terrorist strike, but could something really happen at the AUF summer camp on Utøya? Christian Brændshøi, executive editor of the online edition of the newspaper *VG*, sat by his computer inside the newspaper's shattered offices. Somebody had to keep the wheels in motion, publishing pictures and stories while editing the live feed. On Twitter, somebody claimed that *VG* had been the target. At least they could deny that rumour.

A red message from the NTB agency appeared on Brændshøi's screen, an important, high-priority news item. It referred to the *New York Times* having reported that an Islamist group had taken responsibility for the terrorist attack in Oslo. Brændshøi read the message. The source was good, but, even though everybody in Oslo thought it was Islamists, the facts were thin – too thin. Brændshøi chose not to publish it. *VG* also avoided interviewing experts in the early phases. News first. Many potential leads turned out not to be true, fortunately. The rumours of a train derailment in Drammen, countless suspected bombs in Oslo and an explosion in Festningstunnelen, the motorway tunnel below the city centre, all turned out to be false.

A policeman came up the stairs and looked in at where Brændshøi was. He explained that he was checking the building. The radio on the policeman's shoulder was set to receive. There was a crackling, then Brændshøi suddenly heard a voice say something about a shooting. A colleague picked up that the location mentioned for the shooting was in Buskerud county. *Buskerud*? The policeman left, but, at the same time, Brændshøi's colleagues found several tweets and Facebook messages about shooting on Utøya. Another lead to check out. One of the summer temps was a member of the AUF and so phoned friends who were at the summer camp. Another journalist phoned Eskil Pedersen. It was a short conversation. 'We're under attack,' said Pedersen, hanging up.

The journalist realized it was an ongoing situation. Clearly it was risky to call the AUF members on the island. There were tweets about shooting, people dying and escaping. Was there a connection with the explosion in Oslo? The police were evidently on their way. How would the newspaper cover what was happening right then on the island?

A few hundred metres above Oslo, Marius Arnesen, a cameraman with the public broadcaster NRK, was bobbing up and down like a cork floating on the waves. The camera he was holding was pointed towards the city centre, just like the eyes of the rest of Norway. Smoke was rising from the government district. The helicopter's door was open, which made the filming easier but also meant that the wind and turbulence could get an even better hold of the small craft. Since the airspace above the centre of Oslo was restricted, and had been since 2001, they were far away from the scene, and the pictures Marius was getting were not great. Marius spotted a missed call from the duty manager at NRK. The time was 17:58. A text message came in from him instead: 'You must to fly to Utøya ASAP! Shots being fired there! AUF summer camp. Be careful! But fly there and call as soon as you can.'

'Utøya', Marius told the pilot, 'on the Tyrifjord. Somebody's shooting there!'

They looked at each other.

'Huh?' said the pilot, voicing both their feelings.

The story had started off being about international terrorism, so it seemed, and it was now something to do with Utøya? It was as unexpected as a shark in a field of turnips. Utøya was just so Norwegian; a foreigner would probably not even be able to find the way there, even supposing that for some peculiar reason or another he or she had found out about the AUF summer camp. Both the pilot and Marius had assumed that this had to do with some form or another of Islamist terrorism, but now they had been told to go to Utøya. Was this some kind of attack on the Labour Party? If something really was happening on Utøya, the Labour Party was the only thing the two places had in common that Arnesen or the pilot could think of.

The helicopter leapt and bounced in the rough weather, small and cramped, like an electric car with rotary blades. Arnesen was unsure what to expect. He was better prepared for what might be waiting in the barren valleys of western Afghanistan than then, as he flew westwards from Oslo under low clouds towards the Tyrifjord.

Marius Arnesen was one of NRK's most experienced photographers when it came to war and crisis situations. He had worked for a long time with the Norwegian forces in Afghanistan. Arnesen was cheerful and inquisitive, renowned as a tough guy. The helicopter rushed off over Bærum towards Sollihøgda to the north. The fog was like a wall up there. The forest of Krokskogen had disappeared into a thick grey soup, which the unsophisticated helicopter had no chance of getting through. Instead the pilot turned left and flew south along the edge of the sea of fog.

It felt as if the helicopter were being boxed on the ear by the fog as they brushed past the wisps of cloud hanging above the treetops. The pilot was dependent on visual contact with the ground. After a tough ride over the tops of the spruce trees, the pilot finally found a gap in the solid fog right at the southern tip of the Tyrifjord.

The helicopter continued on across the surface of the water, beneath the low sky. The clouds were 200 to 300 metres above the water. The pilot pointed ahead. 'There's the island,' he said.

A small, flat speck on the grey mass of the fjord. Arnesen pulled his camera up onto his shoulder and started filming. He had never seen the island before and went for general shots first, which a helicopter is best suited for. While his lens captured the nightmarish situation down to the smallest detail, Arnesen tried to understand what was going on down there: shades of green, a large campsite, some buildings here and there, including a large T-shaped one in the centre of the island. There were traces of people everywhere, but the island was strangely empty, like an abandoned campsite. It was completely still. Had it been evacuated?

The roar of the helicopter drowned out all other sounds apart from the pilot's restrained comments coming through the headset, but there was something wrong down there that Arnesen was struggling to grasp. Normally he would have asked the pilot to go lower, but they stayed flying relatively high up just under the clouds, while Arnesen hung out of the door with his small safety belt on, trying to control his camera between the gusts of wind. 'Do a circuit over the main shore,' he said.

Perhaps something was happening there. There were blue lights everywhere and tailbacks on the main road, but the ambulances stood still, lined up. It looked as if they were waiting. He could not see any activity. 'Circle the island,' Arnesen said.

He wanted to get more panoramic shots and was also trying to find his bearings. He spotted people in the water on all sides of the island. Had they gone for a swim? Something was happening here, but what? What kind of a shooting was this?

He noticed spots of colour all around the island. Clothes? People? In some places he saw clusters of people. Why were they so still? Everyone in the water was swimming straight out from the island, not along the shore, not across or in circles. Straight out, straight away. They were escaping. That had to be it. Escape. They were fleeing the island. At the southern end there was something amiss. The splashes of colour there resembled both people and piles of clothing. Arnesen zoomed in. It was hard to keep the camera still. He saw the outlines of people, but it was difficult to make out details. Some of them were moving right out in the water, others lay completely still, while one figure stood out. Arnesen noticed it. The figure was dark and standing up.

'Can you hover?' Arnesen asked, as he wanted to study the southern end more closely.

'Not a chance,' the pilot answered.

The wind was behind them, pushing them towards the south-east, away from the island. The helicopter did another circuit and came in over the island from the east. A boat came alongside at the ferry landing, and Arnesen zoomed in on the dark figures running ashore at the dock. Police. It was like a choreographed dance or a sequence from a film. The policemen took up positions on the jetty and then moved tactically towards the centre of the island. Had the Delta Unit only just got there? Yet another piece fell into place in Arnesen's mind. This had to mean that what was happening was still going on.

'Low fuel,' said the pilot, pointing at the indicator.

Arnesen was filming the rescue operation on the fjord, with young people being dragged onto a white boat naked by a man in a blue jacket. 'OK,' he answered.

On their final trip over the island, he saw more policemen at the ferry landing. This time, they ran towards the white building and the large orange mattress on the lawn, where two figures lay completely still. The policemen did not seem to notice them. Arnesen filmed for eighteen minutes in total, without seeing the faces of the people down on the island. Frightened youngsters were wondering who was in the helicopter, while the murderer glanced at it sceptically.

When Arnesen lowered the camera between his legs and leant back in his seat, as the helicopter veered off south back towards the city, he was completely unaware that he had shot iconic images that would be seen around the world.

What the Camera Saw

If NRK had known what was happening on Utøya, they would not have sent the helicopter. If Arnesen had understood what was happening, he would have kept a good distance from the island, even if just for the sake of his and the pilot's own safety. Instead, in the prevailing confusion, he interpreted the emptiness of the campsite to mean that the island had been evacuated. Meanwhile Ida Spjelkavik, hidden in the so-called Love Grottos, concluded that the NRK helicopter had to be part of the operation against Utøya. Both conclusions were based on concrete observations and reasoning that were understandable in context, but they were both mistaken.

While Arnesen gradually realized that he had ended up in the middle of a situation that had not yet been resolved, his lens picked up the dead bodies lying by the campsite, in front of the main building and by the rock at Stoltenberget. Dispassionately, the camera documented a huddle of six dead young people by the pump house, showing that the water in the cove was red with blood – 20 to 30 square metres of water as dark red as a rose. It looked as if the island was bleeding.

The camera had picked up the Delta Unit's arrival on the island, although Arnesen had not spotted it. The first group of policemen (in Allan's neighbour's boat) came ashore at the ferry landing at about 18:25. The first policemen ran northwards along the island. The next boat arrived barely a minute later. A team of five policemen from the Delta Unit and Northern Buskerud police district heard shots and ran towards the south of the island. They apprehended Breivik at some point between 18:32 and 18:34. It took well over half an hour from when the first policemen were in position at the *Thorbjørn*'s pier on the mainland until the first policemen landed on Utøya, and another eight minutes until he was arrested. It was not a long time, but every minute was precious that day.

At the southern tip of the island, the camera picked up the final sequences of the massacre. At that point, Delta had already landed on the island. A boy is sitting in the water, raising his arms towards an armed figure dressed in black. Pleading, perhaps, or attempting to shield himself. Lying at the feet of the dark male figure with his gun is a tangled mass of clothes and people. Two bodies lie on their sides on the shore in the background. It can be seen that the boy in the water is exhausted, possibly injured. He is completely powerless against the executioner in front of him. The dark figure holds up his weapon with the muzzle aimed towards the sky. The white reflective bands around his trouser legs can be seen, as well as a badge at the top of his arm. He looks at the boy in the water. Then he turns round, walks away and back towards land. As he turns, the bald patch on the back of his head comes into view, as well as a white stripe at the top of his back. The boy in the water lowers his head and drops his arm.

He survived that day.

NRK did not realize what Arnesen had filmed but lent the video to TV2, who passed it on to the Swedish newspaper *Aftonbladet*. The next day, *Aftonbladet* published the image of the dark-clothed executioner on its front page, a frame grab from the sequence at the southern tip of the island when Arnesen zoomed in without realizing what he was filming. It was a shocking tableau, with the boy begging for his life. In Afghanistan, Marius Arnesen had worked on anticipating and thinking through a number of scenarios and had learnt to be prepared for the unexpected. This time he was on home ground and was suddenly reacting far more slowly. His instincts made him keep the helicopter high and zoom in on the southern tip, but at the same time he did not realize what he had witnessed or that he was filming the details of a massacre that was still ongoing.

A message posted on Twitter at 18:54 put it best: '9/11 and Columbine on the same day – in little Norway'. There were no points of reference in recent Norwegian history that could be used to understand what happened on 22 July 2011, so the message referred to events in the USA. The terrorist attack on the H Block, which really had more in common with the bombing in Oklahoma City than with the attacks of 11 September 2001, was followed by what seemed like a school shooting, and perhaps on some level it was. While the events touched Norway's soul and affected thousands of relatives, friends and colleagues, the macabre dramaturgy captivated the whole world. The images of the shattered government district seemed familiar after a decade of terror. The mutilated buildings evoked associations with similar bombings around the world and created the expectation that an Islamist terrorist action had taken place in peaceful Norway. The eyes of the world were on Oslo.

As a result, the international media and news audiences were immediately drawn into the unfolding drama that lasted just over three hours from when the bomb exploded until the culprit was caught. The massacre took place in front of the whole world's eyes, from the destroyed buildings and bleeding people in the centre of Oslo to the mass murderer hunting at the AUF summer camp. Even if the Norwegian surroundings were exotic, everyone realized what was happening: the unfortunate children were surrounded by cold water and had nowhere to run. It was as if a disaster film had been followed by a horror film. First the earth shook in Oslo, and then the devil ran loose among the spruce trees on the island. Preliminary information came during the night that eighty young people had been killed, a macabre world record for a massacre carried out with small firearms by a single person. How could that be possible?

When Fear Takes Over

When were you last afraid? Perhaps when you were driving and a car appeared to swerve towards you. Or perhaps you were in a threatening situation out on the town when an aggressive and intoxicated man approached you. Maybe your heart skipped a beat when your child had a bad fall while skiing. Or maybe you cannot even remember. Fear has been banished to the fringes of our modern society, and we generally experience it only in glimpses. Fear is something you observe in the fish you catch or the animals you startle while walking in the woods. We watch disaster films and horror films, while we immerse ourselves in newspaper articles about terrifying events. What would we do, we wonder, if we were in that situation? When the going gets tough, what would we be like? Perhaps we fantasize about heroic deeds. What would we have done?

Even though our lives are extremely safe in historical terms, fear is still a central part of our biology. From an evolutionary perspective, it is not long since it governed major parts of our lives. Without fear, we would not have survived. To some extent, fear lives on even without any direct reason: anxiety and panic attacks are relatively widespread psychological conditions. Fear has several functions. Memories associated with reactions to fear can be very strong, perhaps because we want to recognize and avoid similar situations in future. Some people say that fear is the best teacher. Or, as Anzor put it, violence is a language all people understand.

When we are afraid, several things immediately happen in our brains and our bodies. The very moment we witness or experience something threatening or frightening, a part of our brains known as the amygdala takes over. Normal thought and interpretation processes are short-circuited, leading to an intense focus on the source of fear, often accompanied by a temporary loss of hearing and what is known as tunnel vision, both of which are a consequence of all non-essential senses being filtered out. The AUF leader Eskil Pedersen, for example, described how he just saw the boat in front of him and did not notice the bodies he ran past when he fled from the white main building on Utøya to the MS *Thorbjørn*, and how everything fell silent 'as if the island were covered by a blanket of death'.[1] Pedersen's reaction to fear probably resulted in auditory exclusion and tunnel vision.

A number of hormonal reactions occur; adrenaline is released in large quantities. Fear is therefore a kind of intoxication, and extreme sports enthusiasts, among others, seek out fear to experience the adrenaline rush and the feeling of having your body on edge. The body is ready for extreme stress. The concentration of glucose in the blood – in other words, the blood sugar level – rises. Both sugar and fat are transferred to the muscles. Blood vessels expand in parts of the muscles, increasing their strength to an optimal level, while the blood vessels in the skin contract, reducing its sensitivity and further raising the threshold of pain, which is perceived as a cooling effect on the body. We say that fear is chilling, but it is actually the opposite. Our body temperature and blood pressure rise, our breathing and pulse speed up. The pupils dilate in order to take in as much light as possible, since dangers came in the dark in prehistoric times. The digestive system is stopped as essential bodily functions are prioritized. It can occur that the bladder automatically empties itself.

All these reactions are meant to help you either to flee or to fight for your life. There is also a third reaction: paralysis, being frozen with fear. When a cat catches a mouse, the mouse will try to escape, but at the point when escape is no longer possible, it will give up and become completely limp. If it is lucky, the cat will lose interest and leave. On the whole it is not so lucky, but thanatosis (feigning death) is nature's very last resort in a dangerous situation. The last reaction to fear is to be scared stiff. When the bomb went off in Oslo, some people lay there in foetal positions, while others ran away.

Some people have argued that there is an opposite reaction to dangerous situations, known as battle trance or aphobia (fearlessness), in which people such as soldiers in combat stop feeling fear and act without regard for themselves. For example, soldiers might throw themselves in front of comrades or officers to save their lives, or people might run into burning buildings to save strangers. There are many examples of this kind of apparently instinctive, unselfish behaviour, which suggests that we have a deeper identity on a reflex level, in which we see ourselves as members of a group, of a herd, and are willing to sacrifice ourselves for the collective good. The boat drivers risked their lives in the rescue operation. According to them, they were acting instinctively.

Fear was the fundamental condition on Utøya. The adrenaline was pumping. Ida ran and climbed with a broken ankle. Fearing death, Stine managed to escape along a steep, craggy shoreline that she normally would have thought was impossible to force her way across. Some of the survivors, and presumably a number of the AUF members who were killed, played dead when the terrorist came, in a conscious effort to avoid the bullets or because they were paralysed with fear. Some, however, reacted differently. Even though panic was breaking out, Anne-Berit Stavenes kept her composure as the terrorist was coming up the steps to the Café Building, and she tried to close the door, maybe because she was used to taking responsibility as the leader of the Norwegian People's Aid team from Hadeland, as a nursery school manager and as an adult on the island. That same experience was possibly the reason why Anne-Berit instinctively put herself in a situation from which she could not escape when she lay under the seriously wounded girl whose life she and the young AUF members probably saved.

As our instincts get the upper hand, fear can reduce our abilities to orientate ourselves or to think clearly, but fear is also an individual matter. We are influenced by our experience, knowledge and training. We wonder what we would have done when we hear about dramatic situations. Fear is primarily an automatic response. The amygdala is part of the reptilian brain, a structure developed 100 million years ago to help dinosaurs to run away from other dinosaurs, forest fires and volcanic eruptions. Even though it is modified by your own experiences, by things you have learnt to fear such as the neighbour's dog or gangs of juvenile thieves, the main point is that you stop being your normal self when you are unexpectedly exposed to extreme fear. That is why few people can really know how they would react in situations like these.

Perhaps that is precisely why people pose themselves that question: 'What would I do?' We go around with another self inside us, and we wonder what kind of person this unfamiliar self is. 'How much can you know about yourself if you've never been in a fight?' Tyler Durden asks in *Fight Club*. From a philosophical perspective, you could question whether you really are yourself at all in situations involving fear. Fear makes you somebody else. The soldier who is cold and rational in combat can be an incorrigible hothead in peacetime. But which person is the real him: the rational warrior or the disturber of the peace? Western societies have been blessed with peace for a couple of generations, and this normality has defined who we are. Norwegians are people with 'many friends in common, and no enemies',[2] as the author Erlend Loe wrote, while Breivik thought that the 'helpless Norwegian youth [. . .] are brought up to be "suicidally" tolerant and therefore [. . .] completely unprepared mentally for attacks such as these.'[3]

Training and preparation are the only things that can improve the way we react when disasters occur. 'You do not rise to the occasion, you sink to your level of training,' as US military officers say. The Norwegian People's Aid team from Hadeland had trained for many different scenarios, including terrorism, and they had a person in charge of crisis management. The group quickly found its bearings and reacted fast. They saved their own lives, as well as those of many young people, by barricading themselves in the Schoolhouse. They worked as a team. Many of the AUF members carried out acts of heroism to save others, some took control and led groups to hiding places, as Ida did, but these were individual reactions when people who were used to having responsibility took responsibility in a given situation. A number of AUF members, such as the late Håvard Vederhus from Oslo, Dana Barzingi from Akershus, Eivind Rindal – who guided the boat *Reiulf* towards land while the terrorist was shooting at it – Secretary General Tonje Brenna and others, performed similar deeds.

The members of the AUF were not trained, prepared or in any way equipped to act as a unit in the situation that arose. When the shooting began, they acted not as a unified group but as 600 individuals. The rational thing for an individual to do was to flee and hope that the police would come. Norwegians are taught not to confront violent people but to inform the police, and that was what the AUF members did. Hundreds of young people called the emergency number 112. The rational thing for a group to do might possibly have been to attack the terrorist, but such a unified reaction would have required some kind of preparation, training or experience, and the AUF was not the Tåsen Gang. Although there is conscription in Norway, most young people have not even been in the armed forces. Perhaps there would have been spontaneous resistance if the terrorist had forced a group into a corner with no way out. He did not.

The Captain and His Ship

If you had Googled the name Eskil Pedersen in August 2011, you would hardly have been able to write 'e–s–k' before options popped up reading 'Eskil Pedersen', 'Eskil Pedersen coward', 'Eskil Pedersen gay', 'Eskil Pedersen boat' and 'Eskil Pedersen ran away'. When people searched for Eskil Pedersen on Google (which logged their searches so that they appeared as suggestions), they were apparently expressing their anger and contempt for the AUF leader having almost immediately 'run away' (not escaped) the island on the MS *Thorbjørn* in the company of seven other AUF members and the ferry captain. The Google suggestions also imply that people searching saw a connection between the AUF leader's sexuality and his alleged cowardice.

The tragedy on Utøya generated intense feelings, and some of the anger was directed at the leader of the AUF. The criticism concerned the fact that the twenty-seven-year-old leader left while the youngsters for whom he was responsible were being murdered. The ferry disappeared with Pedersen on board instead of taking part in the rescue operation. Survivors said that they waved to the MS *Thorbjørn*, hoping to be saved, as the ferry passed the northern end of the island.[4] Pedersen described the time from when he ran onto the boat until he arrived at Northern Buskerud police station. As he lay on the deck of the ferry he thought that, after the bomb in Oslo, Utøya was now 'occupied'. That meant that 'the whole country was under attack' and that Politiets sikkerhetstjeneste [the Norwegian Police Security Service; PST] was involved in an attempt to 'take power' – in other words, an armed coup. The terrorist had introduced himself as an officer from the PST and claimed that another two colleagues were on their way to the ferry landing. As a result, Pedersen thought that nowhere was safe, that people would shoot at them from land, and that other boats might 'board' them.

Pedersen concentrated on calling his many contacts in the Labour Party and in the government to tell them and to ask for help. To the AUF members on Utøya who contacted him, he texted back: 'Swim'. As soon as he was ashore, he hurried up to the main road. While thinking that the PST was carrying out a coup, he stopped a civilian car with a female driver (for some reason he did not feel he could trust men) and asked her to drive him to the police station in Hønefoss. In the meantime, he shouted down the telephone to the Labour Party secretary Raymond Johansen that 'we are under siege'. Even while he was at the police station, he distrusted the police. For a long while he wondered whether he could really trust them, telling them: 'We don't believe you.'

Pedersen himself pointed out holes and contradictions in his reasoning. How could he trust that a murderer who had tricked his way over to the island was the PST officer he claimed to be, or that what he said about two colleagues being on their way was true? If the PST – in other words, the police – was involved in a coup, then why did he call 112, the police emergency number, and why had he gone to Northern Buskerud police station? Pedersen had no explanation of his own to offer apart from the fact he was not thinking logically in that situation. The situation that had developed was inconceivable, and panic reigned on the boat.

When Pedersen had to interpret what he had observed in the few short minutes he was near the terrorist (in other words, the sound of shots, lifeless people outside the building and what the other AUF members on the boat told him about the alleged PST officer), he fell back on notions of war (boarding, being under siege and occupation) and of a right-wing coup featuring the PST in a central role. In a way, Pedersen's notions tell some of the same story as the NRK cameraman Arnesen's situational slowness. There were no references in Norwegian history to help those who were involved in the situation to interpret it. The closest reference to the tragedy of 22 July 2011 was 9 April 1940, the beginning of Norway's involvement in the Second World War, the German occupation and Vidkun Quisling's coup. What Pedersen describes is 9 April 1940. 'You sink to your level of training', and it may appear as if Pedersen had been transported back to his history lessons at the University of Oslo.

Even though Pedersen drew far-reaching conclusions concerning the whole country, a number of the other AUF members had similar ideas independently of each other. Ida suspected the NRK helicopter of being part of the attack, and a large number of the AUF members were sceptical of the people who picked them up in boats, as well as the campers on the jetty at Utvika. Many of them thought that there was more than one gunman on the island and thought that the terrorist had allies on land, on the water, and even in the sky.

Some of the Labour Party leaders with whom Pedersen spoke on the telephone probably tried to explain to him that there was no coup, but a voice on the telephone can do little to influence a person who is on the deck of a boat and thinks that he might be shot at any moment. While AUF members in other situations took charge and became natural leaders, Pedersen and the others were passengers on a boat being steered by an older captain. The captain was Monica Bøsei's partner and had witnessed her becoming the terrorist's second victim on Utøya. He also had a daughter on the island. Given that the captain was in shock and afraid, perhaps it was not so strange that fear and panic spread on the MS *Thorbjørn*.

Some of them were hyperventilating on deck, while others tried to calm them down. In the claustrophobic situation, they discussed frantically where they should take the boat. They did not dare to head to the ferry landing at Utvika for fear of the two PST officers who were allegedly on their way, and they did not count on being able to land anywhere else along the shore. Since Pedersen and the others thought that the whole country was under attack, their escape had only just begun and they felt that they were still being hunted. The ferry eventually put ashore in a cove near Storøya, approximately 3 kilometres north of Utøya, where the captain had a friend he trusted.

While Pedersen and most of the AUF members went up to the main road and hitch-hiked to Hønefoss, the captain was met by his friend, a local resident by the name of Even Frogh. Frogh was employed as a security inspector at Norges Bank, Norway's central bank, he was an officer in Heimevernet [the Norwegian Home Guard], and had served several tours in Kosovo and Afghanistan. He noticed that the captain was deeply affected. After having summarized the situation, the two men and the captain's AUF first mate went down to the camping ground at Utvika to meet the Delta Unit. Frogh thought that the captain might be a valuable first-hand witness for the police. At the same time, Frogh had seen how the fleeing AUF members had moved away from him in fear, seen how the first mate had sceptically asked him who he was, and noticed how shocked the captain was. These impressions defined the atmosphere in the car. Fear is contagious, and, when he heard somebody scream at the camping ground and smelt the stench of gunpowder, Even concluded that there had to be shooting going on there too. He quickly reversed out of there and drove off back towards his house and his boat.

The fact that such an experienced officer could make such an error of perception demonstrated how panic and collective thinking are self-reinforcing and can spread to people who did not even experience the original danger. Once a false perception has grown in a group, it is tremendously difficult for a single individual to challenge, correct or reject that perception, especially if that individual does not personally have access to all the facts and has to trust second-hand information. The captain, together with Frogh and his brother Stian, took part in the rescue operation on Utøya for the rest of the evening, transporting survivors and the wounded ashore on Frogh's bow rider and the captain's ferry.

The way you act also depends on the situation in which you end up. When panic spreads, everybody gets caught up and makes a break for it. In other situations, individuals had an opportunity to think and to act, even in the midst of fear. The intense aggression towards Eskil Pedersen after the massacre seems strangely misplaced, as what could he have done? He could have stayed on the island, but he would have been just as powerless in the face of the terrorist as the others. Perhaps the ferry could have stayed near the island and contributed to the rescue operation. Having originally been a Swedish military landing craft, the MS *Thorbjørn* was armour-plated after all, but, for that very reason, the large, heavy and slow vessel was actually poorly suited to rapid rescue work. The decision to head ashore to fetch help was not necessarily a worse option than trying to save people from the island.

It seems as if the criticism of Pedersen has less to do with what he actually did or might have done than it does with a kind of expectation about leaders, perhaps especially male leaders, left over from other times. As Rudyard Kipling wrote: 'If you can keep your head when all about you / Are losing theirs and blaming it on you; / [. . .] you'll be a Man, my son!'[5] Men's role has evolved considerably since Victorian times. Norwegian political organizations do not choose cold-blooded warriors as their leaders, but people who can communicate and work together, whether they are men or women. Norwegian political organizations choose peace leaders, not war leaders. All the same, there are some residual expectations of a leader in a crisis. The captain should go down with his ship, they say, as if Utøya were a ship.

The disaster on Utøya raises the question of how it was possible for a single terrorist, equipped with a semi-automatic rifle and a pistol, to take the lives of sixty-nine people. But focusing on the unarmed AUF members' inability to resist the terrorist or their leader's inability to keep a cool head are rhetorical dead ends. The AUF leader could hardly have made a difference, while the AUF members on the island would have put up resistance if the situation had allowed them to do so, but the terrorist carefully avoided situations in which he might provoke people to stand up against him. The answer to why the disaster took on such proportions is to be found not with the victims but with the culprit.

13

Anders Behring Breivik's Seventy-Five Minutes on Utøya[1]

> First coming costume party this autumn, dress up as a police officer. Arrive with insignias :-) Will be awesome as people will be very astonished :-)[2]

The Killings at the Main Building, 17:17–17:22

Disguised as 'PST officer Martin Nilsen', Anders Behring Breivik arrived on Utøya with the MS *Thorbjørn* between a quarter past and twenty past five on Friday 22 July 2011, together with, among others, Even Kleppen from Norwegian People's Aid and Monica Bøsei, the camp manager. He had white earplugs and kept taking small sips from the straw leading out of the hydration pack on his back. The ferry docked at the pier below the main building. The captain, who was also Bøsei's partner, lowered the ramp and helped Breivik ashore with his heavy Pelican case, which contained ammunition, diesel fuel and smoke grenades, among other things. The captain put the case in the boot of a car, which he drove a few tens of metres up the track and parked at the back of the main building.

In the meantime, Even Kleppen left the island's security officer and walked across the volleyball court towards the Norwegian People's Aid camp by the Schoolhouse, on the south of the island. Monica Bøsei went over to the security guard and introduced him to Martin Nilsen from the PST. Breivik had asked her to bring together all the guards on the island. The security guard was a policeman and began asking questions, but Breivik interrupted him and suggested that they should walk up to the main building. The three of them walked over the lawn past a large, orange inflatable mattress, with Breivik at the rear. Breivik drew his pistol, a 9 mm Glock 34 semi-automatic handgun, and aimed it at the security guard.

'You mustn't point that at him,' Bøsei said.

Breivik shot the security guard first and then Monica, who tried to run off. They were both shot in the head at close range and immediately fell to the ground. It was 17:21. An AUF guard tried to run away but Breivik shot him and followed up with a head shot.

Over the course of about seventy minutes on Utøya, Anders Behring Breivik caused the death of sixty-nine people, sixty-seven of whom died of gunshot wounds. His victims were aged between fourteen and fifty-one. Thirty-two of them were under eighteen, and the average age of those who died was nineteen. Another thirty-three people were shot and wounded during the massacre. Almost all of the dead and many of the wounded were hit several times, since Breivik fired back-up shots at his victims' heads. The police found 189 empty cartridges on the island and believed that he had fired a total of 297 shots: 176 with the rifle and 121 with the pistol. Breivik killed and injured 100 people (excluding the two who died of other causes) and, according to the charges against him, they were hit by at least 247 shots. Some of the shots may have gone through more than one person, but it appears that the vast majority of the shots Breivik fired must have hit their target. The high percentage of hits is proof of a calm, determined and effective murderer. According to the police, there were 569 people on the island, 12 per cent of whom were killed, which means that approximately one in eight people died. A further 10 per cent were wounded, most of whom were hit by gunfire, while others (such as Ida and Stine) had broken bones, cuts or other injuries serious enough that they were admitted to hospital.

How could the worst peacetime massacre committed by a single person with handguns have been carried out by a person who, in so many other respects, was unable to accomplish things, who was a social, occupational and educational fiasco? On average, Breivik killed one person every single minute during the massacre. There is something puzzling about the massacre on Utøya, something that defies analysis even after the most thorough court case in Norwegian history. It is difficult to scrutinize pure evil calmly and objectively – the impulse is to turn your head away – but perhaps that is precisely why it is important to attempt to understand at least some of the elements that had a role to play in the tragedy.

A combination of factors contributed to the massacre taking on the proportions that it did. One category of factors has to do with Breivik's unique and complex psyche and personality. A second category is made up of tactical reasons, the methods and tools Breivik used on Utøya. Many of these are described in a section of his compendium entitled 'Applying deceptive means in urban guerrilla warfare',[3] in which he also discusses infiltrating Utøya, described as 'the youth camp connected to the largest political party'. A third category of factors consists of circumstances beyond Breivik's control that influenced the course of events, some of which contributed to extending the scope of the massacre, while others limited it.

Breivik later described how he struggled against his will as he stood on the grass together with Bøsei and the security guard, and that he overcame his physical reluctance to kill in order to take the first two lives. 'At that moment, a minute lasted for a decade,' he explained to the court-appointed psychiatrists, as 'in biological terms this is something the body tries to avoid'.[4] In this situation, as with the meticulous planning of the attacks and a series of other situations throughout his life, it is evident that Breivik was capable of brief moments of unusual self-discipline and controlled behaviour.

The most striking aspect of his own statements about Utøya to the police and the court-appointed forensic psychiatrists is how he describes himself as a machine or a robot. After he crossed a boundary with the first deaths, or 'activated', as he called it, he saw the rest of the massacre as 'like a game on TV'.[5] He described comprehensive stress reactions, but in a kind of language as if he were talking about an overloaded computer. His brain was 'bombarded' by impressions and he 'lost access to its databases', images of grotesque details were 'deleted' and he gradually continued on 'autopilot'.[6] Towards the end, he considered 'self-terminating' but surrendered instead.[7]

This robotic, mechanical nature is also linked to the most prominent aspect of Breivik's behaviour as the survivors saw it: he was so calm. Anne-Berit Stavenes described the sound of his footsteps as 'the only calm footsteps on the island'. The other survivors said similar things. The gunman's shots hit their targets because he was calm and composed. The court-appointed psychiatrists Husby and Sørheim related Breivik's peculiar depiction of himself as a machine to a condition known as alexithymia, which means an inability to recognize or describe one's own feelings. Alexithymia is possibly his most characteristic feature (or symptom) and has affected him since childhood. The question is what does this alexithymia entail? Is he unable to articulate his feelings? Has the connection between feelings and language been severed?

On one level he does have feelings, but, when he cried in court or became angry, these emotions were triggered respectively by his avatar (in his propaganda film) and by what he perceived as personal offence ('character assassination', as he put it). Breivik's feelings are evidently linked only to his grandiose self-image, with no trace of any others. If this really was a trait that had persisted from when he was with the child psychiatrists at the SSBU (who noticed that he was unable to express feelings in spite of having well-developed linguistic abilities) until 22 July 2011, it can be questioned whether it is due to a genetic disorder in the brain's development or to damage resulting from the reactive attachment disorder the SSBU believed they had observed in 1983.

When he saw things as 'like a game on TV', this also had to do with Breivik leaping into his avatar, the knight figure he had spent the previous five years constructing. On Utøya, he *became* 'Justiciar Knight Andrew Berwick', or the 'perfect knight', as he described himself to the court-appointed psychiatrists.[8] 'Violence is the mother of change,' as he wrote.[9] 'Humility and modesty are also important virtues,' Breivik told Husby and Sørheim. 'I know of no more perfect knight [than myself].'[10] Even though, according to Breivik, many of his impressions were 'deleted', he did notice details that were not as he had expected. The sound of the head shots was different from impact sounds he knew from TV series or films.[11] Shattered heads and blood pumping out of gunshot wounds also left an impression on him.

The Killings in the Café Building and by the Love Path, 17:22–17:44

After killing the first people by the main building, Breivik went on up the hill towards the Café Building. He was holding a semi-automatic Ruger Mini-14 rifle, he had extra-large thirty-round magazines in his combat vest, and he was wearing his pistol in the holster on his thigh. As he came over the top of the steep slope, he began shooting young people in the yard with his rifle. Many were hit, and panic broke out. At one point, Breivik looked directly at Anzor and shot behind him as the seventeen-year-old from Lillestrøm ran into the woods. Anzor ran to the western tip of the island, but there were not many options to go any further from there.

One of the reasons for the extent of the massacre was of course that Breivik chose to attack an island. This delayed the police response and made it difficult for his victims to escape: many youngsters were killed at the water's edge and on the beaches. At the same time, he hoped, his bomb had focused all attention on Oslo, including the attention of the police and the hospitals. 'Make a sound in the east, then strike in the west,' he wrote in the compendium. 'Hide a knife behind a smile.'[12]

Breivik went on from the yard in front of the kiosk down the gravel track, which went along the side of the large Café Building towards the campsite. At the same moment, Anne-Berit Stavenes went out onto the top step and saw what she thought was a policeman coming along the track. She was about to call out to him but instead witnessed him shooting a girl, who fell to the ground. Anne-Berit went back. But to start with she had felt the same reaction as everyone else on the island: she wanted to turn to the policeman for help and advice.

Breivik used people's trust in the police, and really their trust in society in general, as a weapon. Perhaps this was particularly effective, as most Norwegians have, by global standards, an unusually high level of trust in the police and in one another. Breivik made use of this trust, or social capital. With the help of a police uniform, he obtained access to the island and access to the young people who came to him when he called. When he began shooting, he caused not only death but also deep confusion. By using people's trust as a weapon, he spread disbelief, fear and distrust. As the AUF members thought it was the police shooting at them just after the explosion in Oslo, they began thinking that a coup was taking place and that the camping tourists and rescuers in boats might be involved. While they saw one man shooting, many people thought that the PST or the police in general were attacking them, and that the whole community could be involved. Any camping tourist could be a murderer in disguise.

Breivik went on past the Café Building, where Ida Spjelkavik glanced out of the window in the group meeting room and saw him coming with his rifle raised, shooting a boy in the chest at the corner of the building. The semi-automatic weapons Breivik used were legal, and he had a licence for both of them. The Glock was a competition model, while the Ruger was a .223 calibre flat-shooting hunting weapon, which is legal for hunting roe deer and lynx, but not big game; .223 rounds are relatively small, cheap and easy to carry in large quantities. Breivik used expanding soft-point rounds (bullets with lead tips instead of nickel casing), which inflicted major tissue damage on those who were hit.[13]

It might be thought that an automatic weapon, which has a much faster rate of fire, would have been even more lethal, but, since

Breivik was mainly shooting directed shots and not at random, his semi-automatic weapons were sufficiently effective for his objective. His extra-large magazines reduced the number of times he had to reload, and reloading could put him in a potentially vulnerable position. Furthermore, since he had two weapons, one of them was always loaded. Breivik also had a third weapon, which he called his 'weapon of mass destruction': the Tyrifjord. His plan was to drive the young people into the water so that they would drown. Given the distance to the shore, as well as the air and water temperature that day, it was a plausible scenario. For a long time, Breivik thought that the fjord had taken a large proportion of those who died. When in custody and asked by the psychiatrists about the sixty-nine dead, Breivik estimated that he had shot forty, while twenty-nine had drowned.[14]

Instead of carrying on down towards the campsite, as Anne-Berit and Ida thought, Breivik turned round and went up the concrete steps and into the Café Building. From the doorway between the Little Hall and the corridor, Arshad saw the blond-haired policeman come up the stairs and shoot into the Little Hall. From the window in the group meeting room, Ida saw complete panic break out in the packed hall. Breivik came into the hall and shot the wounded youngsters who were left and those who were playing dead or lying paralysed on the floor. He carried on through the door into the Main Hall. He was surprised that many people did not run when he came in but lay still. Completely calm, he changed his magazine while standing next to the piano in the Main Hall, before continuing to shoot the young people in the head from a distance of 20 to 60 centimetres, according to himself. From the Main Hall, he went into the corridor, back towards the Little Hall, and killed the boy lying outside the toilets where Arshad was hidden behind the wall. Instead of looking behind the door, Breivik carried on into the Little Hall and back out the door to the campsite. Seven people were dead in the Little Hall, and five in the Main Hall.

Throughout the seventy minutes, Breivik was careful not to go into constricted areas. The one time he broke this rule and entered the Café Building, he used people's panic to move them ahead of him so that he avoided ending up in a jumbled mass of people and always kept a distance from the young people as they escaped. His whole appearance was terrifying. He was dressed in black with two visible weapons, one of which was large and military-looking, a hydration pack on his back (he was constantly thirsty) and a bulging combat vest packed with several large magazines, making him appear 'robust' and 'robot-like', as Ida described him.

During the massacre in the Café Building, Breivik used tactics of shock and dominance. He wanted to frighten people and create panic. One of his methods was to shoot salvos with the Ruger, which made more noise and meant that he covered a larger area with bullets. That was how he scared people in front of the Café Building and how he scared people when he went back out into the campsite and shot at the youngsters he saw in the wooded area on the other side. A few times he shouted taunts at the AUF members ('You're going to die today, Marxists!' or 'You're all going to die!') to scare them and drive them off into the water. The effects of his tactics were so great that many people thought there was more than one gunman on the island, which might also have influenced the police to stay on the mainland while the massacre was ongoing. At the same time, Breivik did not lose his head during the massacre, even when he was shouting; he kept calm, did not waste his ammunition and was careful not to get into difficult situations – for example by not checking in the toilets in the Café Building.

The head shots Breivik aimed at the injured and those who were playing dead formed one of the most disturbing aspects of the massacre. The fact that he did this systematically was one of the main reasons that the ratio between the dead and the wounded was two to one (sixty-seven dead and thirty-three wounded), which meant an unusually high proportion of deaths. When James Holmes attacked a cinema in Aurora, Colorado, on 20 July 2012, the ratio was one to five (twelve dead and fifty-eight injured). Breivik's deadly efficiency may appear to be due to his being a good shot. Perhaps he was a good shot, but most of all he was able to keep calm and to get into as favourable a position as possible vis-à-vis his victims – in other words, point-blank range.

A good killer does not necessarily have to be a good shot in the sense that he is good at hitting clay pigeons in the air or small bull's eyes from a hundred metres away. The decisive factor is the killer's mentality. Shooting from a distance at people running away is different to killing young people lying helpless on the ground and begging for their lives. Not many people would be able to do that. Breivik had prepared himself for it in his compendium. In addition to beheading, he was fascinated by head shots. Not only did he describe a range of execution scenes, including 'celebratory lynching', he also painted out the scenarios awaiting him on the island. 'You must therefore embrace and familiarise yourself with the concept of killing women, even very attractive women,' he wrote, advising those who were not capable of doing this to start a blog instead.[15]

When reading the compendium, it is often difficult to determine which parts are neutral preparations for mass murder and which are emotionally or possibly sexually charged fantasies about the same thing. Even though Breivik described the seventy minutes as 'hell',[16] the forensic psychologists noted that he appeared to be pleased with the thought of the massacre he had carried out. What he said about Utøya and what his expressions told were two different things, according to the psychiatrists. Perhaps his smile expressed pride in the massacre, which was a 'military success'.[17] Nevertheless, his behaviour on the island, including his meticulous use of head shots, reinforces the suspicion that a sadistic inclination contributed to the extent of the massacre, as do the many sadistic images in the compendium and his focus on gruesome details when talking with the police and psychiatrists afterwards: the impact sounds of shots, the sight of severe wounds.

'He says that it was "hell", but his emotional response is inadequate,' wrote Husby and Sørheim, 'since he makes a peculiarly stiff and inward-facing smile when he speaks about certain details.'[18] These details were apparently connected to things such as executing people who played dead. 'There was a lot of ammo wasted having to fire so many head shots,' he explained.[19] The smile described by the court-appointed psychiatrists is like an echo of the 'feigned, aversive smile' the SSBU psychologist described in the first portrait of Breivik as a four-year-old child.

After killing the people in the Café Building, Breivik went down the steps and shot at the young people on the other side of the campsite. He had a red dot sight and a scope on his rifle and hit several of the youngsters, even though they were at a range of 50 to 100 metres and he was shooting from the hip. He also had a laser pointer mounted underneath the Glock. A green spot of light marked where the shots would hit, which might have helped him when he fired head shots. Breivik crossed the campsite and went up onto the Love Path. There he encountered eleven young people lying in a close huddle up against the wire mesh fence, squeezed up like a covey of grouse along the path. Breivik shot them from right to left. One of them survived. Among the dead was Bano Rashid.

Breivik carried on south along the path, coming to a steep bank down to the water's edge, down which many AUF members had climbed. Breivik stood up on the path and shot at arms and legs sticking out from behind the rocks. He was trying to get them out of their hiding places. Many were injured; some tumbled out into the open and were killed. 'You hear people hitting the water and rocks,' as one witness who hid on the slope recalled.[20] A number of the AUF survivors described Breivik laughing and shouting while he shot. 'He said "Yesss!" "Yeah!" "Bull's eye!"' as one girl remembered.[21] A player might react like that in a computer game, a well-trained soldier might react like that in combat, and perhaps a sadist would too. Still, Breivik remained calm and did not go down to shoot the victims in the head. Perhaps he was unsure of being able to stay standing upright on the steep slope.

From the Schoolhouse to Stoltenberget, 17:44–18:10

At around a quarter to six, Breivik arrived at the Schoolhouse, where Even Kleppen sat next to the closed door. Even heard the shots coming closer, moving away again and then eventually coming right up to them when Breivik killed a boy and a girl in the woods just outside. The crisis management expert in Norwegian People's Aid had bet that the policeman who was shooting would not risk attacking a barricaded building, and the six People's Aid volunteers from Hadeland had gathered forty-one young people in the building before shutting the door and putting mattresses and tables behind the windows. It was quiet outside, and Even had an unpleasant feeling in his stomach. The window in the door had bars between its panes of grooved glass, a surmountable obstacle for a determined intruder.

Even turned his head and peered out through the glass in the door. All he could see through the grooves was light, shadows and vague contours. A dark silhouette was approaching, treading calmly. 'He's coming,' Even whispered, crawling away from the door and into the corner.

He heard somebody grasp the door handle, then there were two ear-splitting shots. Glass shattered. Breivik shot into the cabin through the door window but without hitting anybody. Even stood half-way up. There was a table nearby and a fire extinguisher on the wall. They were potential weapons. If the gunman came in, the only option was to attack him. Even was tense. It fell completely silent outside. Then he heard more shots, but this time further away.

One of the external causes that limited the extent of the massacre was the conduct of the Hadeland group from Norwegian People's Aid. Their crisis management expert, Guttorm Skovly, was right that Breivik would not risk entering a space where he was not in control. Skovly had taken part in a number of emergency exercises, including a couple to do with terrorism. He had learnt that terrorists rarely attack places where they do not have the full picture. In the Café Building, Breivik had used shock to drive the young people away ahead of him and had made panic do the job for him. It was different in the Schoolhouse, so he left with unfinished business.

One of the weapons in Breivik's tactical arsenal was hope. As long as the youngsters had hope of escaping, they would flee instead of resisting. As long as they fled, he could kill those he caught and chase the rest into the water, where he assumed many of them would drown. He organized the massacre according to this principle, which he described in the compendium thus: 'Cornered prey will often mount a final desperate attack. To prevent this you let the enemy believe he still has a chance for freedom. His will to fight is thus dampened by his desire to escape.'[22]

When he got back to the main building and to the Pelican case in the back of the ferry captain's car, Breivik stocked up on more magazines. He went down to the pier and shot at the *Reiulf*, which was full of fleeing AUF members, and at another boat picking up swimmers. He threw one of his smoke grenades into the barn by the main building. The second grenade exploded outside the main building. The orange smoke rose up above the treetops and could be seen by Allan and Reidun sitting in their cabin on the other side of the water. At around six o'clock, Breivik walked from the Café Building, past the so-called NATO Toilet, in the direction of the small wooded area at Stoltenberget, the cliff at the northern tip of the island. From there he shot at the young people standing on the beach, with bullets hitting the water to the north of the island towards where Erik Øvergaard and his friend were in their boat, approximately 100 metres from land. The efforts of people such as Erik Øvergaard and Allan Søndergaard Jensen were the decisive external factor limiting the extent of the massacre. The spontaneous civilian rescue operation saved a great number of lives that evening.

After having killed another group of young people at Stoltenberget, Breivik called the police to surrender. He picked up the mobile phone of a youngster who had either died or fled and got through on the emergency number 112. Breivik was out of breath and said he wanted to hand himself over. The policeman who answered had no time to enter negotiations before the call was cut off. Breivik did not answer when the policeman tried to call back. One of the external factors that contributed to the massacre not being stopped sooner was the fact that Breivik had forgotten his own phone. He called the police from other phones and did not know the numbers he was calling from. When he phoned from Stoltenberget, or near there, he must have put down or lost the phone he was using, perhaps because he started shooting again. If he had remembered his own phone, the chance of entering real surrender negotiations would have been higher. If Breivik had surrendered when he was on the cliffs at Stoltenberget, around twenty lives would have been spared.

From the Pump House to the Arrest, 18:10–18:34

From Stoltenberget, Breivik crossed the sandy beach in the cove at Bolsjevika and set off on the so-called Love Path, which led south through thick woods and steep, undulating terrain. At about a quarter past six, he emerged out of the woods by the pump house, where there was a large group of young people. He introduced himself again as a policeman, telling them that the culprit had been caught and that they had to gather together to be evacuated. Then he began shooting. While Anne-Berit heard what was happening from her hiding place up in the woods, Stine witnessed the slaughter begin. Breivik carried out the killings very calmly and once again with control shots to the head. He killed fourteen people in very little time before running on past Anne-Berit and in towards the centre of the island by the wash house.

By this point, the killings had been going on for almost sixty minutes. Most of the young people had heard that it was a policeman who was shooting, and many of them had also seen him. Nevertheless, he still managed to trick some (such as Stine) and keep others passive by introducing himself as a policeman when he emerged from the trees. His ruse and his disguise were still able to have an effect because many of the youngsters had either not managed to form a picture of what was happening or were unable to do so. By playing on the natural denial that sets in when something unexpected or inconceivable happens (Ida heard the young ones in the woods wondering out loud: 'What's going on?'), Breivik was able to recycle his baiting method several times over the course of the hour or so he moved around the island.

After a detour towards the centre of the island, Breivik went back onto the Love Path near the steep western tip of the island. Ida Spjelkavik heard him shooting at a boat while she was in the opening of one of the caves in the rock wall, and she saw the boat turn away and disappear out across the water. At this point, Breivik must have realized that the Tyrifjord, his 'weapon of mass destruction', was instead saving many young people, but it is unclear whether he was shooting at the boats in an effort to hit them or to frighten them.

Over the last half hour of the rampage, Breivik moved about quickly and over a wide area. According to his own assertions, he expected that the police might arrive at any moment, at least from when he first called the emergency number to surrender. It might seem as if he did not know how to relate to the police: on the one hand he phoned them to surrender, while on the other hand he moved tactically to avoid them. He kept away from the eastern side of the island because he was afraid of snipers. By moving quickly and over a large area, he created uncertainty about where he was. The first team from the Delta Unit ran north along the island, apparently because of tip-offs from youngsters they met, and they found dead and wounded young people by the rock at Stoltenberget, but not Breivik, who at that point was on his way towards the island's southern end. Breivik's pattern of movement and his attempt to surrender were probably both due to his being afraid. He thought that the police would shoot him. When all was said and done, he was 'not that keen' on dying. His behaviour suggested that he wanted to live.

Breivik got through on the emergency number 112 for a second time at 18:26 and spoke with the control room at Drammen police station. He introduced himself again as 'Commander Breivik' and said that he wished to surrender, but the disorientated policeman was unable to keep the conversation going. He could not call Breivik back either, as the number had not come up on his screen. Breivik was probably calling from a mobile without a functioning SIM card. By this point, the NRK helicopter was circling the island, and Breivik has claimed that he considered shooting at it but decided not to. Through the pine woods and the hazel bushes he spotted a huddle of youngsters at the southern tip of the island.

Marius Arnesen's camera witnessed the final killings Breivik carried out at the island's southern end. The sun broke through the cloud cover just as the figure dressed in black came out of the scrub.

'The madman's been caught,' he said, and then began shooting.

He killed five people at the southern end. A young boy, the son of the security officer, confronted Breivik as he shot. 'You killed my dad,' the eleven-year-old shouted. 'Why do you want to kill me too?'[23]

Yet again, the scene ended with Breivik firing control shots to kill the wounded young people, while he refrained from shooting at the boy in the water or at the eleven-year-old. Why did he spare some of them? When interviewed by police, he explained that he 'skipped two of them who looked very young', presumably the security guard's son and another boy. But he also failed to kill some AUF members. Perhaps it was chance, but, by letting a few people live in between his systematic bouts of slaughter, it could seem that Breivik was further underlining the message that he had command over life and death. Andrew Berwick, the perfect knight: judge, jury and executioner in one. One fundamental precondition for Breivik's terrible actions was his total lack of empathy, or 'serious empathy deficit', as the court-appointed psychiatrists call it. It is difficult to comprehend, but it seems as if the massacre did not affect him psychologically.

Husby and Sørheim indicated that Breivik was conspicuously unmoved during the reconstruction on Utøya, when he retraced the route he followed on 22 July and recalled the killing spree in detail. He appeared as if he were carrying out a 'building site inspection'.[24] When the psychiatrists asked him about the victims he killed, and Breivik probably realized they were hoping to hear about his feelings and ideas about the massacre as well as how he experienced it, he answered: 'I felt traumatized every second, with blood and brain matter spraying everywhere.'[25] He focuses on his own experience, on how it was not easy for him. The notion that he saw the massacre as 'like a game on TV' also paints a picture of his complete inability to see his victims as people.

Breivik's empathy deficit may to some extent have been reinforced by conscious self-suggestion over time, by 'dehumanizing the enemy', as he put it to the psychiatrists.[26] He claimed that he meditated every day, in a similar fashion to al-Qaeda terrorists praying five times daily. His empathy deficit may to some extent have been further reinforced by steroids, excitement and an ephedrine rush during his rampage, but Breivik basically appears to be suffering from what the British psychologist Simon Baron-Cohen calls 'empathy erosion'. According to Baron-Cohen, evil is a function of a complete failure of empathy.[27]

Baron-Cohen describes empathy as consisting of two elements: the ability to interpret the feelings of others and the ability to respond appropriately. People with serious personality disorders can normally interpret other people's feelings but often will not respond in an appropriate, empathic manner. People with autism may not initially be able to interpret the feelings of others but, even though they do not immediately understand that other people have their own feelings and needs, they can learn to respond empathically if they are at least motivated to do so. A lack of empathy does not necessarily mean moral deficiency. People with Asperger's syndrome often have strong feelings about rules and morality. Some personality disorders, however, can lead to destructive and selfish behaviour. The dangerous element of narcissistic personality disorder is precisely the lack of empathy, in the sense of being able to respond appropriately. This is the trait that makes the difference between people with strange thoughts about their own significance and those who are willing to destroy or to kill in order to gain recognition and status.

Some of the days during Breivik's trial in the spring of 2012 were dedicated to the dead and injured from Utøya. The testimonies were moving, and their effect could be seen on everybody present in Courtroom 250, including the judges, the prosecutors and the counsel for the defence. People cried, and only the man in the dock remained unmoved. On one level, a person with impaired empathy is almost invulnerable, as he or she is uninfluenced by the feelings of others. On another level, that person is extremely lonely. The primate brain is equipped with so-called mirror neurons, which are activated both when we perform an action ourselves and when we see others carrying out an action. If you see somebody yawn, it is easy to yawn yourself. A baby will start to cry if it hears other babies crying, and it is the same mirror effect that makes fear contagious.

Baron-Cohen believes that the 'mirror neuron system' is a primitive but important component in human empathy (which is also made up of higher cognitive components).[28] As Breivik was apparently completely unmoved by the strong feelings surrounding him, it could be suspected that his imperturbability might stem from more than Bushido meditation alone. It is, however, not possible to say anything with certainty about whether his behaviour might be due to an impairment in his mirror neuron system or whether it might be connected to weaknesses in what Baron-Cohen calls the brain's 'empathy circuit'.

A video camera on land also captured the killings at the southern end of the island, and how the Delta Unit officers by the pier were startled and ducked when they heard the shots. Five policemen then ran south along the island, across the volleyball court and along the gravel track to the Schoolhouse. Inside the Schoolhouse, from his position by the wall, Even heard several voices shouting warnings and orders.

'Armed police!'

'Freeze!'

'On the ground!'

In the woods outside the Schoolhouse, Breivik put down his gun. Instead of stopping and getting down as he was ordered, Breivik walked towards the five Delta Unit officers. A policeman noticed the cords dangling from Breivik's earplugs, and started to squeeze his trigger. He thought Breivik was wearing an explosive vest, and aimed for the head. Breivik's life was saved at the last moment, when the officer closest to him shouted out that he was only wearing an equipment vest. The police arrested him at approximately 18:34. By then, a little over an hour had passed since the police had first been alerted to gunfire on Utøya, and approximately forty minutes since the first two policemen arrived at the *Thorbjørn*'s pier on the other side of the water. The external factor that contributed most to the massacre taking on such proportions was that the police's immediate action was delayed by their lack of transportation, choice of rendezvous point and unclear areas of responsibility.

'My brothers,' Breivik said to the police as they handcuffed him. As Justiciar Knight Andrew Berwick, he had become a member of the brotherhood of alpha males. 'Have you got a plaster?' he added.

Breivik had a cut on his finger.

The Perfect Executioner

'Cruel but necessary' was how Breivik later summarized his seventy-five minutes on Utøya. It was not just his aesthetics and racial theories that linked Breivik to Nazism. There were clear similarities between his own executioner ethics and the ethical imperative the SS Reichsführer Heinrich Himmler described to his men in connection with the extermination of the Jews. When Breivik writes that 'refusing to apply necessary cruelty is a betrayal of the people whom you wish to protect',[29] it could be the Reichsführer himself talking. The men of the SS had to be tough, pure and '*gnadenlos*' [without mercy], according to Himmler.

In a speech in Poznań in October 1943, which mentioned the extermination of the Jews and was one of the main pieces of evidence against the Nazis in the Nuremberg Trials, Himmler unabashedly described how awful it was to stand next to mass graves 'when 100 bodies lie together, when there are 500, or when there are 1,000'.[30] At the same time, Himmler stresses that such atrocities are both morally just and a duty towards society:

> We have the moral right, we had the duty to our people to do it, to kill this people who wanted to kill us. But we do not have the right to enrich ourselves with even one fur, with one Mark, with one cigarette, with one watch, with anything. That we do not have. Because at the end of this, we don't want, because we exterminated the bacillus, to become sick and die from the same bacillus.
>
> I will never see it happen, that even one bit of putrefaction comes in contact with us, or takes root in us. On the contrary, where it might try to take root, we will burn it out together. But altogether we can say: we have carried out this most difficult task for the love of our people. And we have taken on no defect within us, in our soul, or in our character.[31]

According to Himmler, their work as executioners made the SS tough, but at the same time it was a source of secret honour. Being tough, merciless and pure was the ideal for a man of the SS. This blended aesthetics and ethics together in a notion of the consummate executioner. The execution role of the SS highlighted that they were the chosen superhuman few sacrificing themselves to purge the German *Volkskörper* of the Jews. Breivik's Templar knight is a corresponding form of superhuman living beyond common ethics and morality. Himmler laments that the 80 million 'upright Germans' all know a Jew they like. Even if they accept that Jews are swine to be exterminated, they all know of an exception, but 80 million exceptions would mean the end of the 'necessary' but cruel operation needed to purify the German *Volkskörper* of Jewish contagion.

Himmler favours a consistent policy with no distinctions, exceptions or doubt. Breivik points to a similar problem: 'Many people have a Muslim neighbour who is a fine man, and from this empirical fact they conclude: Islam cannot be all that bad considering our friend Mustapha.'[32] But this conclusion does not take into account the fundamentally aggressive characteristics of Islam, according to Breivik. Even though he dissociates himself from Nazism, many of his ideas are either inspired by or are practically carbon copies of Nazi conceptions of gender, aesthetics, ethics and politics. Regarding the 'cruel nature' of his planned operation, Breivik writes:

> As a Justiciar Knight you are operating as a jury, judge and executioner on behalf of all free Europeans. Never forget that it is not only your right to act against the tyranny of the cultural Marxist/multiculturalist elites of Europe, it is your duty to do so.
>
> There are situations in which cruelty is necessary, and refusing to apply necessary cruelty is a betrayal of the people whom you wish to protect. [. . .] Once you decide to strike, it is better to kill too many than not enough, or you risk reducing the desired ideological impact of the strike. [. . .] In many ways, morality has lost its meaning in our struggle. The question of good and evil is reduced to one simple choice. [. . .] Survive or perish. Some innocent[s] will die in our operations as they are simply at the wrong place at the wrong time. Get used [to] the idea. The needs of the many will always surpass the needs of the few.[33]

Both Breivik and Himmler portray a situation in which common morality has been driven to the wall and self-defence is needed, as their people are on the verge of extinction. As far as they were concerned, the Jews wanted to kill the Germans, and Muslims and cultural Marxists want to kill the free Europeans. Rationalizing murder often entails pleading self-defence. The genocide in Bosnia was partly carried out to prevent what the Serbs saw as a genocide planned against them, or at least that was how some of their leaders explained it. Breivik and Himmler both envisage self-defence on a cosmic scale and hence a corresponding aestheticization and glorification of the role of executioner. The fact that they came to such similar conclusions, in spite of all the historical, social and cultural differences between Hoff in Oslo's West End in 2011 and Poznań in 1943, is to some extent connected to Himmler and Breivik both existing in an occidentalist tradition extending like a dark vein from the Napoleonic Wars to the present day. Their main difference was that, while the Nazis killed as a pack, Breivik acted alone on Utøya.

Evening on Utøya

While the police searched the island for other gunmen and gave first aid to badly wounded youngsters, the rescue operation continued with the boats. At about nine o'clock, the Norwegian Home Guard officer Even Frogh moored his bow rider next to the MS *Thorbjørn* at the pier on Utøya. He went onto the ferry, passing the dead body of a long-haired girl, and met his brother Stian and the ferry captain. Over the last few hours, Even had evacuated young people wounded and in shock from all along the island, and he had seen the twisted hands of the dead bodies along the shoreline. The impressions this left were impossible to imagine. Luckily the ferry captain's daughter had survived and was now in safety on Storøya.

The police had cleared the main building and asked Even and the captain, who were both familiar with the local area, to come inside. They walked past Monica's body on the lawn. While they sat in the office on the ground floor, the outside door opened, and Even heard the tramping of many footsteps. It was Breivik being led inside by the police. His hands were cuffed at the front. As Breivik went up the stairs to the first floor, he looked down at the ferry captain, who was staring back at him from the office. Breivik disappeared into the TV room on the first floor, where he was questioned by the police for the first time.

After having heard the recordings of this first interview, the court-appointed psychiatrists described Breivik as agitated, especially to begin with, while in later interviews and in court he appeared relatively stable. Breivik asked if he would be executed, and said that he thought his family would be executed too. He was fine with being 'tortured for the rest of his life', since his life was over. 'My life ended when I ordained in Knights Templar Europe,' he told the police.[34] He made a number of demands during questioning, including that Norway should introduce the death penalty and the use of torture, as well as that he should be given access to a computer and to Wikipedia while in custody. 'Today I'm the greatest monster since Quisling,' Breivik said.[35]

Breivik's thoughts of suicide and his sadistic focus on torture and execution came across clearly, which was perhaps only natural after shooting young people in the head for over an hour. But he also said these things because he was still his avatar, Andrew Berwick, living out the fantasy he had dreamt of in his room. He expressed his wish to institutionalize torture and execution. Once again he described himself as dead, his 'life ended' when he had ordained as a knight a few years previously. Perhaps the fact he fantasized about his mother being executed (she was the only 'family' he had in Norway) was not so odd, as his compendium touched on the same idea.

Breivik characterized the massacre as 'a stab in the heart for the Labour Party',[36] but he struggled to explain his grounds for killing AUF members. According to the categories he worked with for traitors, they belonged to category C, who were not considered targets to be killed, but on the other hand most of them would eventually move into category B, or maybe even A. He claimed that one of the reasons he had to carry out the massacre and the bombing was that he had been censored by *Aftenposten*.[37] He later told the psychiatrists that the massacre was 'an expression of my love for my own people and country', and that his 'love, empathy and conscience' were over-developed.[38]

In the conversations with the psychiatrists, it is a narcissist speaking, just as it was Breivik the narcissist who wrote the compendium. The narcissistic personality disorder with which Breivik was diagnosed by the second team of psychiatrists, Tørrissen and Aspaas, could explain his eroded empathy and, to some extent, also how he was able to stay calm over seventy-five minutes: it was merely a matter of creating the perfect knight, of becoming his avatar. It was all about him, specifically about his self-image. The young people he killed were just as unreal and insignificant as the monsters he killed when he went questing in *World of Warcraft*. The massacre as such was not essentially different from the times when he graffiti-bombed Skøyen bus depot as a teenager. He wanted to be king; he had to be seen.

Personality disorders are relatively new concepts that are still disputed in psychiatry. There is an ongoing debate as to whether diagnosis of personality disorders should make use of specific categories, such as 'narcissistic personality disorder', or whether it should be based on the extent of dysfunctional or abnormal behaviour and ideas – in other words, creating a kind of composite profile. In Breivik's case, such a profile would probably feature a large dimension of narcissism but would also include dyssocial and paranoid traits, and perhaps elements of sadism, self-dramatization and compulsion as well.

According to the American *Diagnostic and Statistical Manual of Mental Disorders*, narcissistic personality disorder can be defined as:

> A pervasive pattern of grandiosity (in fantasy or behavior), need for admiration, and lack of empathy, beginning by early adulthood and present in a variety of contexts, as indicated by five (or more) of the following:
> (1) has a grandiose sense of self-importance [. . .]
> (2) is preoccupied with fantasies of unlimited success [or] power [. . .]
> (3) believes that he or she is 'special' and unique and can only be understood by, or should associate with, other special or high-status people (or institutions)
> (4) requires excessive admiration
> (5) has a sense of entitlement [. . .]
> (6) is interpersonally exploitative, i.e., takes advantage of others to achieve his or her own ends
> (7) lacks empathy: is unwilling to recognize or identify with the feelings and needs of others
> (8) is often envious of others or believes that others are envious of him or her
> (9) shows arrogant, haughty behaviors or attitudes.[39]

Most of these criteria do seem to fit to some extent, with the possible exception of the eighth criterion, envy. Modern psychoanalysts such as Heinz Kohut have demonstrated that narcissism can have positive aspects and represents a necessary stage of personality development. People should like themselves. At the same time, a number of psychoanalysts and psychiatrists have linked so-called malignant narcissism to extreme cruelty. Everything in moderation, as the saying goes. Erich Fromm, who coined the term, called malignant narcissism 'the quintessence of evil'.[40]

The influential psychoanalyst Otto Kernberg suggested that malignant narcissism should be understood as a blend of grandiosity and sadism, often linked with paranoid and antisocial elements (which the second pair of court-appointed psychiatrists found with Breivik), in which sadistic and destructive behaviour confirms a grandiose self-image. Malignant narcissism has not been included as a category in its own right in any of the major official diagnostic standards, but 'sadistic psychopath' is probably the popular expression that best reflects the essence of Fromm and Kernberg's term.

The American criminal justice experts Ronald Holmes and Stephen Holmes have tested Kernberg's theories against empirical data and have demonstrated a connection between narcissistic personality disorder and serial killers, who are among the most extreme of criminals.[41] They distinguish between four kinds of serial killers (who are chiefly men). Visionary serial killers are psychotic and kill as directed by God or the devil. Mission killers see it as their duty to take the lives of certain categories of people – for example, prostitutes or homosexual people. Hedonistic killers have either sexual or financial motives, or both. The fourth type is more unusual and often appears to be driven by a desire to avenge childhood abuse. Power-control serial killers kill in order to affirm their control over victims. Murder is the most extreme form of demonstrating power, and the feeling of total control gives power-control serial killers satisfaction. The average serial killer has narcissistic personality disorder and a difficult family background, and might demonstrate traits from more than one of the categories mentioned above. His father is usually absent, but might also be authoritarian. His mother combines distance, allure and over-protectiveness.

From an early age, the average serial killer is interested in death, blood and violence. He is motivated primarily by his shame, which usually originates from a form of sexual conflict with his mother. 'The backgrounds of many serial killers show a mother who was promiscuous, seductive, incestuous, and/or abusive,' write Charles Brooks and Michael Church. 'As a result, the killer is preoccupied with maternal sexuality and morality, which makes him feel ashamed of the mother. The killer then transforms this shame into rage and kills to erase painful memories from childhood.'[42]

The causes for personality disorders are generally complex, but there is a 'robust' connection between personality pathology and childhood abuse, according to Karterud, Wilberg and Urnes.[43] The researchers point out some factors in particular that seem to be linked to the development of narcissistic personality disorder, including an unstable emotional attachment to parents in early childhood, emotional abuse, incest (especially between mother and son), a lack of boundary setting and being spoilt as a child.

The policemen who photographed Breivik on the first floor of the main building, wearing handcuffs and with his legs slightly apart, had no idea how much of this profile fitted him. Darkness was falling over the island, and their job was to find out if further attacks were imminent and whether Breivik had accomplices. Any further terrorist actions needed to be stopped.

While Breivik was being questioned, Even Frogh left the island for the last time shortly before eleven in the evening. He had assisted the ferry captain in evacuating young people from the island on the MS *Thorbjørn*; now he had to fetch his youngest daughter from friends. The civilian operation on Utøya was over. Darkness fell over the Tyrifjord and the slopes of Krokkleiva, wiping out the colours and contours in the landscape. Behind the bright light on the pier, Even glimpsed Utøya as a vague dark shape, a rupture on the surface of the water. When the helicopters left every now and then, he could hear the sound of dogs barking from the shoreline below the building. The police search was still ongoing.

When the helicopter with the thermal imaging camera disappeared at around midnight, it was completely dark. But mobile phones lit up around the island like fireflies; some in the grass, others among the rocks and on the cliffs. Various ringtones broke the silence and mobiles on silent rumbled as they vibrated on the stony ground. The displays carried on lighting up all night, like candles flickering erratically in the dark.[44]

14

Hatred

The Utøya Generation

'It's interesting that he's so preoccupied with 9/11,' said Arshad.

On 17 April 2012, the trial of Anders Behring Breivik was just beginning. Arshad, wearing washed-out jeans, a white jumper and brown shoes, looked up at the big screen in Room 269 of Oslo Courthouse. His accreditation card hung round his thin neck. On the back of the card was a sticker with 'No interviews, please' written in English. Again Arshad saw the murderer he had glimpsed outside the Little Hall and had heard in the corridor in the Café Building. Prableen was sitting next to him. The room was full of lawyers and AUF members, many of whom were still wearing their red wristbands from Utøya.

'And his admiration for al-Qaeda. As for the rest . . . ,' Arshad smiled and shook his head.

As early as the evening of 22 July 2011, shortly after Prime Minister Stoltenberg had made his declaration about responding with 'more democracy and more openness', it became clear that the culprit had nothing to do with al-Qaeda, Gaddafi or 'Norway's foreign military adventures'.[1] When Tove had finished cleaning up after spending the evening with her friends, an evening which had been marred by the attacks in Oslo and on Utøya, she turned on the television. It was after midnight, and she wondered who was behind the tragedy. A man had been arrested on Utøya, after all. A picture of Anders appeared on the screen. He was posing in an orange shirt. Tove felt it like a hammer-blow to the head. She sat paralysed in front of the television. The questions came only some while later. Why did you do this? Where did your hatred come from? What kind of person are you, Anders Behring Breivik?

'I'll never have any more contact with him,' Jens Breivik said from France. 'Instead of killing so many people, he should have taken his own life.'

Tove deleted the pictures of Anders from her camera.

When the trial began, the prosecutors played Breivik's YouTube film. Helene Bøksle sang during the film's third part, 'Hope', which was about the Justiciar Knights – in other words, about Breivik himself. Breivik was moved and started sobbing in the dock. The next day began with his reading out a self-written text keenly and enthusiastically. An 'unbearable injustice' had led him to Utøya. He was a cellar man by disposition and had settled into the prison regime well. He spoke of Ila Detention and Security Prison as his 'home'. But as the prosecutor, Inga Bejer Engh, dissected the story he had made up about himself, he turned pale and crumbled, almost like the punctured wreck of the *Hindenburg*. According to the police, there was no such thing as the PCCTS or a Knights Templar network. Muslims had not broken his nose.

'Trying to make fun of me,' said Breivik. 'Asking trick questions.'

He had been 'pompous', he explained, modifying his avatar. Andrew Berwick disappeared. The knight became a 'foot soldier', the 'masterpiece' compendium was 'a rough draft', 'Commander Breivik' was reduced to a 'militant nationalist', and the PCCTS was just 'four sweaty men in a cellar'. As Breivik's self-dramatizing traits were gradually ground down, his paranoid side emerged more clearly. 'Asbjørnsen and Moe' was what he called the first pair of court-appointed psychiatrists, after the famous Norwegian collectors of folktales and legends, accusing Husby and Sørheim of malicious lies. Even though he appreciated humour and could be witty, Breivik's garish narcissism was constant, unchanging and completely beyond the control of his intellect. His defence counsels cited his best friend's brother's funeral as an example that Breivik did have feelings, and he answered the question as if it were a kind of competition. 'I probably cried more than anybody else at that funeral,' he said.

In the functional layout of Courtroom 250, the psychiatrists had a prominent position on the bench in front of the judges. The question of Breivik's soundness of mind was central, and it occasionally appeared as if the four forensic psychiatrists were also standing trial. Husby and Sørheim insisted that Breivik was a paranoid schizophrenic, psychotic and criminally insane. Aspaas and Tørrissen thought that he was criminally sane, but that he had a complex personality disorder, narcissistic, antisocial and with elements of paranoia. How could the experts arrive at such contradictory conclusions? It was reminiscent of the difference between how the SSBU and child welfare had interpreted Anders' smile twenty-eight years earlier. According to the SSBU, it was feigned and aversive; child welfare concluded it was warm. A split personality, but which side was a façade, and which was real?

Behind the psychiatrists towered the lead judge, Wenche Elizabeth Arntzen, whose grandfather was director of public prosecutions and a central figure in the trial of Vidkun Quisling. Her eyes gleamed sharply behind her glasses, but she let Breivik make his monotonous defence speeches largely without interruption. At her side sat the judge Arne Lyng, grandson of John Lyng, who acted as the prosecutor in the trial of Henry Oliver Rinnan, a Gestapo agent who operated around Trondheim. Breivik had already taken his place next to Quisling and Rinnan in the pantheon of Norwegian supervillains long before the trial. In a way, he combined the qualities of the fantasist Quisling and the sadist Rinnan. Around him, the judges, prosecutors, counsels for the aggrieved and defence counsels all struggled to keep a cool head. The sweat glistened on the forehead of the lead defence counsel, Geir Lippestad, while Bejer Engh stared listlessly into space.

Trials are supposed to have two sides, but in Courtroom 250 there was a unity between the legal practitioners in their black robes, whether they were judges, defence counsels or prosecutors. Everyone who was in the courthouse that spring felt fear and compassion, and even the experienced lawyers stared down into the abyss with disbelief. Sometimes their eyes glazed over while evidence was given about the dead and the survivors. Other times, the court turned a collective shade of pale when seeing pictures from Utøya: dead youngsters, sometimes in groups, with horrible wounds. Only Breivik sat calmly, apparently unmoved in his nature as a radical outsider, an alien on planet Earth. Making slow movements, he filled his glass with water from the jug in front of him and held it up to his lips, gazing into the distance, but he pricked up his ears when the experts on forensic medicine described how the lead-tipped bullets had fragmented inside the bodies of the dead before criss-crossing through tissue and bones. It is the functioning of the till that interests him, as the SSBU once observed, not relations or emotions.

The 189 minutes of hell, from the explosion in Grubbegata to the arrest outside the Schoolhouse on Utøya, were turned inside out and relived in detail. The post-mortem reports were illustrated by the forensic experts indicating on a mannequin where the bullets struck.

Some of the young people were shot through their hands when trying to shield their heads. One of the victims had been shot through her open mouth, with the entry wound going through her palate. Perhaps she had been pleading for her life. The survivors told about how loud noises startled them, how they had difficulty sleeping and were trying to adjust to living with the injuries the bomb and Breivik's lead-tipped ammunition had inflicted on them.

'If the number 20 bus stops where the number 26 bus should stop, then I react very badly,' one girl said.

For most Norwegians, those 189 minutes were an interruption to their normal lives, but many of the survivors struggled to return to normality. They had lost that invisible trust that holds up Norwegian society. But, for the rest of Norwegian society, the opposite applied. Trust between people and people's trust in the state, which were already very high in Norway, grew even more. People were roused by the violent events and joined together in rose marches and Facebook campaigns.

'The community we had after 22 July was not a state-organized collective, but a spontaneous civil society,' as Jonas Gahr Støre summarized the response. 'The group feeling that manifested itself in the rose marches and on social media was an expression of social capital.'

Norway was rich in more than oil, and 22 July 2011 became a symbol – not of division or weakness, but of strength and solidarity. At the same time, many people wondered how this community would have reacted if the culprit had been a Muslim from a foreign background: would Norwegians have had enough social capital to avoid conflict and suspicion then?

Arshad was one of those who had moved on since Utøya, even if not entirely without repercussions such as difficulty with sleeping and concentrating. He still thought that 2006 had been worse for him than the period after 22 July 2011. The point of being involved in politics became even clearer, and at university he immersed himself in King Harald Fairhair's journey towards power. The boy from the family of migrants was about to put down roots in Norway as deep as the sword sculptures in the stone at Hafrsfjord. In February 2012 he wrote a piece for *Stavanger Aftenblad* after Arfan Bhatti's demonstration in Oslo in January, when the old thug demanded in front of a handful of people that Norwegian soldiers should be pulled out of Afghanistan 'for the sake of Norway's security'. Arshad felt it was important that extremists should not have a monopoly on defining Islam and Muslims. 'What some of these bearded brothers and veiled sisters have in common is apparently their ability to judge who are devout, practising Muslims, and who are infidels,' Arshad wrote.[2]

Breivik's terrorist acts changed Norway in several ways that were, above all, contrary to his declared intentions. In the months after 22 July 2011, debates about Islam took place mainly between Muslims, in contrast to the previous decade, when Mullah Krekar and the Progress Party politician Carl I. Hagen were often each other's best enemies. It became clear to most people that Fjordman's assertions that Muslims were like orcs might be slightly inaccurate. At Bano Rashid's funeral, her coffin was followed to her grave by both a priest and an imam, while a whole nation watched on.

'This girl, who came to Norway as a refugee, had enough within her to fill Gro's shoes,' Jonas Gahr Støre said in his eulogy in church, 'just as Gro gladly filled hers.'

On television, Muslims discussed one another's views on democracy and religion in the same hot-tempered fashion as other groups in society. A girl with an Algerian surname came forward in the newspaper *VG* as a victim of rape, breaking with the expectations of girls from Muslim and Arab backgrounds. When she later received threats, she infiltrated her critics' Facebook groups and shared their threatening, insulting and bizarre religious statements publicly. 'You deserve to be raped hard, you *murtad* [apostate] trash woman!' was one of the messages she received.

The 'bearded brothers' came under pressure from all sides, and only a handful turned up at Bhatti's demonstration in the snow outside the Storting. The winter of 2012 was quite simply not a good time to be an extremist in Norway. Krekar ended up in prison for making threats, while Fjordman, 'the dark prophet of Norway', lost some of his mystique when he turned out to be quite a normal thirty-six-year-old with curly hair and glasses who wrote letters to the local newspaper. Who was leading the struggle against the extremists? Even the girl with the Algerian surname was affiliated to the AUF and the Labour Party.

The year that followed 22 July 2011 showed that the youth organization was something more than a saccharine, state-subsidized utopia in the Tyrifjord. The old action group stepped into the breach in the battle against extremism and hatred. It seemed as if the Norwegian labour movement was still able to offer a standpoint for the oppressed of the world even in the modern age of migration, while at the same time drawing renewed energy and fresh talent from the growing pains of society. Norway changed in such a way that new groups of Norwegians took a definitive step into the 'new Norwegian we' about which Støre had written. 22 July 2011 is perhaps the one single incident that will be associated with what in reality was the result of 'long-term hard work', to quote Stine Håheim.

During the long days in the courthouse, the portraits of the dead were shown and their eulogies were read out. The same faces had been smiling at the nation from the newspapers ever since 22 July, and their names were read out during the national memorial ceremony at the Oslo Spektrum arena on 22 August 2011, in a television sequence that moved the whole country – faces of typical Norwegians and other happy faces with Caucasian, Arab, Kurdish, African, South-East Asian and Polynesian features. Jens Stoltenberg had the support of over 90 per cent of the population in the weeks after the massacre.

'In a way, it's as if all those who were killed [. . .] represented all of us,' as the widower of the administrative secretary who died in Einar Gerhardsens Plass put it.

The parade of faces with backgrounds from around the world represented today's Norway, just as the names on the memorial stone at Ris had represented Norway in the post-war era. The death announcements reflected the same tendency. One of those killed 'gave his life for his ideals and for democracy in the tragedy on Utøya', as it said in a local newspaper.

At the courthouse, they stood across from each other again, Breivik and Arshad, 'the old and then the new time', as the poet Per Sivle once put it, 'that which would fall, against that which would rise'.[3] Arshad himself represented the new national unification, the forerunner of which he was studying at the University of Oslo. Bano died on the island's Love Path, but perhaps the day was approaching after all when the prime minister of Norway would be a woman in a turban or a man with a Chechen surname.

The Heart of Darkness

There did, however, still remain a fragment of doubt as to where this eruption of hatred had really come from. Something was clearly rotten in the state of Norway. One of 'our own' had attacked us. Some people discussed the destructive effect of computer games, while others thought that extreme right-wing ideologies and anti-Islamic doomsday rhetoric were to blame, that the Internet and social media could radicalize people, turning them into monsters, or that there was a hidden class of hateful male losers in Norway. Were there invisible rifts in Norwegian society that could reopen and spit out the glowing red lava of hate again?

Different psychiatric diagnoses were discussed in court. Breivik's abilities to make thorough plans and handle various practical challenges, his largely quite ordinary political views (for the counter-jihadist community), and his ability to control himself in order to avoid being ridiculed all weighed against his being seriously detached from reality with a form of paranoid schizophrenia. Since very few people could see any psychosis in Breivik, narcissistic personality disorder was the description that most experts endorsed: mad, but not criminally insane.

As I saw him in court while I followed the trial from the benches of Courtroom 250 or via a screen in other rooms in Oslo Courthouse, he was continuously making reassessments and constantly making decisions. He chose his words, he chose his tactics, and he had chosen a strategy that he carried out over ten long weeks. The question of whether people have free will becomes particularly acute in the case of a traumatized and disturbed person such as Breivik. He is clearly damaged, clearly different, but a person who can make judgements, explain himself and adjust his behaviour according to his surroundings does appear to be sane. The doubt to which Husby and Sørheim gave rise with their diagnosis of paranoid schizophrenia was still of such a nature that the prosecution argued, perhaps a little half-heartedly, that he was criminally insane. This meant that the parties were at least able to engage in a process of contradiction, since the defence counsel Lippestad argued that Breivik was criminally sane and (without much hope or enthusiasm) that he should be acquitted.

When the court ruled that Breivik was sane at the moment of the crime, rejecting Husby and Sørheim's evaluations point by point, Norway breathed a sigh of relief. The 22 July Commission's report and the judgement put things in their place and determined where the responsibility lay. It was time to move on. At the same time, the question remained: who was Anders Behring Breivik?

The experts who did not believe that Breivik was psychotic explained his avatar and the PCCTS on the basis of his self-dramatizing personality. 'Pseudologia fantastica', said Terje Tørrissen, going on to refer to a German textbook:

> manifests itself in incredible accounts of major occurrences and particular strokes of bad luck. Only a fraction, at most, of what is included in these accounts has actually taken place. The events described are elaborated in a fantastical style, and the depictions become increasingly dramatized with each repetition. The desired notion is so vivid and suited to confirmation by the personality in question, and eventually so indispensible, that the hysterical individual half believes in it themselves.[4]

A psychologist at Ila Prison suggested that Breivik might have acted out of a motivation of jealousy 'that the Labour Party epitomizes a degree of power and community that [Breivik] desires, and Utøya represents a degree of social belonging in which enthusiastic young people can share their political ideas and passions.'[5] It was not a major surprise that Breivik rejected this. Even though he was not schizophrenic, he could have other kinds of congenital mental disorder: was his smile perhaps a tic?

Just like one of Breivik's former tagging colleagues, Professor Ulrik Fredrik Malt, an expert in psychiatry, also speculated about whether a general developmental disorder, Asperger's syndrome, might explain parts of his story. Asperger's syndrome (a high-functioning form of autism) is a developmental disorder that begins to manifest itself at the age of two or three – in other words, at the time Breivik's mother was complaining about his unpredictable, hyperactive and aggressive behaviour. People with Asperger's syndrome are mentally reproductive but not reflective, which might explain the compendium's cut-and-paste feel. His slightly peculiar language, characterized by repetition and frequent quantifying of everything in percentages, his aptitude for logistics, his monomaniacal interest in certain topics (such as bomb recipes and orders of Templar knights) and compensating conformism: Malt related all these things to developmental disorders – in other words, genetically determined disturbance of the mind.

Malt also thought that there might be a connection between Asperger's syndrome and Breivik's puzzling, possibly unique ability to kill mechanically. But, even though Breivik exhibited these traits, his friends and the SSBU concluded that he had 'contact abilities'. Even Malt did not try to determine where Breivik's hatred came from: people with Asperger's syndrome have no documented inclination to kill and are, on the contrary, generally very moral people.

The white flash of the explosion was followed by a cloud of smoke. At times, the trial fumbled through a haze, as if the smoke were still hanging over the centre of Oslo. When I walked home through Marienlystparken during the afternoon of 22 July 2011, before it was known who was responsible for the bomb, I assumed that it was a political attack that had struck my city. I later wrote in *Aftenposten* about Occidentalism, online radicalization and the danger of 'monsters from the blogosphere'.[6] In September 2011, in my application to Fritt Ord [the Freedom of Expression Foundation], I described this book project as starting from the assertion 'that the disaster was not only the result of an individual's mental illness (as the former editor of *The Times*, Simon Jenkins, had claimed in

The Guardian), but also an expression of a reaction to globalization and modernity'.

In my effort to work out 22 July 2011, I headed in several directions. I have been charting human rights violations and war crimes abroad for almost twenty years and have spoken with many refugees, survivors and eyewitnesses to serious crimes. Even though the Norwegian victims saw the criminal arrested and put in prison – criminals elsewhere have been appointed president – I encountered the same rigid expressions, drifting gazes and dark powerlessness in the survivors of Utøya as I had previously seen in the Balkans and the Caucasus. Their anger leaked out and looked for accomplices in the massacre of their friends. The Labour Party were the 'victors' of the twentieth century, to cite the Norwegian author Roy Jacobsen. The multicultural Utøya generation are the victors of the twenty-first century. But the victors carry a burden of sorrow and anger which may not yet have been fully declared.

I interviewed former taggers and people who were young lads in the West End of Oslo during the nineties to get closer to Breivik's adolescence. It was not easy. The same haze descended over the West End as soon as Breivik's name was mentioned; people did not want to talk about him or to be connected to the case. *Omertà* at Ris: the manor house locked its doors, but some people did talk. Some witnesses were able to tell me about Breivik's childhood and family. At the same time, I immersed myself in his compendium. This peculiar mammoth of a text was the very key to my work. I read it several times. I eventually realized that the compendium really made sense only if read as a response to experiences and conflicts in his own life, especially in his childhood. 1,300 years of conflict between the West and Islam emerged as a cover story, and the trial confirmed this impression. Breivik fumbled and appeared unenthusiastic when accounting for the political and historical sides of his project but came around as soon as there was talk of terrorism. His radicalization emerged as a manifestation of his pseudologia fantastica: accounts of fictional confrontations with Muslims mixed with merely trivial incidents. His childhood, on the other hand, was not something he wanted to talk about.

There are many people with whom I would have liked to speak but have not met. There are many police interviews, records and case papers to which I would have liked to have had access. All the same, when I eventually read the reports by the two teams of court-appointed psychiatrists in their uncensored versions, they answered many of the questions I was left with after reading the compendium and studying Breivik's 189-minute-long killing orgy. If the fundamental story in the compendium concerns constructing an avatar to bring back an absent father and dispose of mothers for good, why was it essential to control women's sexuality and bodies? And why did Breivik assert in Oslo District Court that 'the media and the prosecution [. . .] have claimed that I have an incestuous relationship with my own mother',[7] when no such claims had been made?

A person is not an island. It is impossible to write the story of a person without including the individual's immediate family. The problem with trying to explain Breivik's hatred is that the explanation inevitably has to touch on the deficit of care to which he was subjected in his early childhood. 'Irrespective of the eventual formal diagnoses, formal diagnostics will be insufficient to understand ABB and his actions on 22/07,' Professor Malt wrote in a memo to the defence counsel in June 2012. 'An understanding requires the addition of a psychiatric-psychological analysis stressing his upbringing and family relationships.' Breivik's mother did not want this story to be known. The question is whether her wish to protect her private life weighed more heavily than the public interest in understanding what formed Anders Behring Breivik. The media has been cautious in this regard, even though the newspaper *VG* published the psychiatrists' reports in almost complete versions, censoring only a few pages that they thought went too far into the private sphere of Breivik's family, primarily concerning his mother. NRK published an article in November 2011 saying that former neighbours from Silkestrå thought that he had been exposed to experiences of a sexual nature.[8] The article went on to say that 'two independent sources have confirmed to NRK that the psychological report suggested abuse of a sexual nature' towards Breivik when he was a little boy. But no more was heard of this shocking information.

Norwegian news desks probably felt that the story of child abuse depicted in the censored pages is not significant enough in the court case for its publication to be justified. Furthermore, some of the details are so extraordinary and unusual that it is a journalistic challenge to describe them without appearing sensationalist. As a result, even after seventy-seven funerals, the details of Breivik's deficit of care and the mental problems that affected his childhood are still unmentioned. In a way it is commendable that the Norwegian media protects individuals, even in the most extreme cases. At the same time, it can be queried whether the media is working as it should in the interests of the public if this information is central to the case. Shedding light on this story is not really a matter of exposing Breivik's mother to criticism, but of asking why she did not receive help when she asked for it.

In the material the media (specifically the *VG* website) published, there were descriptions and conclusions about the deficit of care to which the SSBU believed Breivik had been subjected, as well as references to his maternal grandmother's mental illness. The censored parts of the report concerned his mother's medical history and the evaluation of her as well as descriptions of how she harassed the young boy – in other words, a detailed depiction of the deficit of care. Hundreds of policemen, reporters, lawyers, bereaved family members and people directly affected have access to this information. People whisper in Oslo Courthouse and at late nights in town. Perhaps it is a classic West End story: blacked-out family secrets living their own lives and growing into a monster of rumours and theories. Perhaps the 'truth', as it appears in the SSBU's records, is less spectacular than the speculations fed by silence.

The publication of the report by the first team of psychiatrists had consequences. The criticism of the report contributed to another team of psychiatrists being appointed, which was a good example of Stoltenberg's wish for openness meaning that public discourse could indirectly become part of the legal process, as well as of the attempt to understand what had happened. Without the public debate, there would probably have been only one psychiatric report, and Breivik would have been found criminally insane.

As the trial progressed, it had little to do with 'a psychiatric-psychological analysis' of Breivik. It was only the question of sanity that was of direct significance to the criminal proceedings, and Breivik and his mother did not give their consent for access to the confidential SSBU material. Witnesses from the SSBU were called, but none were heard in court. Furthermore, the four forensic psychiatrists did not even read the whole compendium, with even the otherwise very scrupulous Aspaas and Tørrissen relying on the PST's quite telegraphic summary of the document that had been Breivik's great passion over the past few years. As a result, the judgement on 24 August 2012 said little about where the hatred stemmed from, even if it indicated that the unclear distance between mother and son did not necessarily constitute an expression of psychosis, as Husby and Sørheim claimed, but could be a feature of their relationship. Perhaps it is easier to address this problem in the context of a book in which the deficit of care is part of a larger story or analysis, and so an author's evaluation differs from that of a news editor. The decisive difference is perhaps mainly that I believe there are traces of Breivik's childhood trauma in the compendium and therefore also in his crimes.

22 July 2011 was a tragedy of such proportions that it takes a lot to remain silent when you are in possession of information shedding

light on the case. It is difficult to live with uncertainty and conjecture about a case that is being discussed around the world, which shook Norway and which directly affects so many people and families. Many of the parents who are left without children, and some of the children who will grow up without parents, want or will want to know why they were targeted. I believe that the elements of the deficit of care to which Breivik was subjected in his first years (if not every single detail) do belong in any serious attempt to explain why things happened the way they did. That is why I have chosen to describe and to quote some of the material that is not generally known and which concerns Breivik's relationship with his mother and her background. This entails entering the private sphere of Breivik and his immediate family, but I believe some of this information is so important that the picture of the case is incomplete if it is left out. I believe there is a justified need for information about Breivik's childhood. I have, however, omitted or altered information describing indirect relatives or third parties, as this is less important for the case at hand.

Many people are subjected to a deficit of care, and few of them become mass murderers. There is no psychological determinism meaning that Breivik's background had to lead him to Utøya, but when his story is plotted back in time with the evidence to hand of how it ended, and especially if the compendium is used as a key, you end up in his early childhood. It will take a long time to establish a complete explanatory hierarchy in which the various circumstances that made Breivik into a terrorist are accounted for and the key factors highlighted. This book is merely a contribution to that process. Explaining Breivik does not mean defending him. Denouncing him as a monster is a natural reaction, and many people want to forget him and move on, but understanding is important, not only to offer answers to the victims. Knowledge can mean that society learns from the tragedy, while at the same time preventing a moral panic from gaining ground and accusations or aggression being misdirected.

The censored extracts from the SSBU dossier on the Behring Breivik family indicate that Breivik was subjected to a far-reaching deficit of care. He was seriously mistreated, and this appears to be linked to some of the darkest themes of the compendium.

The SSBU carried out reports on children with a view to improving the situation of the children and of their families. Would things have gone differently if child welfare or the court had listened to their recommendations and placed Breivik in a foster home when he was four years old? Or with his father and Tove? His attachment disorder would probably have had consequences anyway, one member of the SSBU team thought, while his colleague answered that things would probably have gone better for the boy. The question is compelling, even if it cannot be answered.

The SSBU's sources were first and foremost their own observations, followed by information from the mother and from the family welfare centre in Christies Gate, including information from the respite care family and concerned neighbours at Silkestrå. The SSBU described the mother as 'a woman with an extremely challenging upbringing [. . .] a borderline personality structure and extensive if partly negative depression'. In their descriptions, it appears as if the mother made a deep impression on the observation team, who occasionally used terms to describe her that do not appear to have a professional basis, such as 'primitive'.

What is most striking about her treatment of the four-year-old Anders, based on the extracts from the SSBU case papers, is how she sexualized him and told him that she wished he were dead. In the case summary, the mother is described as 'confused' and 'uncritical', in actuality a woman with an unsound grasp of reality and everyday life:

> While in the unit [at SSBU], she spoke somewhat uncritically about sexualized and aggressive fantasies and fears and exhibited a very ambivalent attitude towards the male staff. During her stay, she composed herself and became considerably calmer. Psychological testing of the mother (Rorschach) indicates a woman living in her own inner, private world with poorly developed relationships to fellow human beings. She is highly anxiety-ridden in her close relationships and emotionally affected by negative depression. She is threatened by chaotic conflicts and shows signs of illogical thought in pressured situations. She has a borderline disposition as a woman who functions very unpredictably. Given structured external circumstances in life, she can function well, but she becomes very vulnerable in crises.

The background to Breivik's mother contacting the family advice centre was that her problems had been piling up during 1982 in connection with the move to Nedre Silkestrå. She had made some scattered attempts to work after she had become single, but had given up, and in their small flat it became too much for her to cope with the children as well as her own needs. The SSBU did not link her problems primarily to stress in connection with the move or to long-term post-natal depression, but to 'the highly pathological [abnormal] relationship between Anders and his mother'.

> A large part of the reason that the mother has had increasing difficulties over the past few years is connected to her extremely unusual

> relationship with Anders. She projects her primitive aggressive and sexualized fantasies onto him, everything that she perceives as dangerous and aggressive in men. Her daily interaction with him is characterized to a great degree by double communication; on the one hand she is symbiotic, while at the same time rejecting him with her body language and can suddenly shift between speaking with him in an overly sweet manner and openly expressing death wishes.

So, according to the SSBU, Anders was a 'victim of his mother's projections of paranoid aggressive and sexualized fear of men in general'. Of course, it is impossible to establish any entirely clear connections, but perhaps there is an echo of his mother's 'aggressive and sexualized fantasies', into which Anders was unwillingly drawn, in his own sadistic notions and behaviour. The double communication between them also had a physical side. 'Symbiotic' was how the SSBU characterized their relationship. It was as if mother and son were one body: 'In the period since they became alone, Anders has slept in his mother's bed at night with close bodily contact. His mother has made small, sporadic attempts to end this, but perhaps she does not really want to.'

Unclear distance, rejection one moment and intimacy the next. This feature of their relationship did perhaps continue in a certain form later in life. The joke gift Breivik gave his mother in 2004, when she and her partner broke up, was allegedly a vibrator.[9] After Anders moved home in 2006, his mother complained that he either would not want to come out of his room or would sit right up next to her on the sofa, once kissing her.

Psychiatric definitions of child sexual abuse often focus on the culprit drawing the child into acts or ideas in order to get sexual gratification. Other definitions are broader, focusing more on the child's experience of being unwillingly sexualized. The Norwegian Penal Code's focus on the molester's own satisfaction and concrete sexual acts does not quite fit into the picture painted by the SSBU, even though they referred to an incident when his mother allegedly asked Anders to perform a sexual act on a person from outside the family.

The SSBU did not really describe a woman using her child to seek sexual satisfaction, but instead a disturbed and depressed woman incapable of setting boundaries between fantasy and reality or between herself and her son. Children who have been subjected to sexual abuse are generally at a higher risk of developing psychiatric illnesses, and, if the abuser is the mother, there is an increased chance of being damaged. 'When the mother performs the abuse, it appears to cause more damage,' write the psychiatrists Grøholt, Sommerschild and Garløv. 'This is probably because children are, as a rule, more dependent on women, and because female abusers as a group are more psychiatrically disturbed. They are often infantile with extreme dependency needs and are frequently alcoholics. A mother's abuse of her child might entail embraces with sexual overtones or intense body contact, but it might also include genital manipulation or mutual masturbation.'[10] There does not appear to be anything in the SSBU material resembling concrete abuse of that nature, but Breivik was without doubt subjected by his mother to an invasive and confusing sexualization. She held the four-year-old tightly at night and, during the day, accused him of being a threat towards his sister. According to police interviews, neighbours at Silkestrå were also concerned that the mother's sexualized language and ideas were being transferred to her children, that she did not always take care of Anders, and that there was noise in the flat that sounded like sexual activity while the children were at home.

It is difficult not to see some connection here too between the SSBU's description and Breivik's attack in his compendium on his mother's sexual morality, which had brought shame on him. His wish to control female sexuality and the female body, as well as replacing mothers with artificial wombs, may have to do less with his career as a loser on the sexual market and more with traumatic experiences from his childhood of being unwillingly sexualized by his only caregiver. Perhaps the problem was not his lack of access to the female body in adolescence or later but his experience of having been invaded by it as a child.

In the early eighties, attention to child sexual abuse and views on incest were of a different nature from today. There was less focus on this in society and less knowledge among academics. In spite of their great professional expertise and modern focus on the child, the SSBU had no methods for charting sexual abuse or procedures for alerting the police when violations of the law in this regard were suspected. 'We had no idea, and we didn't think about it like that,' said a former SSBU employee who participated in the report on the Behring Breivik family.

It was only in later years that the SSBU seriously began to focus on this field and that psychiatry began to have an idea of the consequences of sexual abuse. The connection between childhood abuse and personality pathology, as pointed out by Karterud, Wilberg and Urnes, is especially pronounced in connection with sexual abuse. Mentalizing ability (in other words, the ability to think about oneself and others) can be impaired, leading to an 'estranged self-experience', a kind of splitting of the self, in which 'there is an attempt to cast loose [negative] experiences, so that they can live their own lives as disturbing and frightening presences in the psyche. [. . .] With an estranged self-experience that is burdened with destructiveness and cruelty, there can also be an attempt to externalize it through projective identification. [. . .] This entails the individual trying to find somebody else to bear the burden of the cruelty for them.'[11] The term 'projective identification' is related to Ronald Holmes and Stephen Holmes' research on serial killers and the 'power-control' behaviour they described: violence against others becomes a method of alleviating the person's own feelings of shame and self-contempt.

According to the SSBU's case history – the mother's own account of her medical record – she wanted an abortion when she was pregnant with Anders because of problems in her marriage, but she could not make up her mind to apply before the time limit was up. During her pregnancy, she already 'perceived Anders as a difficult child who was restless and kicked her, almost deliberately. [. . .] Jens was present [at the birth], which she felt was unpleasant and loathsome. "Anders was hers!" [. . .] She breastfed the child for ten months, before stopping because she felt that his sucking was so strong and aggressive that it was destroying her.'

Anders was a normal child in terms of his motor and linguistic development, but after they moved back to Oslo his mother thought he became 'very demanding. [She] lived/lives in constant anxiety about what bad deeds he might get up to, both alone and with regard to his sister.' It seems strange that a mother should be afraid of what a two-year-old boy might do to his eight-year-old big sister, but she consistently expressed herself with little sense of proportion. It seems as if, in a way, she saw the boy as a grown man with sinister intentions. Thirty years later, this fantasy would become reality, but there is little to suggest that Anders had always been as difficult and aggressive as his mother described him. The mother's fantasies and reality seemed to run into each other, her mentalizing ability had apparently collapsed, and she occasionally described the little boy as a kind of manipulative and invulnerable villain.

Indeed it was also clear to the SSBU that she did not have control of her wandering little boy. 'Anders' reaction to his mother's relatively ambivalent attempts to set boundaries is to smirk and laugh,' the SSBU wrote. 'His mother says that "he just tip-toes around and smirks slyly". When she smacks him, he says: "It doesn't hurt, it doesn't hurt."' Breivik's unusual smile was clearly something else to which his mother reacted negatively. The fact that he said it did not hurt when she hit him could be a reaction of defiance, but it could also be true. At his nursery school, they were concerned that Anders did not cry or show any signs of pain even when he fell down hard. This could suggest that Breivik had a form of analgesia, an absence of the ability to feel pain. This condition, or its symptoms, is normal among traumatized children, especially among those who have been subjected to physical abuse.

To the caseworker at the social care office, Anders' mother said that she wanted 'to get rid' of him. It is a little unclear as to whether that meant she wanted him to be adopted or whether she meant he should disappear in another way. She told the SSBU that she felt 'like peeling him off me'. The mother's view of a boy who 'kicked her' before he was born, 'destroyed her' as a breastfeeding baby and grew up to be 'aggressive', 'hyperactive' and 'clingy' seems to have been accompanied by a pattern of declared wishes to have an abortion, 'to get rid' of the boy and to 'peel him off', as well as expressions of 'death wishes'. The little boy would have heard at least some of this.

If empathy is developed by imagining what our primary care-giver feels and thinks, as attachment theory claims, and if it is correct that children will not develop empathy or an understanding of others if they are not safe to imagine what their care-giver thinks or feels, perhaps it is not so puzzling that all the psychiatric experts thought Breivik was characterized by a total lack of empathy. Since his only care-giver said that she wanted him dead, neither is it perhaps strange that his adult perception of himself is as a zombie, one of the living dead, or that his great project is a kind of masked suicide attempt in the form of a spectacular act of terrorism.

The abuse to which Anders was subjected by the only care-giver he had, in the critical attachment phase during the second and third years of his life, was of an emotional nature and also contained a sexual component. Even if the SSBU mentioned that Anders was 'smacked' and repeatedly used the word 'aggressive' about his mother, and even if some of the details about Breivik might suggest that he had analgesia, it is not possible to conclude that he was also abused physically. Analgesia can have other causes, and in the material to which I have had access there are no grounds to suggest that Breivik was subjected to physical abuse. It could be expected that the nursery and child welfare, which were following the case after all, would notice if that had been happening, but of course it is only a morsel of Breivik's childhood that emerges in the documents from the SSBU and child welfare. Probably nobody will ever tell what really went on behind the walls in Fritzners Gate and at Silkestrå in the early eighties. It was difficult to work out even at the time.

One of the mysteries is how differently the SSBU assessed the case compared to child welfare, who perceived the problems as situational. It could be envisaged that the SSBU might have seen a distorted image of the family and let their assessment be influenced by their experience of poor co-operation with the mother, who had 'a very ambivalent attitude to the male staff'. It could be imagined that they saw the family when they were at rock-bottom, and that the situation at home was different and better than in the unfamiliar SSBU premises at Gaustad. Still, there are a number of reasons to opt for the SSBU version.

The observation was carried out over time (for three weeks) and not based on three short home visits and some office consultations with the mother (which was the sum total of child welfare's oversight of the case during the period from the custody trial in October 1983 until they shelved the case in June 1984). The SSBU observation was carried out by a team of eight specialists, while child welfare based their report on the impressions of a home visitor from the social care office at Vika. The SSBU had access to quite a wide range of material when making their evaluation and reviewed the family's situation and background a lot more thoroughly than the home visitor's slightly superficial description of a 'harmonious' family with a 'calm' mother, a 'well-mannered' daughter and a 'pleasant, relaxed' son. In a way, the family depended on putting up a strong façade, as there was no internal framework to keep them together, and perhaps the façade was so well tended that it convinced not only child welfare but often the mother herself too. Some of the neighbours at Silkestrå, on the other hand, shared the SSBU's views of the family and their concerns.

Behind the SSBU's alarm call is the mother's own 'extremely challenging upbringing', which they believed was now having consequences for her son, in line with the theory about attachment disorders as a kind of psychiatric ancestral sin. The SSBU ostensibly based their description of the mother's upbringing on information she provided herself. Since she often appears imprecise, perhaps we should be cautious in believing all the details of her case history. Maybe she also felt a need to construct her past, in a similar fashion to her dramatizing son. But the key points were emotional and physical abuse, bullying, a father who died early and an extremely difficult relationship with a mother afflicted by polio, who apparently fell ill while she was pregnant, blamed Breivik's mother for her physical disability and was controlling, spiteful and jealous of her daughter.

She describes her relationship with her mother as a version of the tale of Snow White. The evil queen became jealous of Snow White as she grew up and entered puberty. Wenche 'never had the feeling of belonging to a family', according to the SSBU report. The story of Breivik's mother appears to reflect that of her own mother. Just as Breivik's mother broke away from her family and fled from Kragerø to Oslo when seventeen years old, her own mother had travelled in the opposite direction many years earlier. Apart from her relationship with her father, her association with men was very difficult. A man in her life allegedly abused her physically, while another 'forced himself on her'.

Keeping up their façade was important, and there were many family secrets that Breivik's mother came to learn only later, including that she herself had spent a couple of years in a children's home and that there were half-siblings in her family at a time when decent people did not get divorced or have children outside marriage. 'The family [in Kragerø] bore traces of mystification and downward social mobility,' the SSBU wrote. 'As a result of this, she developed defective abilities in contact and attachment.' 'Mystification' was the SSBU's word for suppressed secrets. Breivik's mother broke off contact with her mother, who towards the end of her life developed 'paranoia and hallucinations'.

Mystification, maintaining a façade and downward social mobility are terms that could also describe the small family in Hoffsveien after 2006. Themes are repeated in the family across decades and over generations. How many generations back in time have poor attachment patterns persisted? To what extent is this generational transmission of trauma and mental illness due to genetic factors or to a repetition of poor attachment patterns?[12]

The SSBU saw this as an important case and recommended that Anders should be taken into care. Perhaps those in the SSBU were ahead of their time; perhaps they were regarded by other state agencies as a group of left-wing windbags. Both child welfare and the court ignored the SSBU's repeated warnings, notes of concern and reports. The judge asked for another review to be carried out, postponing the clearly difficult case. Child welfare concluded that the family's home situation had changed and closed the case just half a year after the SSBU's last letter on the matter. This could certainly not be called technocracy if the professionals' views were disregarded time after time.

The presumption of maternal custody, and what we now call the biological principle, apparently overrode the professionals' evaluation. Consideration of the family's unity, the belief that the mother has a particular significance for the child, and perhaps the notion that a mother could not commit abuse weighed more heavily than attachment theory and the SSBU's passionate report and dramatic conclusions. In most people's eyes, Breivik's mother appeared strange and pitiful, but, of the witnesses in Oslo District Court in 2012, it was only Breivik's best friend who saw her as a directly negative influence in connection with what he thought was Anders' depression, and it was only the SSBU who described her as dangerous. This was a 'very important case', the SSBU insisted, but this fell on deaf ears. Anders stayed with his mother. The family was more important than the child. Mothers want only what is best for their children. Wenche Behring certainly wanted the same for her children, but could she manage?

The Lost Child

'The hand that rocks the cradle is the hand that rules the world,' Breivik told Husby and Sørheim in a conversation at Ila Prison, illustrating his world of thought and his most important concern.[13] Husby and Sørheim asked him to comment on the SSBU papers and the custody case. Breivik apparently had no memory of his earliest years but still ascertained that 'it would have been best if my father and step-mother had won' the case.[14]

> The subject then begins a long discussion concerning potential changes to the law in terms of 'parenting rights. My mother is not intellectually capable,' he says. 'She is average, and against Islamization. But women do not understand codes of honour, and 90 per cent of them are emotionally unstable. That's why we support a change in the law so that fathers will automatically be given parenting rights,' he says. 'The hand that rocks the cradle is the hand that rules the world. It will reduce the divorce rate.'
>
> The psychiatrists ask the subject to explain further. 'I detest Marxism for my own parents' divorce and for matriarchy. That's why women's role should be in the home. [. . .] They should not be allowed to divorce, and fathers should have parenting rights.'[15]

It is typical of Breivik how he projected his individual experience to apply to the whole world. His mother was 'emotionally unstable', so it followed that all women, or at least 90 per cent of them (perhaps the former salesman cut off 10 per cent so as not to offend Sørheim), were 'emotionally unstable' and did 'not understand codes of honour'. The opposite of honour is shame, and for Breivik women were linked to shame. He was unable to distinguish between his own inner world and the external world, between his own, possibly forgotten, trauma and the varied and nuanced landscape that is society. Everything was equal, and nothing existed outside his own mind.

The compendium appeared as an adaptation of his own upbringing, with personal trauma and experiences blown up to an enormous scale, projected onto a broad canvas of civilization and finding their historical solutions through the intervention of his avatar, which reflected the isolated world of his thoughts. Superficially, the compendium appears to be a political text, and perhaps Breivik saw it as such, but it was also an expression of an intense focus on the brutal, boundary-transgressing and frightening experiences to which he had been subjected as a child.

The final volume in Johan Borgen's trilogy of novels about Wilfred 'Little Lord' Sagen is entitled *Vi har ham nå!* [We've got him now!]. The bombastic title is, on one level, a warning against believing that it is possible to define and understand a person entirely. The Little Lord defies simple categorizations or analyses, and so does Anders Behring Breivik, as was demonstrated during the trial by the confusion of the two forensic psychiatric reports. Still, there are some perspectives on Breivik's hatred and rage that appear more fruitful than others. Perhaps the hatred that hung over the city that Friday afternoon did not stem mainly from online aggression and doomsday notions, from violent computer games, the structural violence of consumer culture, class angst in the West End of Oslo, the gang culture of the nineties, friction in a multicultural society or a male feeling of frustration in the vaginal state. I believe that the dark impulse came from his childhood, not from counter-jihadism.

Through my work on this book I have moved away from seeing 22 July 2011 as a reflection of a greater 'reaction to globalization and modernity' and far in the direction towards seeing the acts of terrorism that day as the outcome of a deficit of family care, the intergenerational transferral of poor attachment patterns and a resultant individual mental illness. I no longer believe that Breivik's radicalization, his hatred, was due mainly to mass suggestion or to the ideological greenhouse effect of the counter-jihadist online community. That does not mean that the terrorist attacks were not a political act, or that we do not all have a responsibility as citizens to react against extremist remarks and acts in our own society. Mental illness and politics have been closely linked to each other from Caligula to Hitler. Breivik used his extreme right-wing ideas of an ongoing civil war, in which the Muslims were the enemy and the elites were traitors, primarily to justify his bloody vision and deeds. He probably felt part of a collective as he sat by his screen, constructing his avatar.

During the trial, it became clear that Breivik was capable of adapting his avatar to quite a significant degree. This shows that he was sensitive to influence from others, so it is easy to imagine that he was equally keen to find support and a firm foundation when he was constructing his avatar too, and that the fervour of politicians about the dangers of multiculturalism and 'sneaking Islamization' strengthened his belief that he was about to create a 'masterpiece'. As the blogger Bjørn Stærk articulated it the week after the attacks: 'There are many of us now who have thought long and hard over the past few days about whether anything we might have written about Islam or immigration might have made the terrorist feel less alone while he sat there for years, planning this evil deed. The honest answer: probably.'[16] In his New Year speech, Prime Minister Stoltenberg urged people to be 'digital watchdogs' in order to counteract the growth of online hatred and aggressive subcultures.[17] The AUF girl with an Algerian background who infiltrated the Muslim extremist groups on Facebook embodied the new public spirit.

At the same time, there is an old adage among online debaters: 'Don't feed the troll.' Trying to argue against hateful outbursts by replying online or in readers' comments sections is not always productive. If you give the online trolls your attention, they only get angrier. The counter-jihadists are close to a genre in which exaggeration is key: the genre of tirades. A rapper in a dissing battle might tell his adversary that he plans to shove fifty baseball bats up his backside without necessarily meaning it literally. Even if they are not meant to be comical, exaggerations are an important part of anti-Islamic tirades too; on Document.no, Breivik wrote that the branding of 'cultural conservatives' was 'just as bad as the persecution of the Jews in the thirties or during the Inquisition'.

When Fjordman writes that there is a civil war, that Europeans have the right to defend themselves and should consider procuring weapons, the impression comes across that the statement might have more to do with creating a mood of elevated and epic gravity than being an actual declaration of war. But, even if for most people Occidentalism is a matter of sticking their tongues out and saying a heartfelt 'Bleah!' to the elites, the *Zeitgeist* and society in general, it is from this field that political violence has come to Norway in the years since the Second World War. Unfortunately, it is not a bold prediction to say that Norway has probably not heard the last of the occidentalist tradition.

In my opinion, however, the most important lesson from this tragedy is not about integration policy, the Internet, ideology or the police's operating methods and resources, in spite of the harsh and far-reaching criticism of the police by the 22 July Commission. It is about child and family welfare policy.

The 22 July Commission concluded that the 'perpetrator could have been stopped earlier on 22 July'.[18] But could Breivik have been stopped before that fateful day? Yes, maybe he could. Not by the police security agency, the PST, who acquitted themselves in their own comprehensive evaluation of the case, even though they were also criticized by the 22 July Commission for not following up tip-offs on Breivik. But perhaps child welfare could have intervened in the years 1983–4. The banality of evil in the case of Breivik is the significance of childhood trauma in the hatred of a grown man. Countering hatred, radicalization and terrorism is also a matter of preventing children from being abused by their parents – a banal insight, perhaps, possibly so banal that it has been overlooked. The wide-ranging report by the 22 July Commission did not look into this: 'We have foregone issues related to the perpetrator's motive, childhood and state of health, and we have not explored the measures society puts in place for the early prevention of radicalisation.'[19]

Nevertheless, this is an important matter for debate, not least in this case. The question of where the boundary lies between the state and the family, and how society can best protect children growing up in broken homes is also just as topical now as it was in 1983.

In the summer of 2012, the Ministry of Children, Equality and Social Inclusion published the report 'Bedre beskyttelse av barns utvikling' [Better protection of children's development]. The official report summarizes the massive consequences of deficit of care (defined as physical abuse, sexual abuse, emotional torment and neglect). Research indicates that a deficit of care causes extensive damage to the brain and nervous system and a series of lifelong psychological problems such as aggression, anxiety and a lack of social skills. 'An American study demonstrates that traumatic experiences from childhood through adult life cost society as much as HIV and cancer put together, but that the ratio of resources allocated is 1:100. [. . . C]hildhood trauma is perhaps the greatest health problem of our times, and probably the main cause of mental problems while growing up and in adulthood.'[20]

Attachment theory and neurological research are changing our views of the family. The most important thing for children is to have a good basis for attachment. Whether the care-giver is a biological parent or not, man or woman, homosexual or heterosexual, is less relevant. The report investigated how the biological principle is administered by child welfare and concluded that child welfare may have too high a threshold for presenting cases to put children into care. The biological principle still weighs heavily, the committee thought, meaning that the child's interests are perhaps not always seen as the most crucial element in difficult cases.

The committee therefore recommended introducing a new principle, defined as 'the principle of developmentally beneficial attachment', which should contribute to governing the work of child welfare and ensuring that children are not left in intolerable situations just because their tormentors are members of their family. 'The principle of developmentally beneficial attachment' might not exactly be a catchy term, but it can have major consequences. If this principle is added to the Children Act, it will be applied when assessing whether to place children into care.

> The committee recommends that the threshold for taking children into care be assessed according to the following three factors:
> a. whether or not the quality of attachment and relationships between the care-givers and the child supports the child's development;
> b. how serious and stable the deficit of care is (omission of care, failure to undergo therapy or instruction, maltreatment or abuse);
> c. whether the care-giver's personal traits (mental impairment, mental illness, intoxication) are of a long- or short-term nature.[21]

In Anders Behring Breivik's case, there is little doubt that, if 'the principle of developmentally beneficial attachment' and the method of assessment based on it had been in use in the early eighties, this would have meant that child welfare had to support putting him in care, in line with the SSBU's recommendation.

With the evidence to hand of how it all ended, it is easy to feel indignant towards child welfare and the court. How could they let the little boy stay with his poor, sick mother?! Why did she not receive help when she asked for it? It is important to remember that it was a different time. Views of mental illnesses and abuse in the family were different. Gro Harlem Brundtland had just become Norway's first female prime minister a few short months earlier, but the long-term hard work needed to redefine gender roles – so that men could also be care-givers in the family and women could also be leaders in public life – was far from complete.

Nevertheless, the system did realize that Breivik was at risk of ending up as an outsider. Owing to the judgement of individuals leaning on judicial precedent and contemporary views of the family, the state let go of him again. Doors were still open for Breivik. Another life was possible. One by one, those doors were locked. He did not want to conform, or was unable to do so. He was unable to ask for help either. 'Nothing worked out for him,' as his mother said. He turned thirty. As he hardly had a life at all, he had nothing to lose. Finally he decided to construct a grotesque avatar and take the route to Utøya.

Today, Anders Behring Breivik is sitting in his cell, convicted, isolated and under guard. He may never get out, but paradoxically he may nevertheless be in a better situation now than he was before 22 July 2011. He was isolated then too, and was laughed at when he went out on the town. Now he has become famous and exchanges letters with like-minded people and admirers from across the world. In that regard, his operation was a success, as he claimed, like other Herostratic crimes: politically counter-productive, but on a deeper, darker and personal level a success just the same. While the zombie has acquired some kind of life, the bereaved will never see their dead children, brothers, sisters, partners or parents again. Many of the survivors will be forever affected by the catastrophe. There is no justice in this.

No punishment in the world would have been proportionate to the harm Breivik caused, but perhaps what constitutes the strength of Norwegian society has become clearer. Over the course of the year I have been working on this book, I have spoken with many people. One quotation in particular stays with me, to do with trust.

'Maybe we have been naïve,' Allan Søndergaard Jensen said. 'But it's not wrong to see the best in people.'

The 'Morg' tag on Kirkeveien in Oslo

If I had looked left up the street in Kirkeveien while I was on my way home on the afternoon of 22 July, wondering who had attacked my city, I would have seen an old, almost completely faded piece of graffiti beneath a window with a mesh grating in front. If I had gone closer, I would have been able to make out the large, unattractive and irregular letters. At the foot of the ochre-painted block of flats facing out towards Kirkeveien and the number 20 bus, there was the tag in thick black ink: 'Morg'.

Sometimes the solution is closer than you think, and the warnings are written on the wall where nobody notices them. A hesitant smile, narrow eyes beneath his light-coloured fringe: it was the guy who used to write 'Morg'.

Notes

All translated quotations from non-English-language texts are the translator's own, unless indicated otherwise. Quotations from Breivik's compendium are reproduced as in the original English text, although some minor changes have been made to punctuation and capitalization.

Chapter 1 The Explosion

1 These comments were made on a blog post by Edward S. May (Baron Bodissey), 'Terror Attack in Central Oslo', *Gates of Vienna*, 22 July 2011, http://gatesofvienna.blogspot.co.uk/2011/07/terror-attack-in-central-oslo.html, cited in Øyvind Strømmen, *Det mørke nettet* [The Dark Net] (Oslo: Cappelen Damm, 2011), p. 17.

Chapter 2 Bacardi Razz

1 Torgeir P. Krokfjord, Anders Holth Johansen, Sindre Granly Meldalen and Frode Hansen, 'Breivik festet på kjendisbar natta før massemordet' [Breivik partied at celebrity bar the night before the mass murder], *Dagbladet*, 19 August 2011, www.dagbladet.no/2011/08/19/nyheter/anders_behring_breivik/innenriks/terror/terrorangrepet/17724429/. According to one of the *Dagbladet* journalists who worked on the story, their source later told them that Breivik had not been at Skaugum the evening before, as the article states, but another day that week.

2 Breivik's entries on the forum of the Progress Party youth wing (Fremskrittspartiets Ungdom; FPU) were to be found online but have since been removed: http://fpu.no/2011/08/anders-behring-breiviks-debattinnlegg/.
3 Torgeir Husby and Synne Sørheim, 'Rettspsykriatisk erklæring' [Forensic psychiatric report], 29 November 2011 (the first psychiatric report), reproduced by *VG*: www.vg.no/nyheter/innenriks/22-juli/psykiatrisk_vurdering/, pp. 36, 38, 105–6.
4 See note 1 above. The depiction of Breivik is based on Husby and Sørheim's description of his body language.
5 Andrew Berwick [Anders Behring Breivik], *2083 – A European Declaration of Independence* (hereinafter referred to as *2083*), p. 1401.
6 Ibid., p. 687.
7 Ibid., p. 1171.
8 Ibid., pp. 1424–5.
9 This literary scholar is an acquaintance of mine.
10 *2083*, pp. 1406, 1434.
11 Ibid., pp. 1401–2.
12 This episode is retold based on an interview with the literary scholar who met Breivik that evening.
13 *2083*, p. 1424.
14 Ibid., p. 839.
15 To borrow a term from the court-appointed psychiatrists Husby and Sørheim.
16 In a comment on Document.no. Breivik's comments on Document.no can be found at www.document.no/anders-behring-breivik/.
17 André Glucksmann, *Dostoïevski à Manhattan* (Paris: Robert Laffont, 2002), p. 24.
18 Yukio Mishima, *The Temple of the Golden Pavilion*, trans. Ivan Morris (London: Vintage, 2001), p. 5.
19 Ibid., p. 204.
20 Albert Borowitz, *Terrorism for Self-Glorification: The Herostratos Syndrome* (Kent, OH: Kent State University Press, 2005), p. 79.
21 Ibid., p. 82.
22 Ibid., p. 104.
23 Ibid., p. 52.
24 *2083*, p. 1371.
25 Ibid., p. 1424.

Chapter 3 A West End Family

1 This chapter is based on written and oral sources, principally interviews with Tove, who was married to Breivik's father from 1983 to 1993, and two members of the observation team from Statens senter for barne- og ungdomspsykiatri [the State Centre for Child and Youth Psychiatry]

which reported on Breivik, his mother and his sister in 1983 (both are bound by their duty of confidentiality but were able to describe the report in general terms), as well as two other sources who were closely acquainted with the family during this period. I have also made use of material from the reports by the two pairs of court-appointed psychiatrists that have been reproduced by *VG* in a redacted form: www.vg.no/nyheter/innenriks/22-juli/psykiatrisk_vurdering/.

2 One of the texts in Anders' compendium is entitled 'The Fatherless Civilisation'. It was written by his favourite blogger, the extreme right-winger from Ålesund, Peder Are Nøstvold Jensen, alias Fjordman.

3 Agnar Aspaas and Terje Tørrissen, 'Rettspsykiatrisk erklæring' [Forensic psychiatric report], 10 April 2012 (the second psychiatric report), reproduced by *VG*: www.vg.no/nyheter/innenriks/22-juli/psykiatrisk_vurdering/, p. 8.

4 Interview with Tove.

5 Aspaas and Tørrissen, p. 151. It is not clear what the source was for this description.

6 Interview with Tove.

7 Interview with source closely acquainted with the family.

8 Ibid.

9 Ibid.

10 Ibid.

11 Ibid.

12 The following is partly based on Berit Grøholt, Hilchen Sommerschild and Ida Garløv, *Lærebok i barnepsykiatri* [Child psychiatry textbook], 4th edn (Oslo: Universitetsforlaget, 2008).

13 Sigmund Karterud, Theresa Wilberg and Øyvind Urnes, *Personlighetspsykiatri* [Personality psychiatry] (Oslo: Gyldendal Akademisk, 2010), p. 65.

14 One member of the SSBU team thought that this was the diagnosis they would have given him in 1983, if such a diagnosis had existed then. The SSBU was, for that matter, perhaps more preoccupied with providing thorough individual descriptions of cases than making diagnoses that can often be slightly imprecise instruments: reality is more nuanced than the diagnostic manual, as the psychiatric reports on Breivik demonstrated. Moreover, many of the most central diagnostic tools and test methods in child psychiatry have been developed since 1983.

15 Peter Fonagy, 'Transgenerational Consistencies of Attachment: A New Theory', Paper presented to the Developmental and Psychoanalytic Discussion Group, American Psychoanalytic Association Meeting, Washington, DC, 13 May 1999, http://dspp.com/papers/fonagy2.htm.

16 Karterud, Wilberg and Urnes, p. 58.

17 Grøholt, Sommerschild and Garløv, p. 348.

18 Ibid.

19 Interview with source closely acquainted with the family.

20 Interview with source from the SSBU who followed the court case.

21 *2083*, p. 1387.

22 According to the Norwegian tax administration, the average income for thirty-year-olds in Skøyen (Nedre Silkestrå, 0375 Oslo) in 2009 was just under 400,000 kroner (approximately £45,000), which was almost double the national average for all age groups.
23 *2083*, p. 1371.
24 Ibid., p. 854.
25 Ibid., p. 1170. It is quite doubtful whether Breivik was correct that an 'alarming number of young girls' in Oslo's primary schools are 'giving' (or having) oral sex. According to the statistics from the 2003 *Ung i Norge* [Young in Norway] survey, 12 per cent of fourteen-year-old girls stated that they had had intercourse, 16 per cent had carried out sexual acts in the sense of touching sexual organs, while 52 per cent had French kissed or 'snogged'.
26 Ibid., p. 1171.
27 Ibid., p. 1387.
28 Ibid., p. 1172.

Chapter 4 Morning on Utøya

1 *2083*, p. 854.
2 Jonas Gahr Støre, 'Urolige tider' [Uneasy times], *Bergens Tidende*, 21 July 2011, www.bt.no/meninger/kommentar/Urolige-tider-2540395.html.
3 Ibid.
4 Erlend Loe, *L* (Oslo: Cappelen, 1999), p. 23.
5 Nordahl Grieg, 'Til ungdommen' [To the youth], in *Samlede dikt* (Oslo: Gyldendal, 2011), pp. 138–9.

Chapter 5 Morg the Graffiti Bomber

1 This chapter is based on interviews with acquaintances of Breivik from Ris Lower Secondary School, Hartvig Nissen Upper Secondary School and Oslo Commerce School, as well as from the tagging community and the 'Tåsen Gang'. They have all been anonymized according to their own wishes. Contributions were made by four of Breivik's contemporaries from Ris, three people from the tagging community and two people from the Tåsen Gang, in addition to a few other sources. I have also made use of legal statements and police statements from some of Breivik's friends, as they were reproduced in the forensic psychiatrists' reports published online by *VG*: www.vg.no/nyheter/innenriks/22-juli/psykiatrisk_vurdering/.
2 'Heinrich Himmler på R.O.O.M.!' [Heinrich Himmler at R.O.O.M.!], *Ris avis: Ris Ungdomsskoles nettavis*, 2008, www.risavis.net/Himmler_pa_room.htm.

3 Harald Ulvestad, 'Om Ris skole under okkupasjonen' [About Ris School during the occupation], *Medlemsblad for Vinderen historielag*, 16/1 (2007), 2–5.
4 Statistisk sentralbyrå [Statistics Norway], 'Hjulet: Styrings- og informasjonshjulet for helse- og sosialtjenesten i kommunene, 1996 [The hub: Management and information hub for health and social services in the municipalities, 1996], 31 December 1996, www.ssb.no/helse/statistikker/hjulet/aar/1996-12-31. See also similar statistical reports from 1995 to 1998.
5 Aslak Nore, 'Kommentar: Oslo Noir' [Comment: Oslo Noir], *VG*, 28 August 2011, www.vg.no/nyheter/meninger/artikkel.php?artid=10098241.
6 This description is based on Tore Bjørgo and Thomas Haaland, *Vold, konflikt og gjenger: En undersøkelse blant ungdomsskoleelever i Skedsmo kommune* [Violence, conflict and gangs: An investigation among lower secondary school pupils in Skedsmo municipality] ([Oslo]: NIBR, 2001).
7 Torgeir Husby and Synne Sørheim, 'Rettspsykriatisk erklæring' [Forensic psychiatric report], 29 November 2011 (the first psychiatric report), reproduced by *VG*: www.vg.no/nyheter/innenriks/22-juli/psykiatrisk_vurdering/, p. 103.
8 It is difficult to find figures to substantiate this, but researchers who have studied juvenile crime confirm this impression, including Tore Bjørgo of the Norwegian Police University College in a discussion with me in early 2012.
9 Husby and Sørheim, p. 96.
10 Ibid., p. 36.
11 According to a source from Tåsen who knew Breivik in 1997.
12 *2083*, pp. 1389–90.
13 Ibid., p. 1394.
14 Sigmund Karterud, Theresa Wilberg and Øyvind Urnes, *Personlighetspsykiatri* [Personality psychiatry] (Oslo: Gyldendal Akademisk, 2010), p. 63.

Chapter 6 The 'Mother of the Nation' Returns to Utøya

1 Hadia Tajik, 'Snart på Utøya for å høre på Gro Harlem Brundtland. Funfact: Vi er like høye :)' [Heading to Utøya to listen to Gro Harlem Brundtland. Fun fact: We're the same height :)], *Twitter.com*, 22 July 2011, https://twitter.com/HadiaTajik/status/94314303951351808.
2 Einar Lie Slangsvold, 'Røde homoer' [Red and gay], *Gaysir.no*, 5 March 2008, www.gaysir.no/artikkel.cfm?CID=12799.
3 Sigbjørn Obstfelder, 'Jeg ser' [I see], in *Digte* (Bergen: John Grieg, 1893), pp. 15–16.
4 Ian Buruma and Avishai Margalit, *Occidentalism: A Short History of Anti-Westernism* (London: Atlantic Books, 2004), p. 11.

5 Cited ibid., p. 13.
6 Nasjonal Samling, 'Orden, rettferd og fred: Program for Nasjonal Samling' [Order, justice and peace: Nasjonal Samling programme], 1934, www.nsd.uib.no/polsys/data/filer/parti/10279.rtf.
7 Cited in Oddvar K. Hoidal, *Quisling: A Study in Treason* (Oslo: Norwegian University Press, 1989), p. 72.
8 Jon Alfred Mjøen, *Rasehygiene* [Racial hygiene], 2nd edn (Oslo: Jacob Dybwad, 1938), pp. 235–8.
9 Hans Rustad, 'Ap-representant går ved Medina-universitetet' [Labour Party representative attends university in Medina], Document.no, 17 February 2010, www.document.no/2010/02/ogsa_ap-representant_ved_medin/.
10 Arshad Mubarak Ali, 'Jødehets er ikke et særskilt muslimsk problem' [Anti-Semitism is not a uniquely Muslim problem], *Stavanger Aftenblad*, 27 June 2011: www.aftenbladet.no/meninger/kommentar/Jdehets-er-ikke-et-srskilt-muslimsk-problem-2829275.html.

Chapter 7 Andrew Berwick and Avatar Syndrome

1 Morten Hopperstad et al., 'Moren hvitvasket penger for Breivik' [Breivik's mother laundered money for him], *VG*, 1 April 2012, www.vg.no/nyheter/innenriks/22-juli/artikkel.php?artid=10072811.
2 Conservatism [Anders Behring Breivik], Forum post under topic 'Lemasive, internet famous!', *World of Warcraft* Silvermoon Realm Forum, 5 February 2011: http://eu.battle.net/wow/en/forum/topic/1622897808#6.
3 Faltin Karlsen, 'Emergent Perspectives on Multiplayer Online Games: A Study of *Discworld* and *World of Warcraft*', PhD thesis (Oslo: University of Oslo, 2009), p. 174. Karlsen's thesis includes a clear description of *World of Warcraft* (as well as hardcore gamers) and how the game from Blizzard Entertainment developed from 2006 to 2008.
4 See the threads 'Just for those who didn't know', *World of Warcraft* Nordrassil Realm Forum: http://eu.battle.net/wow/en/forum/topic/2423044016; 'Andersnordic', *Last Legion* Forum: http://lastlegion.shivtr.com/forum_threads/877599.
5 Offler, forum post under topic 'Andersnordic', 24 July 2011, ibid.
6 Cited in Jason Schreier, 'Norway Mass Murderer Was "Unremarkable", Says Former *World of Warcraft* Guildmate', *Kotaku*, 23 April 2012, http://kotaku.com/5904338/norway-mass-murderer-was-unremarkable-says-former-world-of-warcraft-guildmate.
7 *2083*, p. 1344.
8 Ibid., p. 1472.
9 'If we look at it analytically, if we look at it historically, we quickly find out exactly what it is. Political Correctness is cultural Marxism. It is Marxism translated from economic into cultural terms. It is an effort that goes back not to the 1960s and the hippies and the peace

movement, but back to World War I.' From a lecture by Bill [William S.] Lind, 'The Origins of Political Correctness', *Accuracy in Academia*: www.academia.org/the-origins-of-political-correctness/.

10 Kent Andersen and Christian Tybring-Gjedde, 'Drøm fra Disneyland' [Dream from Disneyland], *Aftenposten*, 25 August 2010, www .aftenposten.no/meninger/kronikker/article3783373.ece.

11 Even though the three-volume epic *The Lord of the Rings* has been loved and revered for over fifty years, the books also have their critics. '[A]ll the characters [. . .] are boys masquerading as adult heroes. [. . . H]ardly one of them knows anything about women [and they] will never come to puberty,' wrote the poet Edwin Muir in his review of *The Return of the King*: 'A Boy's World', *The Observer*, 27 November 1955, p. 11.

12 According to the report by Politiets sikkerhetstjeneste [the Norwegian Police Security Service; PST] delivered in Oslo District Court on 30 May 2012.

13 Fjordman, 'Native Revolt: A European Declaration of Independence', *The Brussels Journal*, 16 March 2007, www.brusselsjournal.com/node/ 1980.

14 Fjordman, 'Defeating Eurabia, Part 5', *Gates of Vienna*, 31 October 2008, http://gatesofvienna.net/2008/10/defeating-eurabia-part-5/.

15 *2083*, p. 1254.

16 Fjordman, 'Fjordman – The First Five Years', *Gates of Vienna*, 20 February 2010, http://gatesofvienna.blogspot.co.uk/2010/02/fjordman -first-five-years.html.

17 Cited in Morten Hopperstad et al., 'Peder Jensen er drapsmannens forbilde "Fjordman"' [Peder Jensen is the killer's role model 'Fjordman'], *VG*, 5 August 2011, www.vg.no/nyheter/innenriks/22-juli/artikkel .php?artid=10089389.

18 The following is based, *inter alia*, on an interview with the editor and journalist Hans Rustad in October 2011.

19 Cited in Johann Hari, 'In Enemy Territory? An Interview with Christopher Hitchens', 23 September 2004, http://johannhari.com/2004/09/23/ in-enemy-territory-an-interview-with-christopher-hitchens/.

20 All Breivik's comments on Document.no are presented here: www .document.no/anders-behring-breivik/.

21 Hans Rustad, 'Ekstremistan IV: Sex som våpen' [Extremistan IV: Sex as a weapon], Document.no, 18 December 2009, www.document.no/ 2009/12/ekstremistan_iv_nye_ekstremist/.

22 Bjørn Stærk, 'En nettreise gjennom islamkritikkens tiår' [A decade of Islam critique on the web], *Samtiden*, 4 (2011), 32–49. Bjørn Stærk's own blog took another direction, becoming one of the most prominent sites for criticism of conspiracy theories and of right-wing fear and hate rhetoric.

23 Cited in Ørjan Torheim, '– Som en liten gutt' ['Like a little boy'], *Bergens Tidende*, 23 July 2011, www.bt.no/nyheter/innenriks/–Som-en -liten-gutt-2542176.html.

24 Ibid.
25 See note 20 above.
26 *2083*, p. 666.
27 See note 20 above.
28 *2083*, p. 1416.
29 Torgeir Husby and Synne Sørheim, 'Rettspsykriatisk erklæring' [Forensic psychiatric report], 29 November 2011 (the first psychiatric report), reproduced by *VG*: www.vg.no/nyheter/innenriks/22-juli/psykiatrisk_vurdering/, p. 40.
30 Ibid., p. 39.
31 Ibid., p. 78.
32 Ibid.
33 Ibid., p. 36.
34 Ibid., p. 68.
35 Ibid., p. 74.
36 Ibid., p. 76.
37 Perhaps the most striking aspect of Breivik's mother's conversation with the court-appointed psychiatrists, as it is reproduced in Husby and Sørheim's report, is that she never mentioned anything about her son's deeds or victims. It is as if that part of the story did not exist. On the other hand, she said that the case had been 'a terrible strain' on her (p. 73) – after 22 July 2011 she was admitted to a psychiatric unit for some time – and said that she was 'upset and angry' (ibid.) because of inaccurate reports by journalists. A picture emerges from the report, as in the SSBU reports from 1983, of a person who has difficulties understanding and taking seriously other perspectives than her own, including her son's, and who sees herself solely as a victim. 'He lied and deceived me,' she said, crying (p. 82), but she said nothing of the suffering her son had caused to others.
38 Husby and Sørheim, p. 78.
39 Ibid., p. 41.
40 Ibid., p. 78.
41 Ibid., p. 77.
42 Ibid., p. 79.
43 Ibid.
44 *2083*, p. 856.
45 Husby and Sørheim, p. 80.
46 Ibid., p. 82.
47 Ibid., p. 81.
48 Ibid., p. 77.
49 According to Breivik's testimony in Oslo District Court, 20 April 2012.
50 Husby and Sørheim, p. 37.
51 Ibid., p. 44.
52 *2083*, p. 1154.
53 Ibid., p. 1434.

Chapter 8 The Safest Place in Norway

1 Statistisk sentralbyrå [Statistics Norway], 'Attitudes towards seven statements on immigrants and immigration, 2002–2011', 5 December 2011, www.ssb.no/a/english/kortnavn/innvhold_en/tab-2011-12-05-01-en.html.
2 Statistisk sentralbyrå [Statistics Norway], 'Population 1 January 2010 and 2011 and changes in 2010, by immigration category and country background', 28 April 2011, www.ssb.no/a/english/kortnavn/innvbef_en/tab-2011-04-28-01-en.html.
3 Integrerings- og mangfoldsdirektoratet [Directorate of Integration and Diversity], 'Integreringsbarometeret 2010' [Integration barometer 2010], June 2011, www.imdi.no/Documents/Rapporter/Integreringsbarometeret_2010.pdf.

Chapter 9 The Book Launch

1 According to Breivik's testimony in Oslo District Court, 19 April 2012.
2 *2083*, pp. 1411–12.
3 Ibid., p. 1409.
4 Ibid., p. 767.
5 Ibid., p. 1164.
6 Ibid., p. 1472.
7 According to Breivik's testimony in Oslo District Court, 19 April 2012.
8 Fjordman, 'The Failure of Western Feminism', *Gates of Vienna*, 31 August 2008: http://gatesofvienna.net/2008/08/the-failure-of-western-feminism/, cited in *2083*, p. 343.
9 *2083*, pp. 959–60.
10 See, e.g., *2083*, p. 1261. In court, Breivik described al-Qaeda as the world's most successful terrorist organization.
11 Ibid., pp. 820, 931, 1115.
12 Ibid., p. 1065.
13 Ibid., p. 836.
14 Ibid., p. 1298.
15 Ibid., p. 802.
16 Ibid., p. 806.
17 Ibid., p. 1435.
18 Ibid., pp. 1144–5.
19 Ibid., p. 894.
20 Ibid., p. 1457.
21 Ibid., pp. 1158–9.
22 Ibid., p. 1155.
23 From cross-examination in Oslo District Court, 17 April 2012.
24 *2083*, p. 820.

25 Ibid., p. 935. This quotation is perhaps also inspired by Bushido, the way of the warrior, a form of life philosophy or practical faith that was popularized in the Tom Cruise film *Samurai*. According to William Scott Wilson's translation of Tsunemoto Yamamoto's *Hagakure: The Book of the Samurai* (Tokyo: Kodansha, 1979), a description of Bushido from the 1700s, a warrior must meditate frequently in order to overcome his fear of death: 'If by setting one's heart right every morning and evening, one is able to live as though his body were already dead, he gains freedom in the Way. His whole life will be without blame, and he will succeed in his calling' (p. 18). Breivik explained to Aspaas and Tørrissen that his Bushido meditation could be compared to the five daily prayers of Salafi terrorists.
26 *2083*, p. 849. The trial demonstrated how strongly this music affected Breivik. In court on 16 April 2012, during the prosecution's presentation of the propaganda film he had uploaded on the morning of 22 July 2011, which features Bøksle's song as part of the soundtrack, Breivik burst into tears.
27 Ibid., p. 940.
28 Ibid., p. 1276.
29 Ibid., p. 1378.
30 Red Army Faction, 'The Black September Action in Munich: Regarding the Strategy for Anti-Imperialist Struggle', November 1972, trans. André Moncourt and J. Smith, in *The Red Army Faction: A Documentary History*, vol. 1*: Projectiles for the People*, ed. J. Smith and André Moncourt (Montreal: Kersplebedeb, 2009) pp. 205–36 (at p. 223).
31 *2083*, p. 1168.
32 Øystein Sørensen, 'En totalitær mentalitet' [A totalitarian mentality], *Dagbladet*, 1 August 2011: www.dagbladet.no/2011/08/01/kultur/debatt/kronikk/2083/breivik/17511868/.
33 *2083*, p. 1404.
34 Ibid., p. 1219.
35 Ibid.
36 Ibid., p. 338.
37 Ibid., p. 1219.
38 Ibid., p. 29.
39 Ibid., p. 697.
40 Ibid., p. 1387.
41 Ibid., p. 1177.
42 Ibid., p. 1181.
43 Ibid., p. 1182.
44 Ibid., p. 1187.
45 Torgeir Husby and Synne Sørheim, 'Rettspsykriatisk erklæring' [Forensic psychiatric report], 29 November 2011 (the first psychiatric report), reproduced by *VG*: www.vg.no/nyheter/innenriks/22-juli/psykiatrisk_vurdering/, p. 200.
46 Agnar Aspaas and Terje Tørrissen, 'Rettspsykiatrisk erklæring' [Forensic psychiatric report], 10 April 2012 (the second psychiatric report),

reproduced by *VG*: www.vg.no/nyheter/innenriks/22-juli/psykiatrisk_vurdering/, p. 199.

47 Husby and Sørheim, p. 80.
48 *2083*, p. 1454.
49 Ibid., p. 933.
50 From Breivik's testimony in Oslo District Court, 19 April 2012.
51 From Breivik's testimony in Oslo District Court, 25 April 2012.
52 Thor, his hammer Mjölnir (or 'Mjolnir', as it was inscribed on Breivik's pistol), Odin and his spear Gungnir all make extensive guest appearances in the Marvel Universe too, for example in the 2011 film *Thor*.
53 See Aspaas and Tørrissen, p. 38.

Chapter 12 What Is Happening in Norway?

1 Eskil Pedersen's story is drawn from the TV2 documentary *Fire fortellinger fra Utøya* [Four stories from Utøya].
2 Erlend Loe, *L* (Oslo: Cappelen, 1999), p. 23.
3 *2083*, pp. 1389–90.
4 Kjetil Stormark, *Da terroren rammet Norge: 189 minutter som rystet verden* [When terror struck Norway: 189 minutes that shook the world] (Oslo: Kagge, 2011), p. 183.
5 Rudyard Kipling, 'If–', in *Rewards and Fairies* (London: Macmillan, 1910), pp. 175–6.

Chapter 13 Anders Behring Breivik's Seventy-Five Minutes on Utøya

1 This chapter is based on Breivik's statements to police and accounts reproduced in Torgier Husby and Synne Sørheim's report ('Rettspsykriatisk erklæring' [Forensic psychiatric report], 29 November 2011 (the first psychiatric report), reproduced by *VG*: www.vg.no/nyheter/innenriks/22-juli/psykiatrisk_vurdering/), on his testimony in court, and on the review of the police investigation on Utøya as presented in court on 3 May 2012.
2 *2083*, p. 1470.
3 Ibid., pp. 917–21.
4 Husby and Sørheim, p. 152.
5 Ibid., p. 30.
6 Ibid., p. 152.
7 Ibid., p. 161.
8 Ibid., p. 122.
9 *2083*, p. 839.
10 Husby and Sørheim, p. 160.

11 Agnar Aspaas and Terje Tørrissen, 'Rettspsykiatrisk erklæring' [Forensic psychiatric report], 10 April 2012 (the second psychiatric report), reproduced by *VG*: www.vg.no/nyheter/innenriks/22-juli/psykiatrisk_vurdering/, pp. 39–40.
12 *2083*, p. 918.
13 Ibid., p. 1465; Husby and Sørheim, p. 152.
14 Husby and Sørheim, p. 153.
15 *2083*, p. 933.
16 Husby and Sørheim, p. 30.
17 Ibid., p. 21.
18 Ibid., p. 30.
19 Ibid.
20 Cited in Kristopher Schau, 'Rettsnotater: Uke 10' [Trial notes: Week 10], *Morgenbladet*, 21 June 2012, http://morgenbladet.no/samfunn/2012/kristopher_schau_rettsnotater_uke_10.
21 Tonje Brenna in the TV2 documentary *Fire fortellinger fra Utøya* [Four stories from Utøya].
22 *2083*, p. 919.
23 According to a witness who was shot and injured, and who overheard the incident.
24 Husby and Sørheim, p. 30.
25 Ibid., p. 153.
26 Ibid., p. 145.
27 Simon Baron-Cohen, *Zero Degrees of Empathy: A New Theory of Human Cruelty* (London: Allen Lane, 2011).
28 Ibid., pp. 25–6.
29 *2083*, p. 837.
30 The Complete Text of the Poznan Speech, 4 October 1943, *The Holocaust History Project*: www.holocaust-history.org/himmler-poznan/speech-text.shtml. Translation used with the permission of the Holocaust History Project (www.holocaust-history.org).
31 Ibid.
32 *2083*, p. 50.
33 Ibid., p. 837.
34 Husby and Sørheim, p. 15.
35 Ibid., p. 16.
36 Ibid., p. 23.
37 According to the newspaper's chief editor, Hilde Haugsgjerd, it did not appear that *Aftenposten* had received any contributions from Breivik.
38 Husby and Sørheim, pp. 141, 183.
39 *Diagnostic and Statistical Manual of Mental Disorders*, 4th edn, text revision (Washington, DC: American Psychiatric Association, 2000), p. 717.
40 Erich Fromm, *The Heart of Man: Its Genius for Good and Evil* (London: Routledge & Kegan Paul, 1965), p. 37.
41 Ronald M. Holmes and Stephen T. Holmes, *Profiling Violent Crimes: An Investigative Tool*, 3rd edn (Thousand Oaks, CA: Sage, 2002).

42 Charles I. Brooks and Michael A. Church, 'Serial Murder and Mass Murder', in *Encyclopedia of Contemporary American Social Issues*, vol. 2: *Criminal Justice*, ed. Michael Shally-Jensen (Santa Barbara, CA: ABC-CLIO, 2011), pp. 679–88 (at p. 684). See also Louis B. Schlesinger (ed.), *Serial Offenders: Current Thought, Recent Findings* (Boca Raton, FL: CRC Press, 2000).

43 Sigmund Karterud, Theresa Wilberg and Øyvind Urnes, *Personlighet-spsykiatri* [Personality psychiatry] (Oslo: Gyldendal Akademisk, 2010), p. 63.

44 Espen Sandli and Line Brustad, 'Utøya ble lyst opp av mobiltelefoner' [Utøya was lit up by mobile phones], *Dagbladet*, 24 September 2011, www.dagbladet.no/2011/09/24/nyheter/innenriks/terrorangrepet/utoya/politiet/18277022.

Chapter 14 Hatred

1 Helge Lurås, cited in Kamilla Simonnes, 'Analyse i kaos' [Analysis in chaos], *Morgenbladet*, 5 August 2011, http://morgenbladet.no/samfunn/2011/analyse_i_kaos.

2 Arshad M. Ali, 'Skjeggbrødre og plaggsøstres dom over andre' [Bearded brothers and veiled sisters' judgement of others], *Stavanger Aftenblad*, 7 February 2012, www.aftenbladet.no/meninger/kommentar/Skjeggbrodre-og-plaggsostres-dom-over-andre-2926934.html.

3 Per Sivle, 'Tord Foleson', in *Olavs-Kvæde* (Oslo: Bogvennen, 1901).

4 In Oslo District Court, 18 June 2012.

5 Agnar Aspaas and Terje Tørrissen, 'Rettspsykiatrisk erklæring' [Forensic psychiatric report], 10 April 2012 (the second psychiatric report), reproduced by *VG*: www.vg.no/nyheter/innenriks/22-juli/psykiatrisk_vurdering/, p. 128.

6 Aage Storm Borchgrevink, 'Fra bloggosfæren med hat' [From the blogosphere with hate], *Aftenposten*, 24 July 2011, www.aftenposten.no/meninger/kommentarer/article4182214.ece.

7 In Oslo District Court, 17 April 2012. See, for example 'Her er Breiviks ordrette forklaring' [Here is Breivik's testimony word for word], TV2, 17 April 2012, www.tv2.no/nyheter/innenriks/22-juli-terror-oslo-og-utoya/her-er-breiviks-ordrette-forklaring-3757760.html.

8 Annemarte Moland, Ingunn Andersen and Øyvind Bye Skille, 'Breivik kan ha blitt utsatt for overgrep' [Breivik may have been subject to abuse], NRK, 28 November 2011, http://nrk.no/nyheter/norge/1.7894111.

9 This has emerged in police interviews, according to two independent sources.

10 Berit Grøholt, Hilchen Sommerschild and Ida Garløv, *Lærebok i barnepsykiatri* [Child psychiatry textbook], 4th edn (Oslo: Universitetsforlaget, 2008), p. 373.

11 Sigmund Karterud, Theresa Wilberg and Øyvind Urnes, *Personlighetspsykiatri* [Personality psychiatry] (Oslo: Gyldendal Akademisk, 2010), p. 63.
12 The personality disorder with which Breivik was diagnosed is a serious mental illness, and the mother's 'borderline personality structure' can be interpreted as if the SSBU believed they had identified in her a borderline personality disorder.
13 Torgeir Husby and Synne Sørheim, 'Rettspsykriatisk erklæring' [Forensic psychiatric report], 29 November 2011 (the first psychiatric report), reproduced by *VG*: www.vg.no/nyheter/innenriks/22-juli/psykiatrisk_vurdering/, p. 187.
14 Ibid.
15 Ibid.
16 Bjørn Stærk, 'Det er en annen tid nå' [It is another time now], *VG Debatt*, 29 July 2011, http://vgdebatt.vgb.no/2011/07/29/det-er-en-annen-tid-na/.
17 Jens Stoltenberg, 'Prime Minister Jens Stoltenberg's New Year's Address', 1 January 2012, www.regjeringen.no/en/dep/smk/Whats-new/Speeches-and-articles/statsministeren/statsminister_jens_stoltenberg/2012/prime-minister-jens-stoltenbergs-new-yea.html?id=667848.
18 22. juli-kommisjonen [22 July Commission], 'Rapport fra 22. juli-kommisjonen' [22 July Commission Report], 'Preliminary English Version of Selected Chapters', 13 August 2012, http://22julikommisjonen.no/en/content/download/472/3668/version/2/file/Complete_combined_English_version.pdf, p. 11.
19 Ibid., p. 9.
20 'Bedre beskyttelse av barns utvikling: Ekspertutvalgets utredning om det biologiske prinsipp i barnevernet' [Better protection of children's development: The committee of experts' report on the biological principle in child welfare], Report for the Ministry of Children, Equality and Social Inclusion, NOU 2012: 5, p. 207.
21 Ibid., p. 16.

Acknowledgements

I have received a lot of help and support in writing this book. Many people have taken the time to talk with me about difficult and occasionally hideous experiences. Some chose to speak anonymously, others came forward openly, but many people have contributed in their own way to telling me about a story that was both close to me and distant at the same time.

Arshad Mubarak Ali, Marius Arnesen, Christian Brændshøi, Anzor Djoukaev, Even Frogh, Stine Renate Håheim, Allan Søndergaard Jensen, Even Kleppen, Torstein Tvedt Solberg, Ida Spjelkavik, Anne-Berit Stavenes, Jonas Gahr Støre, Hadia Tajik, Erik Øvergaard and Tove Ø.: thank you all. Thanks also, among others, to Big Al from Hovseter, Dekor from Tåsen, Mono from Smestad and to a number of other people who gave accounts of the eighties and nineties.

Particular thanks go to the editor, Aslak Nore, for his enthusiastic reading and creative suggestions. Thanks also to Jan Swensson, editorial head of non-fiction, and to the publisher Gyldendal Norsk Forlag for getting the project going, and to Stiftelsen Fritt Ord [the Freedom of Expression Foundation] and the Norsk faglitterær forfatter- og oversetterforening [the Norwegian Non-Fiction Writers and Translators Association], who supported me financially.

For their advice, tips and suggestions, thanks also go to Stian Bromark, Ane Farsethås, Cathrine Grøndahl, Sturla Haugsgjerd, Andreas Hompland, Sigmund Karterud, Prableen Kaur, Ole Andreas Holm, Faltin Karlsen, Charlotte Lundgren, Jane Nordhagen, John Erik Riley, Finn Skårderud, Hilchen Sommerschild and Svein Østerud.

Even though many people have helped me en route, I take sole responsibility for the content of this book.

Index

The extra vowels *æ*, *ø* and *å* belong at the end of the Norwegian alphabet but, for the purposes of word order in this index, *æ* and å have been treated the same way as *a*, and *ø* has been treated as *o*.